QUEERING VISUAL CULTURES

QUEERING VISUAL CULTURES

RE-PRESENTING SEXUAL POLITICS ON STAGE AND SCREEN

Edited by Subashish Bhattacharjee

Universitas Press
Montreal

Universitas Press
Montreal

www.universitaspress.com

First published in August 2018

Cover art: Francisco Zorieuq, *O Principio* (*The Beginning*),
enamel paint, 1m x 0.8m
franciscozorieuq.wix.com/quadros

Library and Archives Canada Cataloguing in Publication

Queering visual cultures : re-presenting sexual politics on stage and screen / edited by Subashish Bhattacharjee.

Includes bibliographical references.
ISBN 978-0-9950291-3-2 (paperback)

1. Homosexuality and the arts. I. Bhattacharjee, Subashish, editor

NX180.H6Q83 2018 700'.453 C2016-904017-8

Table of Contents

Introduction: Placing Visual Cultures in a Queer Context

SUBASHISH BHATTACHARJEE

Art is not linked to some intrinsic relation to one's own body but exactly the opposite: it is linked to those processes of distancing and the production of a plane of composition that abstracts sensation from the body.

Elizabeth Grosz, *Chaos, Territory, Art*

The visual arts genres have been under critical and theoretical scrutiny for a substantial length of time, although not quite as long as the literary arts have been on the receiving end of scholarly attention. The wide spectrum of the visual arts genres—painting, theatre, dance, and cinema among others—has encouraged the possibility of a similarly wide range of critical measures to anticipate the direction of social 'performance'. LGBTQA theories too have had increasingly significant bearings (or even the other way round) on visual culture artifacts over the decades since the mid-twentieth century. The present state of 'crisis' that necessitates an excursion into reading visual culture in the backdrop of 'queer theorizations' can be summed up in the words of David V. Ruffalo from 2009 in the context of the recent developments in terms of cultural assimilation of tropes that were previously denied polity and parity and may still be viewed as abject:

> Queer has reached a political peak. Its theoretical movements have become limited by its incessant investment in identity politics and its political outlook has in many ways attained dormant status due to its narrowed interest in heteronormativity. . . . Over the past two decades, a significant body of work has contributed to what is referred to as queer studies. Queer theorizations are at the heart of this anti-canonical genre where the intersection of bodies, identities, and cultures continue to be a central focus. (1)

The visual arts possess a unique possibility of transgressing heteronormative boundaries by pushing the liminal spaces between theorizing and practicing tactics of resistance. The location of such resistant artifacts is necessary as they ensure the displacement of an abstract hegemonic normative interface. Renate Lorenz refers to this transgression into the heteronormative space through representations of the queer in art, or queer art, when she writes that "these [queer-oriented visual culture artifacts] artistic works are precisely in the position to break off interpellations, producing a temporal and spatial distance—a deferral and a gap—between an experience and any possible effect on the process of subjectification. These works thematize embodied categories such as gender, tracing their history and making them non-self-evident, but they do not offer them up to identification. Instead, they make material beyond gender available for reflection and experimentation" (18).

It is necessary to have the reactionary counter-measure of enabling the queer frequency of visual cultures as the heterosocial paradigms repress the non-normative with prominent repressive measures such as the use of shame. The queer performer/producer and the audience of such product are considered beyond the normal parameters of society: incomprehensible and distasteful. Despite the auteur output in cinema and *avant garde* productions in painting, the stigma attached to queer presentations is tenaciously resistant to the alternative offered for normative sexuality in the arts. To contextualize the 'shame principle' affected by queer portrayals particularly in cinema, one could state that "cinema is flooded and flooding with affect; its absorptions move the viewing subject, to tears or laughter or fear or sadness, and shame is no exception. But if shame is so individuating, so contagious, what are the negotiations by which we can actually look at a movie that involves shame and negative affects?" (Johnson 1381). Shame, or the experience of abject dissociation upon viewing the alternative visual object, is an immanent factorization in the context of queer visual cultures. While artistic depictions of heterosexual acts have been an accepted norm, the portrayal of lesbian sexual acts on screen, on stage or as art is appropriated by patrinormative[1] society as pornographically charged, whereas the visual presentation of male gay sexual acts is depicted within the frame of perversion.

Furthermore, queer subcultures, which integrate the various visual culture genres that portray the queer, have existed beyond a historiographical or sociological phenomenon of reading into popular culture and the arts. Their co-existence has been uncontested because

[1] "The inculcation of norms through paternal authority" (Shoham 299).

they have operated militantly to reorganize the generic formula that has schematized the 'production of culture' (Bourdieu). With the growing acceptance of a parallel cultural paradigm of the queer, the prefix 'sub-' may be questioned and argued as being redundant; obsolete because it does not faithfully determine the spatiality of the post-gender/post-sexual/post-queer complex. However, the subculturation is a necessary methodology as "[q]ueer subcultures produce alternative temporalities by allowing their participants to believe that their futures can be imagined according to logics that lie outside of those paradigmatic markers of life experience—namely, birth, marriage, reproduction, and death" (Halberstam 2). The very association to the 'sub-'-ness of culturalism has its renditions in the form of manifest and emancipated representations instead of a continued regime of coded implications of sexual differentiation in the classification of socially accepted sexualities and their portrayals.

Donald E. Hall has stated that "a 'queer text' that reveals mutability, mutuality, possibilities for exceeding or abrading that binary must be met with a queer reading and critical response practice (or set of practices) that similarly recognizes and allows for such excess" (165). The readability of the visual arts displaying a queer possibility too possess such characteristic 'mutability, mutuality' that must be read with allowance for an excess. Cinematic movements such as New Queer Cinema, and specifically films such as those by Apichatpong Weerasethakul, Bruce LaBruce, whose work also displays effects of Queercore, Casper Andreas, Françoise Doherty, Gregg Araki, Todd Haynes and Gus Van Sant, prior work by Derek Jarman and Andy Warhol, both in cinema and painting, the gay theatre movement and its allied groups such as the Gay Theatre Alliance, plays by playwrights such as Larry Kramer, William M. Hoffman, Tony Kushner, Bryony Lavery, Alexi Kaye Campbell and Nicholas de Jongh, artwork by Kimberly Austin, Francis Bacon, Lyle Ashton Harris, Bhupen Khakhar, Paul Cadmus, David Wojnarowicz and Nahum B. Zenil, plastic artists and sculptors such as Jesse Harrod, Pierre Fouché, Allen Porter, Jessica Whitbread, Chiachio & Giannone, Ben Cuevas and Sonny Schneider, queer ballet companies such as the Ballez, and museums dedicated to queer visual arts such as the Leslie Lohman Museum of Gay and Lesbian Art help unpack the excesses that queer counter-normative artistic practices posit against the dominant cultural and societal paradigms.

The contemporary popular cultural space has leveraged the queer in the same format of representation as its presentation in the 1990s.

Although the queer is portrayed in a less perverse light than a decade ago, popular cultural representations of the queer in the visual culture genres are still on the level of the banal. However, with a more inclusive outlook, queer politics may find more welcoming access into the popular cultural genres, especially the visual arts. It can be argued that despite the "[p]roliferating queer representations in popular culture, however various and diverse . . . the problem of heteronormativity or antiqueer violence" has not been eliminated (Peele 5). While popular culture has become more encouraging towards the queer, the broader cultural opinion about the queer has been progressively more skeptical, compromised by the idea that the queer is encroaching on spaces reserved exclusively for heteronormative recreation. It is imperative that analyses of popular cultural depictions and presentations of the queer are performed with the extensive intent towards encouraging a politics of inclusion and towards deterring the abjection of the queer subject in popular cultural portrayals. These analyses must also factor into its conclusions that the queer is attempting to carve out its own niche and not to displace heterosexuality; the responses to such readings must also not seek regimental opposition to sexual practices practised and normalized by societies over centuries.

The performativity of visualization has been a driving factor in its assimilation of queer politics. While the literary arts can allow for a subtler activation of the queer subcultural narratives, the more reactionary statements can be projected chiefly through visual media. This places an immense responsibility on visual artists bringing in queer politics as a manifest or latent narrative. Judith Butler has stated in *Gender Trouble* that "[in] the theatre, one can say, 'this is just an act,' and de-realize the act, make acting into something quite distinct from what is real. Because of this distinction, one can maintain one's sense of reality in the face of this temporary challenge to our existing ontological assumptions about gender arrangements; the various conventions which announce that 'this is only a play' allows strict lines to be drawn between the performance and life" (278). This distinction and differentiation has received critical attention because performance here is viewed as a purely isolated event, leading critics of performance studies and aesthetics to speculate that the performer and the act are confined to their own specific locations without the possibility of overlap. This posits a serious performative and ethical disability on the part of the actor and the acted. Recent studies in performance analysis have shown a leaning towards re-representation of the binaries that are likely to separate the screen and the off-screen.

The visual cultural narratives assessed here are also intent on erasing such binary classifications to merge more carefully with Butler's later conceptual enframing of performativity and social performance. This position can be further expanded upon and explained through James Loxley's reading of Butler's statement:

> If our identities offstage are the product of the various acts through which we become who and what we are, then the notion of an essential person underlying those acts turns out to be merely a socially dominant dissimulation of that process of performative constitution. In which case, the ontological criterion for distinguishing between onstage and offstage, the invocation of this kind of fundamental difference between role-playing and just being ourselves, cannot be upheld. Derrida sought to undermine what had been assumed to be an ontological rendering of the distinction between serious and non-serious performatives; Butler later appropriated this deconstructive intervention for her own purposes. (Loxley 142-3)

The concern of the critic and the viewer of queer visual cultures can be poised within a new binary of validity and rejection of certain paradigms that are dismantled or newly constructed. Colebrook asks, "what do we do with what remains of the archive: do we stop reading all the works of fiction and cinema that are structured around gender binaries, do we (we theorists or literary critics) place ourselves in a world other than that of a still present and insistent gender binary?" (167). Although the query could possibly possess no specific answers, it is necessary to not view the queer subject in visual cultures as a displacing alternative. The archive of cultural artifacts will proliferate endlessly, and it is only through inclusion that the possibilities and continued relevance of such transcultural multi-genre, multidisciplinary and post-global forms of visual cultures can be ensured.

James H. Sanders' comments provide an essential standpoint for the idea behind the development of the volume, although the specifics of his comments are largely restricted to fluid visuals and overlap with the other arts through association:

> Broadcast, motion picture and advertising industries create market demand for queer and straight folks alike, in part constructing the consumers' reading of social reality through their products. Each is complicit in supporting the status quo, as are art educators when failing to instruct students in how to critically read visual cultural texts and cross-platform

> promotions, including product placement in major motion pictures and media personality spokespersons. . . . The arts and sexuality are bed partners in the 20th century. Art educators can make sure this relationship is not considered an indecent exposure, but a fertile site for critically reading contemporary culture and understanding social change. (47-48, 53)

The areas of inspection have generally widened over the course of the less than two decades since the publication of Sanders' essay. It is no longer the responsibility of art educators to encourage or inculcate a sense of propriety in studying queer visual arts practices, but rather a pressing social need. The impetus to be more inclusive and accommodating in both theory and practice of proactive queer visual cultures is interdisciplinary and not caught within the periphery of limited measures of existing sexual normative.

However, the thrust of the volume is not to establish a strict codec for theorizing visual cultural presentations of the queer. There, quite possibly, cannot exist in isolation a severely imposed schematic of interpretation of the parallel non-normative visual arts production. There is no distinct homogeneous concept for a unified interpretation or approach to the wide variety of visual cultural genres and the stratifications within the term queer itself. To cite David Halperin:

> The last thing we should do, then, is to devise and distribute a kind of cultural resistance meter, a test to determine how radically transformative, or *truly queer*, one practice or another *really* is. . . . Without advancing a notion of political ascesis so minimal and empty that it might include shopping for the right outfit, in other words, what we really need to do is to avoid formulating a set of criteria for resistance so rigorous and systematic that they would absolutely exclude the possibility that resistance could *ever* take the form of shopping for the right outfit. (113-15)

The majority of the following essays focus on cinema, which is, unsurprisingly, the most widely circulated and mediated visual cultural genre for the counter-positions proposed by queer re-presentations. The sentiment is widely attested to in other works that broach a similar aspect of research or study. Robert Lang, citing Stephen Neale, presents the relevance of the cinematic arts within a wider perspective of gender studies and vice versa thus: "As 'systems of orientations, expectations, and conventions that circulate between industry, text, and subject,' cinematic genres offer the critic a uniquely accessible approach to a large and complicated object of study" (4). Two decades ago, Jack Stevenson caught onto the evolving nature of 'gay cinema' as it tended towards more progressive forms of expression rather than merely reactionary or revolutionary when he stated that "[t]oday a discernible breaking-down of barriers has been achieved, liberating film-makers to some degree from the compartmentalization of strict genre classification and affording them more creative freedom. Gay film-makers are no longer automatically considered soldiers in the battle for gay liberation, but can be creative, apolitical artists making movies that play to wider audiences and which are not even necessarily 'gay films'" (31). The contemporary queer artist or filmmaker does not have to eke out the response of the viewer on a similar plane as when reacting to a righteous crusade. The viewer has evolved simultaneously, although not always positively, but now possesses the possibilities of processing the visual culture artifact in a better way than the previous generations of 'consumers' of the visual arts.

The present volume is at once a study of performance as well as of performativity, in that it has its roots in philosophy as well as in theatrical concepts. However, this performativity is not restricted to moving images or stage performances only, but it also addresses visual cultures that operate on static images. The essays selected in the volume succeed in mapping the queer cartographic possibilities of visual cultures. An overview of the essays should successfully convey the vast scope and prospects of the volume.

William J. Simmons analyzes Lars von Trier's cinematic 'duology'—*Nymphomaniac Part I* and *Part II*. His study is an interesting intervention on the ideas of female sexualities, sexual attraction, and alternative sexual practices, ideas of physical oppression, bondage, and even torture, and sexual addiction as represented in the two parts of the film. The essay is a performative reading of the sexualities performed in the films, just as Elke Krasny's essay in this volume is reading of the spatial/platial politics in the performances of the collective Queering Yerevan. Her study of the discourse of performance, of politicizing space and place puts into perspective how sexuality is itself politicized through similar spatial conditions.

Rohit K. Dasgupta writes about the portrayal of gay relationship in the Bollywood film *Dostana*. The essay analyzes the concepts of 'dosti' and 'yaarana' and charts an area of familiarity between friendship and homosociality, and simultaneously looks into the representation of the artificial gay relationship in the film as well as responses of the Indian cinema-going audience to the portrayal of queer relationship on screen. Fernando Gabriel Pagnoni Berns, Canela Ailen Rodriguez Fontao and Mariana Zárate's essay presents a close inspection of the subtextual queer element in slasher films of the 1980s. The essay takes into consideration the three films *Terror Train* (1980), *The Burning* (1981) and *Sleepaway Camp* (1983) to unravel the queer politics operational behind the setting of such violences.

Lara S. Narcisi looks into the visualizations of queer and the specter of AIDS, and the auto-affiliate of 'safe-sex'. The essay is an analytic as well as a historiographic study that presents an evolutionary trajectory of AIDS theatrical portrayals, the processes of dissociation that such portrayals evoke in the audience, as well as a prospective statement for the future. Fanny Beuré presents a reading of the queer elements in the TV series *Glee*. Her reading not only validates an academic engagement with clearly defined homosexual characters in the series, but also brings into sharper and more acute focus the presumably or tacitly homosexual or bisexual characters in the show.

Daniel Klein Martins's essay is an extension of a study of 1980s slasher films, extending its focus on thriller/horror spectacles of the 1980s that directly address the issue of homosexuality or transsexuality. The films in this study are *Cruising* and *Dressed to Kill*, both from 1980, and both films presenting the queerness of sexual 'deviance', and how a patriarchal oppression of sexual preferences can culminate in violence. Anna Fåhraeus discusses the issue of 'shaming' of actual or assumed homosexual individuals and the impact of such accusations in a heterosocial culture. In order to contextualize her study, she analyzes Lillian Hellman's hit play *The Children's Hour*, focusing on the impact of the shaming on said individuals. The chapter makes use of contemporary theoretical developments in studying social shaming in the play. Argha Banerjee focusus on the theatrical and filmic portrayals of Oscar Wilde's trial. Read as a 'queer spectacle,' the idea of queer shaming is brought into sharper focus with varying amplitudes showcasing the variance in attitudes historically in the subsequent portrayals and adaptations. The parallels between queer aethetics and the paradigm of legality are explored in detail through the mediation of the historicity of Wilde's trial in cinema and theatre in the exhaustively researched essay.

Florian Zitzelsberger contextualizes his reading on the period film *Pride* (2014), and brings to his use the twofold study of an actual historical event as well as its depiction on screen. Rather than critiquing the film from a queer cinematic perspective wholly, the chapter draws the attention of the readers to the corporeal interactions between queer and non-queer collectives.

Works Cited

Bourdieu, Pierre. *The Field of Cultural Production: Essays on Art and Literature*. Edited and Introduced by Randal Johnson. Cambridge: Polity, 1993.

Butler, Judith. *Gender Trouble: Feminism and the Subversion of Identity*. New York: Routledge, 1990.

Colebrook, Claire. *Sex After Life: Essays on Extinction*. Vol. 2. Ann Arbor: Open Humanities Press, 2014.

Halberstam, Judith. *In Queer Time and Place: Transgender Bodies, Subcultural Lives*. New York and London: New York University Press, 2005.

Hall, Donald E. *Queer Theories*. New York: Palgrave Macmillan, 2003.

Halperin, David. *St. Foucault: Towards a Gay Hagiography*. New York: Oxford University Press, 1995.

Johnson, Liza. "Perverse Angle: Feminist Film, Queer Film, Shame." *Signs* 30.1 (Autumn 2004): 1361-1384.

Lang, Robert. *Masculine Interests: Homoerotics in Hollywood Film*. New York: Columbia University Press, 2002.

Lorenz, Renate. *Queer Art: A Freak Theory*. Bielefeld: transcript Verlag, 2012.

Loxley, James. *Performativity*. New York and Oxford: Routledge, 2007.

Peele, Thomas. "Introduction: Popular Culture, Queer Culture." *Queer Popular Culture: Literature, Media, Film, and Television*. Ed. Thomas Peele. New York: Palgrave Macmillan, 2007. 1-8.

Ruffalo, David V. *Post-Queer Politics*. Farnham: Ashgate, 2009.

Sanders III, James H. "Visual Culture Texts." *Visual Arts Research* 33.1 (2007): 44-55.

Shoham, Shlomo Giora. *To Test the Limits of Our Endurance*. Newcastle upon Tyne: Cambridge Scholars Publishing, 2010.

Stevenson, Jack. "From the Bedroom to the Bijou: A Secret History of American Gay Sex Cinema." *Film Quarterly* 51.1 (Autumn, 1997): pp. 24-31.

Queerness and the Limits of Criticism in Lars von Trier's *Nymphomaniac*

William J. Simmons

On the Abuse of Women

This essay is an intensely personal one, and I would like to indulge a moment of biography, as I believe that being precise about the intent of this essay is essential to it being a useful document.[1] For some time, Lars von Trier has fascinated me from formal, compositional, and historical viewpoints. As most film scholars and art historians would agree, he has changed the course of international cinema. He is moreover notable for his use of astoundingly skilled female actors, and there is nothing more satisfying than his films' overwrought, but deeply affecting and complex, melodramas that allow me, as a gay man, to project certain fantasies about myself onto these dynamic female protagonists. For this reason, I originally proposed for this volume a highly academic reading of instances of queerness in von Trier's oeuvre.

However, I consider myself to be a queer feminist art historian, and there is an inherent problem here—most of von Trier's films center on the abuse of women. I presented the problem most clearly in a conversation with my friend, the filmmaker Coleen Fitzgibbon, about David Lynch's paintings and films: "Lynch's work is predicated on violence against women's bodies, but there is also a very frail and fragile male ego on display. Where is the line between ironic and incorrigible? What can be said for the fact that Lynch's films could be a trigger for people who have experienced real sexual violence?" (Fitzgibbon and Simmons). How could I consider myself a feminist or advocate of queer and trans theory when I find myself engrossed by Lynch or von Trier?

[1] I would like to thank Ian Simon-Curry, Ashley Garrett, Coleen Fitzgibbon, Michael Thomas Vassalo, Paula Hayes, Sue de Beer, and Khary Simon for the many valuable discussions we had about Lynch and von Trier prior to and during the drafting of this essay. My analysis of *Lars von Trier's Women* here has been expanded in an online book review for the Canadian Society of Continental Philosophy. See Simmons, William J. "Rex Butler and David Denny (eds.), *Lars von Trier's Women.*" *Symposium* (2017). http://www.c-scp.org/2017/02/23/rex-butler-and-david-denny-eds-lars-von-triers-women.html.

I imagine that others have had a similar crisis of faith, considering that two books about von Trier and women have come out only in the past year—an edited volume entitled *Lars von Trier's Women* by Rex Butler and David Denny, as well as Ahmed Elbeshlawy's *Women in Lars von Trier's Cinema: 1996–2014*. These are all men, if I might state the obvious.

This explosion of writing might be a result of von Trier's latest film *Nymphomaniac* (2013), which is widely heralded as wantonly sexist. The film opens with the battered body of Joe (Charlotte Gainsbourg) in an alleyway, whereupon Seligman (Stellan Skarsgård) takes her in and offers her a chance to rest and heal. The film progresses in the style of therapy or analysis, in which Joe tells her story of sexual awakenings and traumas while Seligman listens and interjects with explanations for her behaviour. What most critics miss is that the drive of the film is not the sexual anecdotes themselves, but Joe trying to prove, and Seligman trying to disprove, that she is a fundamentally evil person because of her highly active sexuality. *Nymphomaniac* could be said to be about much more than sex, but it is sex that is most spectacularly put on display, and thus takes up most of the critical conversation. It is true, however, to return to the fundamental issues of safety, triggers, and the abuse of women, that Joe is sexually abused again and again—but the film argues, as Joe does, that this was all on her own terms.

In the wake of *Nymphomaniac* and von Trier's reprehensible comments about Nazism at the Cannes Film Festival, *Lars von Trier's Women* tentatively defines its mission as presenting von Trier as a feminist director, or at least a director who is in conversation with feminist themes. The editors state in the introduction, "von Trier's thoughtful manipulation of this relation [of trust and chance in *Nymphomaniac*] sets up moments of resistance that intensify aesthetic appreciation and thereby complicate the controversy around his treatment of his female protagonist, allowing for a more nuanced and troubled reading" (Butler an Denny 12). This implies that any analyses that call von Trier sexist are neither nuanced nor troubled. In fact, Butler and Denny go to unusually polemical lengths to discount anyone who would say that von Trier is unilaterally sexist. Butler and Denny ultimately conclude, "Whether this [von Trier's identification with his female characters] is a simple sadism and hatred of women or a reflected masochism and hatred of himself, it does not ultimately matter" (Butler and Denny 3). Only male artists get this kind of sensitive insight into the psyche, and such comments are endemic to the trope of the "troubled male artist." After all, if a woman's motives are questioned, it usually comes down to the assumption of a sexist and simplified hysteria.

Despite the editors' bold claim, it does matter if von Trier's films reflect a hatred of women, but it is the male historian's prerogative, in his mind, to maintain a quasi-neutral stance. I am not a sociologist, so I will not go into the rampant violence against women across the globe, but suffice it to say that *it does matter* because these are deeply corporeal, lived emotions that must be attended to with sincere empathy and not academic remove. Von Trier himself refutes this kind of masculinist distancing in *Nymphomaniac.* Joe tells her confidant Seligman of the pain she must have caused a foetus after giving herself an abortion without anaesthesia, for when the mother is not anaesthetized the foetus is not either. When Seligman replies that he cannot judge her because he is a man, and therefore has no insight into the complexities of abortion (a typical liberal progressive man's answer), Joe replies, "First you say that, as a man, you cannot understand a woman's feelings with regard to abortion. Well, that's a bit like saying I couldn't understand the victims of earthquakes because they were Chinese. I thought we agreed that empathy is the foundation of all humanism. But I can see that it's very convenient for men to leave all that abortion stuff to women, that way they don't have to deal with the guilt." Amy Simmons in her essay on *Nymphomaniac* rightly calls this phenomenon "Seligman and the Crimes of the Sympathetic Liberal"—I might only add "Male" to that title (Simmons 2016). Von Trier and Joe seem to discount the equivocation that surrounds the issue of feminism in film, and maybe we should take their words to heart. To quote Linda Badley in her analysis of von Trier's *Antichrist*, "Perhaps as per *Breaking the Waves*, Trier exploits and simultaneously confronts the taboo by unearthing a persistent, half-conscious misogyny that passes without comment in a glib, consumerist "post-feminist" era, exposing it for what it is" (Badley 149).

So what am I doing here, in this space that I believe is irrevocably anti-feminist and anti-queer? The only way to get at the heart of postmodern criticality's failure is to illustrate it. This paper considers the importance of lesbian desire in *Nymphomaniac* as an analytical tool, but I hope also to refute this hypothesis, and in so doing create an example of the paradoxes inherent in postmodern criticism that makes claims about identity politics. In this way, I hope to tentatively illustrate in my own writing Linda Badley's argument that von Trier is engaged in both filmic performance and self-performance as they relate to or complicate the return of the (repressed, battered, and newly earnest) subject in late postmodernism (Badley 16). Though historians of art and film must fervently claim objectivity, each authorial venture—by artists and theorists alike—is a self-archival act. Von Trier's films represent an end point of criticism wherein academic objectivity fails, wherein the intellectual desire to make meaning where there may be none is no longer a political act.

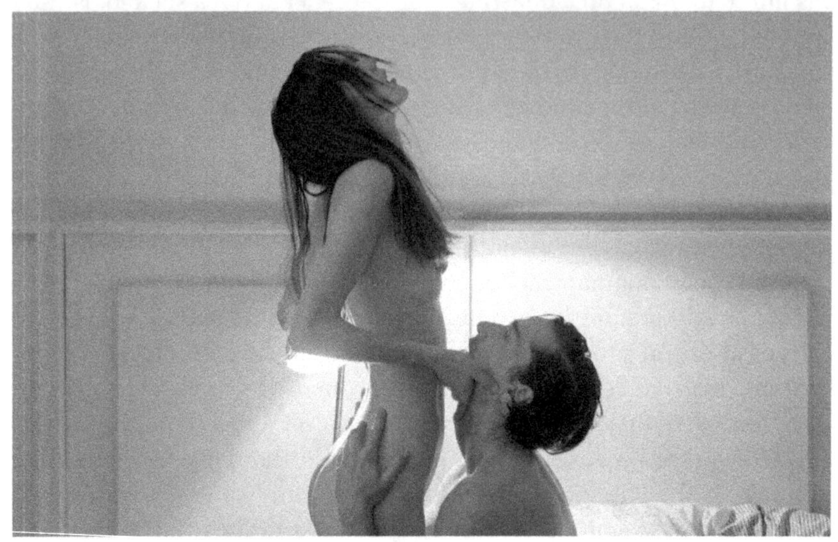

Stacy Martin and Shia LaBeouf in NYMPHOMANIAC: VOLUME I, a Magnolia Pictures release. Photo courtesy of Magnolia Pictures. Photo credit: Christian Geisnaes

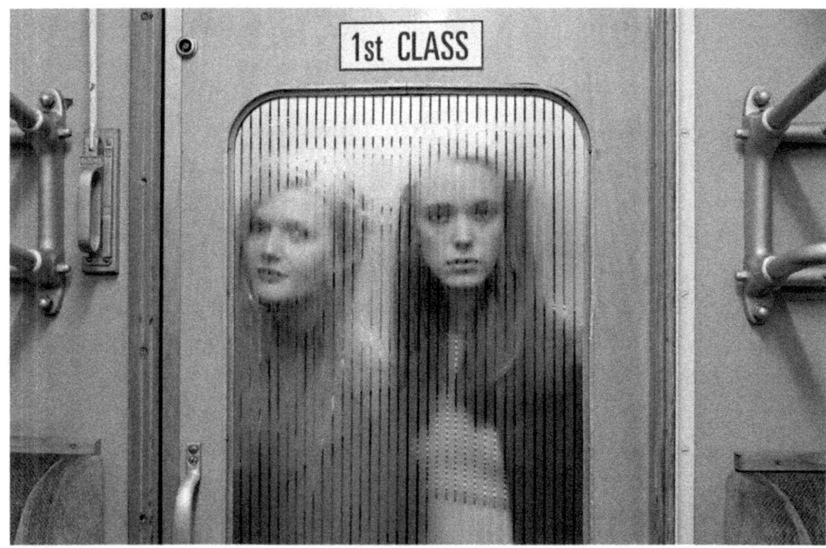

Sophie Kennedy Clark and Stacy Martin in NYMPHOMANIAC: VOLUME I, a Magnolia Pictures release. Photo courtesy of Magnolia Pictures. Photo credit: Christian Geisnaes

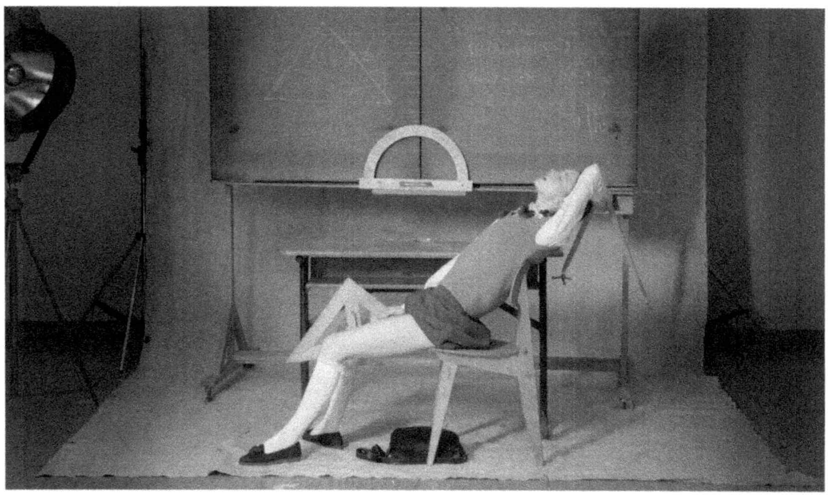

Stacy Martin in NYMPHOMANIAC: VOLUME I, a Magnolia Pictures release. Photo courtesy of Magnolia Pictures. Photo credit: Christian Geisnaes

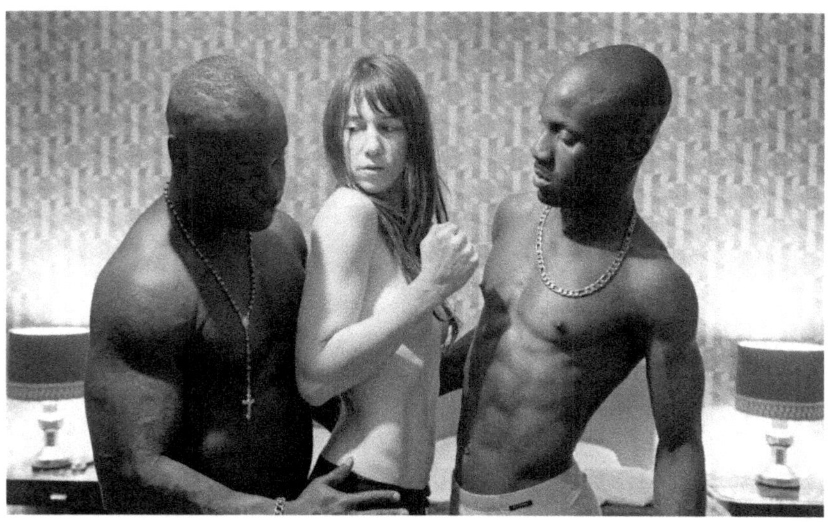

Kookie Ryan, Charlotte Gainsbourg and Papou in NYMPHOMANIAC: VOLUME II, a Magnolia Pictures release. Photo courtesy of Magnolia Pictures. Photo credit: Christian Geisnaes

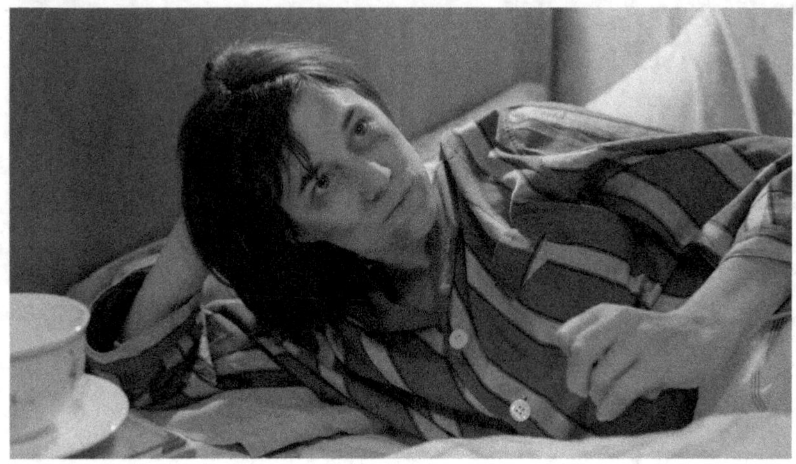

Charlotte Gainsbourg in NYMPHOMANIAC: VOLUME II, a Magnolia Pictures release. Photo courtesy of Magnolia Pictures. Photo credit: Christian Geisnaes

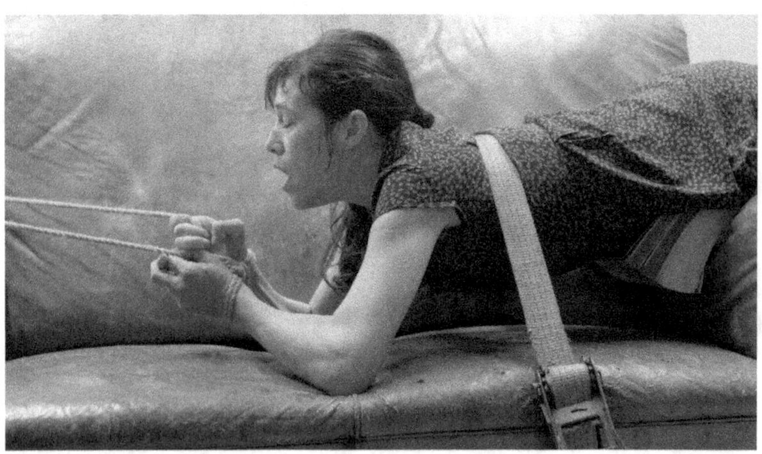

Charlotte Gainsbourg in NYMPHOMANIAC: VOLUME II, a Magnolia Pictures release. Photo courtesy of Magnolia Pictures. Photo credit: Christian Geisnaes

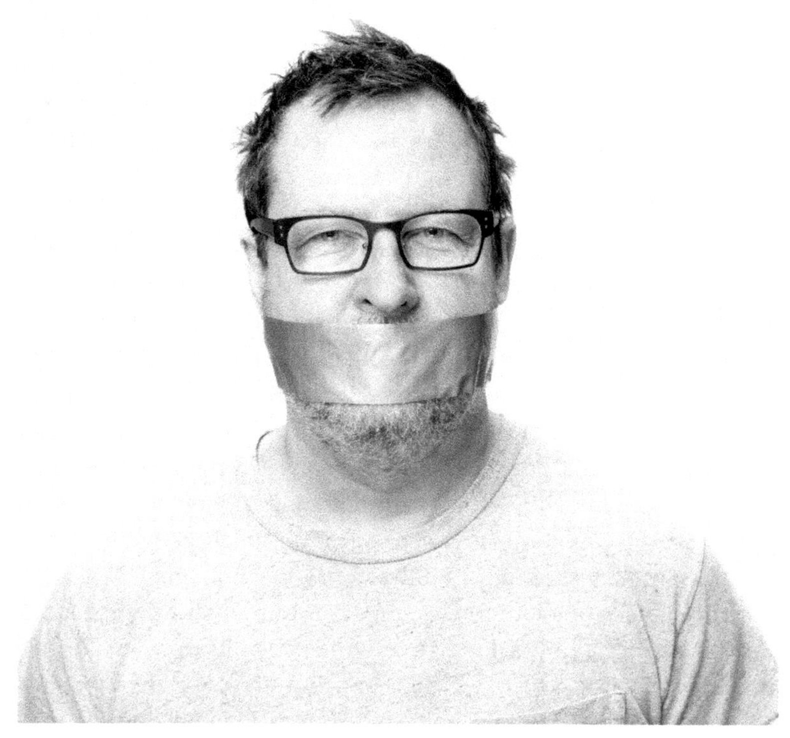

Lars von Trier, director of NYMPHOMANIAC: VOLUME I and VOLUME II, a Magnolia Pictures release. Photo courtesy of Magnolia Pictures

The Absent Queer in *Nymphomaniac*

The turning point in *Nymphomaniac* is, in fact, a lesbian relationship, something that not a single commentator has discussed, and it is here that we might find a progressive von Trier. After Joe finds herself involved with organized crime because of her unique ability to persuade men, her boss L (Willem Dafoe) instructs her to find a protégée. The criteria for her selection are a young woman who has no family, has low self-esteem, and is lonely so that Joe and L can mould her into a loyal partner. Joe comes upon P (Mia Goth) and grooms her by attending P's basketball games and cheering her on, and later professing the beauty of P's deformed ear that causes her to be bullied at school. This, of course, is a deeply troubling and emotionally manipulative arrangement, but the film suggests that this changes over the course of months and years. The relationship slowly turns sexual even as Joe's depression intensifies. In one of the most beautiful scenes in the film, Joe is abed and deeply unwell while P attempts to remove Joe's clothing. P, in what she sees as an act of compassion, implores, "I want to see you," to which Joe replies, "No, I have a wound." P counters, "I have that thing with my ear." She removes Joe's robe, and we see her vulva bruised and scabbed from masturbation and her self-induced abortion.[2] The sex that ensues is tender and illustrates a mutuality of desire; P respects Joe's wishes and finds other pleasurable outlets that leave her battered vulva untouched.

Joe's relationship with P, however, ends in disaster, when P, entirely by chance, becomes involved with the man who took Joe's virginity—the sleazy Jerôme (Shia LeBouf). When Joe and P walk up to an anonymous home in order to collect a debt, Joe realizes it is Jerôme's house and insists that P do the job on her own. This kind of coincidence is frequent in *Nymphomaniac*, which creates a kind of queer time; queerness is, after all, based on the coincidence of missed or consummated encounters among constantly shifting identities. P worries Joe by taking a long time with the collection, and then by returning again and again to Jerôme's house on the pretense of business. Joe discovers in due course that her first lover and her most recent lover, one male and one female, have begun having sex; so overcome with grief is she that she wanders out into the country—the archetypal place where earlier in the film she describes a transcendent childhood orgasm—and gazes upon a windblown and gnarled tree whose base has grown apart into two trunks.

We immediately cut back to Seligman's room and Joe muses, "I understand dictators who commit murder. What was Hitler, when it all boils down, other than a man to whom society gave free reins?" Seligman balks at a response, and Joe continues, "What I mean is—it's said to be difficult to take someone's life. I would assert that it's more difficult not to, when, as the dictator *or as me*, you have nothing to lose. For a human being, killing is the most natural thing in the world. We're created for it" (emphasis mine). Joe finds herself in communion with Hitler—a figure whose boundless atrocities certainly do not have any relationship to anything Joe could even imagine. Still, this comes across not as hyperbole but as sincere self-awareness, a final assertion that (homosexual) love has made her evil.

[2] A full shot of the damage is only shown in the extended version of *Nymphomaniac Volume II*. In the theatrical version it is only alluded to.

Joe then waits for Jerôme and P in the same alleyway where the film began, and as she emerges from behind a wall to shoot them with P's own gun, she pulls the trigger and there is a reverberating click, but nothing happens. Joe puts it away, embarrassed and afraid, and without an exchange of words, Jerôme beats her mercilessly in a cruel and anti-orgasmic rehearsal of her whippings in a dungeon earlier on in the film. BDSM taught Joe to respond to pain with silence, and she does hardly more than sigh as Jerôme kicks her in the ribs and punches her face again and again. P and Jerôme proceed to fuck in front of her, and P stands over Joe and pisses on her. This act of fetish play (urination, also known as 'watersports') is potentially cruel or pleasurable, and though many consider this to be an act of defilement, in the context of this film it might not need to be.[3] As her attackers/lovers leave her to die, Joe whispers, "Fill all my holes, please," a phrase she uttered when she first realized she was in love with Jerôme. In a glorious turn to normative melodrama, it begins to snow, and we are finally at the point where Joe's story and the film's narrative meet. Homosexuality and the loss of same-sex love bring the story full circle.

Would Joe have killed P and Jerôme, or would she have spared her the innocent young woman who had become a friend and sexual companion? Joe assumes that the malfunctioning gun was simply a technical error, but Seligman reminds her that she (and P before her) had forgotten to rack it, which he associates with a subconscious resistance to her murderous impulse. It is at this point that Joe decides her story has concluded and that she is too tired to continue the conversation/ analysis. Before she goes to sleep, Joe begins to weep for the first time. She proclaims that she will "[rid] herself of her sexuality" and "start up against all odds, just like a deformed tree on a hill"—which suggests that her lesbian relationship had finally given her some clarity. As she sleeps, Seligman attempts to rape her. When she awakes to his advance, the screen goes black. Joe grabs her gun, racks it, and Seligman begs with less eroticism than dry reason, "But you've fucked thousands of *men*" (emphasis mine). Joe shoots him, the body thuds, and we hear her run out into the alley.

Seligman's last words privilege heterosexuality, and it is this that finally sets Joe off. Some have interpreted the scene as the death of rational humanism, or the resurgence of the patriarchy, or an example

[3] Amy Simmons, for example, suggests in her essay that, "As a completing gesture, P then sadistically urinates on top of Joe, in what appears to be an attempt to seal Joe's fate."

of Joe's sexual limits (but never, interestingly, as a woman protecting herself against a rapist). What is really at issue here is that Seligman entirely dismisses the same-sex eroticism of Joe's final tale, as have critics and historians. The beauty of Joe's relationship with P goes unnoticed, and she reacts violently, as this is the only part of the story that has not truly been heard or discussed. She shoots Seligman so that we might know that, while she has fucked thousands of men, there was a woman too, and she was different. This interpretation may slide into romanticism, but it nevertheless remains that the full range of Joe's sexual experiences and desires have gone unacknowledged.

The astonishing lack of acknowledgement of this queer moment in *Nymphomaniac* is perplexing. This lacuna might be a result of lesbianism's normalization within a larger set of self-consciously extreme sexualities, so, in this way, critics and historians may not see it as worthy of comment. Still, in an act of unsubtle conservatism, many historians and critics also understand Joe's actions to be deviant, and this mindset, one might assume, would also apply to the "deviance" of lesbianism. Elbeshlawy, for instance, opines, "Joe's ultimate loneliness is stressed by her openness to countless sexual relationships with countless *men* and her view of her own sexual organs as one of those doors with sensors that open at the slightest spur" (193, emphasis mine). Note firstly that the author, as does Seligman at the end of the film, uses "men" instead of "people," despite the obvious presence of a lesbian relationship. Moreover, although Joe herself characterizes her vulva as a door (with more humour than anything), the author nevertheless attributes loneliness that she never claims for herself. Are promiscuous people inherently lonely? Of course not. Who is to say that Joe is ultimately lonely? Might her relationship with P have been satisfying even though it was grotesquely painful? After all, Joe has a period of bliss with someone—but this person is a woman, and she is therefore rendered invisible. Indeed, even the most retrograde critics will not discuss lesbianism, as if to say that its impropriety is too obvious for comment.

Perhaps people have interpolated a homophobic element of the film without realizing it, and this could have perhaps been von Trier's intention. In one of the film's strange asides, Joe notices that both Seligman and Jerôme use a cake fork to eat breakfast pastries, which she considers "unmanly" and "feminine." Seligman then defends his choice by recalling the Bolshevik Revolution and the accoutrements—like cake forks—that were associated with the bourgeoisie. He claims that the cake fork is "at worst, bourgeois." Joe's disgust with a cake fork seems misplaced, but it highlights Seligman's intellectualism as something tacitly queer. Though Seligman describes himself as asexual, the aesthete—whether asexual, queer, or straight—has always been associated with a "queer" relationship to the body. In fact, for much of the modern era, the female nude in painting and sculpture was considered indiscreet for a woman's gaze, but entirely appropriate for the aesthete, whose intellectualism allowed him to have an "asexual" and critical view of the nude body.[4] Joe's diatribe about cake forks is certainly anti-intellectual and anti-bourgeois, but it is also anti-queer. Perhaps those who have attempted to write about *Nymphomaniac* have taken on Joe's homophobia and applied it to the film as a whole.

Given the forcefulness of same-sex discourses in *Nymphomaniac*, I see the absence of queerness in the literature not as a mistake, but as an active dismissal. Imagine if a man who had wanted to fuck Joe had taken her in; the story would be over as soon as it started. Queerness therefore drives the film's plot. The discomfort with Joe's same-sex love is likely an issue with the entirety of film criticism's and art history's disciplinary confines. The suffocating presence of Jacques Lacan in film criticism is one of its greatest pitfalls. The heteronormativity of Lacan has been explicated endlessly elsewhere, and it is more useful to consider the question of lesbianism specifically. Caroline Bainbridge, for instance, in her discussion of *Antonia's Line* (1995) suggests that "desire between women is not easily made visible in narrative cinema" (Bainbridge 53). In Bainbridge's reading of Luce Irigaray, same-sex desire as a form of self-love becomes essential to Woman, since it aids in "establishing the conditions in which alternative feminine subjectivities might emerge" (81). It could be, then, that von Trier has attempted to rectify the occlusion of lesbianism and homosexuality generally from cinema by making them the very foundations of his story at structural and thematic levels.

The Curtain Call of Criticism

It is time to return to the accusations of sexism that have plagued von Trier and take them seriously, as none of the volumes on women in his films deign to do. What can we say with some modicum of conscience

[4] I owe this point to a lecture by James Saslow at the Graduate Center, CUNY in a seminar by Katherine Manthorne on 31 October 2016.

to women who experience films like *Nymphomaniac* and return to their own experiences of sexual violence? What of those women who have had traumatic abortions? What about anti-pornography feminists, who have largely been considered retrograde, but who nevertheless deeply believe, as feminist women, that pornography is degrading? What about Björk and Nicole Kidman, whose discomfort with von Trier caused the former to swear off acting forever and the latter to reject being in a sequel? There is no amount of intellectual effort that can negate these facts of identity politics and women's experiences.

The air of intellectualism that dominates the writing on von Trier does its best to obfuscate feminist, queer, and activist critiques with statements like Elbeshlawy's irresponsible proclamation regarding Joe's foray into BDSM, "The shot in which she experiences her most powerful orgasm under the lashes of the whip is indeed difficult to comprehend without reading all of those books by Lacan, Žižek, and Kafka" (Elbeshlawy 189). This apotheosis of these male and largely anti-feminist writers deliberately privileges the intellectual over the activist, and, tacitly, masculinist criticism over feminist criticism. This is not to say that we should never turn to theory, but to consider theory to be the crux of criticism is a failure on the part of the reclusive academic and the advocate of postmodernism in the visual arts.

However, it could be that my understanding of queerness in *Nymphomaniac* falls into the same traps. Returning to Bainbridge's point about the difficulty of representing lesbianism in narrative cinema, it is painfully true that most instances of same-sex desire in cinema rehearse masculinist fantasies. Notable examples include Roman Polanski's *Bitter Moon* (1992) or Lynch's *Mulholland Dr.* (2001). This is, in fact, true across the visual arts—perhaps most obviously in 18th- and 19th-century Orientalist paintings of harems or contemporaneous bathing scenes. It is entirely possible, then, that the relationship between P and Joe is just another straight man's fantasy projected onscreen, something not meant to empower but to titillate. Even if von Trier wanted to create a realistic and empowering lesbian relationship, it nevertheless does explode into violence, which asserts the primacy of compulsory heterosexuality as the driving force of normative society and filmic romance.

I have thus arrived at a point of disbelief in my own analysis. This is not something that I will attribute to von Trier's genius, because that is an easy way out. We have far too much of the type of criticism that sees ambivalence as avant-garde. What my doubt rather points to is the fundamental disconnect between a postmodern reading of a work of art and the identities with which my analysis and the film itself attempt to contend. This is not a problem with feminist theory. The authors I have noted who bluntly dismiss those who call *Nymphomaniac* sexist might see it this way. It is rather a result of the masculinist assumption that postmodern criticality and feminist theory *necessarily* go hand-in-hand, that the post-structural tropes of self-reflexivity, irony, deconstruction, and performativity are themselves feminist or queer. The problem is, as Sara Ahmed puts it with regard to Craig Owens's foundational texts on postmodernism and feminism, "Here, feminism is defined in terms of—or in the terms of—postmodernism itself" (Ahmed 3). Just because von Trier's films engage in post-structural and postmodern discourses of distancing and pastiche, among other intellectual clichés, does not mean that it is by nature feminist, or that it at its core has anything to do with feminism at all.

All that remains is a discouraging reminder that the language of deconstruction and psychoanalysis championed across the humanities is both essential to and impossibly removed from lived experience. It is the latter that feminism and queer theory has brought to the fore by showing us that affect is as important as intellect. What film studies and art history can do is constantly mine other disciplines for the materials necessary to complicate their inherent assumption that a feminist *explanation* is the same as feminist *critique*. Perhaps most obvious and embarrassing is the concurrent point that a self-aware male (gay or straight) academic is not by nature a feminist academic. Indeed, guilt has never been a viable source for truly generative art histories.

Postscript

I drafted this essay some months before I needed to submit it in its final form, and during that time, as with all things, a multitude of changes occurred. Upon finishing the film for the fourth time, I felt compelled to add a short postscript describing the way my thinking has evolved. Perhaps this particular viewing was different, but it became clear that central to the film, above any optimism I ascribed to it, is a reminder of all that we must exclude from life in order to keep living. Julia Kristeva called this the abject. These are the traumas that both repulse and nourish us. *Nymphomaniac*'s triumph is that it leaves you intimately knowing these traumas; its despair is so complete, so tragic and comical, that one has no choice but to laugh nervously at one's own sentimentality.

There is a reason that Joe denounces this word—*sentimentality*—for it is exactly the postmodern paradigm; a combination of irony, intellectual remove, affect, and the truest emotions humans can feel. It is the former two that have received the most attention, but this is not where the emphasis should be. The conclusion of *Nymphomaniac* kills Seligman and our desire to feel separate from the story. We fall headfirst into the most profound sadness—the knowledge that, as much as we try, we cannot save Joe and we cannot save ourselves. We might find ourselves on the edge of a breakthrough, at the moment where we finally consider ourselves "well," only to be dragged back into the realities of the world; no matter whose fault it is, we hate ourselves for it.

Works Cited

Ahmed, Sara. *Differences That Matter: Feminist Theory and Postmodernism*. Cambridge, UK; New York: Cambridge University Press, 1998.

Badley, Linda. *Lars von Trier*. Urbana, Ill.: University of Illinois Press (Contemporary Film Directors Series), 2011.

Bainbridge, Caroline. *A Feminine Cinematics: Luce Irigaray, Women and Film*. Basingstoke; New York: Palgrave Macmillan, 2008.

Butler, Rex and David Denny, Eds. *Lars von Trier's Women*. New York: Bloomsbury Publishing, 2016.

Elbeshlawy, Ahmed. *Woman in Lars von Trier's Cinema, 1996–2014*. New York: Palgrave Macmillan/Springer International Publishing, 2016.

Fitzgibbon, Coleen and William J. Simmons. "On the Paintings of David Lynch: Masculinity, Melodrama, and the Black Lodge." *BOMB Magazine*. 2 April 2015. https://bombmagazine.org/articles/on-the-paintings-of-david-lynch/

Simmons, Amy. "My Filthy, Dirty Lust: Sex, Agency and Nymphomaniac (Lars Von Trier, 2013)." *Senses of Cinema* 80 (September 2016). http://sensesofcinema.com/2016/feature-articles/nymphomaniac/

Queering Yerevan—Politics of Location: A Feminist Material Analysis of Dis/Orientations and Self-Defined Artistic Labour

ELKE KRASNY

The Queering Yerevan Collective has been active in Yerevan, the capital city of Armenia, since 2007. The collective describe themselves as a "loose network of artists, writers, activists, and cultural critics who use Yerevan as a virtual and experimental space to queer everyday life" (*In and Between the Republic* 157). The three-person core group, around which a fluctuating translocal and diasporic network variously gathers, is based in Yerevan and consists of the two visual artists Arpi Adamyan and lusine talalyan, and the writer-translator Shushan Avagyan. Their artistic practice oscillates between queering and queer, between post-Soviet and diasporic realities, and between performative acts, ephemeral installations, experimenting video works, collective readings, discursive exchanges, and text-based articulations. Their work shifts between unannounced "slant activism" engaging visually and spatially with public space and intimate gatherings allowing for direct exchange with an invited audience ("E-Mails 2007-2011" 242).

This chapter offers an account of the Queering Yerevan Collective with a focus on politics of location in order to articulate their artistic practice through a perspective on the specific historical conditions of Yerevan today as they appear as "orientating" and dis/orientated via their work (see Ahmed 5). Politics of location is a reference to Adrienne Rich's 1984 *Notes toward a Politics of Location* (Rich 210-231). In her essay, she emphasizes the "need to understand how a place on the map is also a place in history in which as a woman, a Jew, a lesbian, a feminist I am created and trying to create" (Rich 212). And, she advises to "begin with the material," to pay attention to "when, where, and under what condition," and to be weary of "abstraction" as it allows "no differences among places, times, cultures, conditions, movements" (Rich 213, 214, 221). Her essay was, of course, written against the backdrop of very different historical conditions, a bipolar Cold War constellation, emerging politics of identity, and increasing tensions between women of colour feminism and white feminism. Today, there is a multipolar, globalized world destabilized by economic and political crises, militant terrorism, and rising xenophobia. And the twenty-first century has turned matters of sexual orientations and LGBTQA issues into a battleground for drawing new ideological lines. At the same time LGBTQA issues inspire mass digital pop cultural expressions and translocally networked activism, including a resurgence of queer, and queer feminist, activism and -ist radical artistic expressions. It is with today's historical conditions in mind that I turn to "how a place on the map is also a place in history" as I consider being mindful of this question highly relevant to an account of queering as collective artistic practice in Yerevan (Rich 212). In theoretical terms, politics of location opens up the move to bring closer together the following two separate strands of theoretical work: feminist art historical materialism and queer phenomenology (Dimitrakaki 2013; Ahmed 2006). The implications of material conditions and the implications of orientations with regard to bodies, space, and time complexly intersect via politics of location. Therefore, politics of location acts as an alert to take into account the given material conditions as they impact on art making, and in particular on dis/orientations expressed via queering, in the local, translocal, and diasporic context of Yerevan. And, queer phenomenology significantly adds to the analysis via politics of location an awareness for orientatedness and dis/orientations as they are expressed in Queering Yerevan's practice through their deep involvement with local urban conditions and their dedication to shaping translocal collectivity.

My account of the collective's artistic practice first introduces their motivations to form a collective and goes on to give a reflection on what their name entails. What follows then is structured around three key locations relevant to their artistic practice: Republican Square in central Yerevan, a private garden at 34 Zarubyan Street in downtown Yerevan, and an e-mail listserv. During New Year's night 2010, the three core members of Queering Yerevan descended into the temporarily dysfunctional water basin at Republican Square and appeared as a 17-minute unannounced public intervention on war, queer sexualities, memory, and time. Over a period of three consecutive summers, starting in 2008 and continuing through 2010, the loose local, translocal, and diasporic Queering Yerevan network turned the garden at 34 Zarubyan into an intimate outdoor art space for installations, happenings, and readings, effectively involving the gathered audience. From 2007 through 2011, a listserv provided a transnational space for expressing the orientations and directions of their forming a collective. E-mail conversations and e-mail debates in English, Armenian, and Russian took place between the local, translocal, and diasporic contributors.

The three examples chosen for my account situate Queering Yerevan's work in three turns relevant to contemporary artistic practice in the twenty-first century: the social turn, the documentary turn, and the archival turn.[1] For this account, I have access to the chosen examples via the documentary and the archival. Their 2010 New Year's act occasioned the following document: a reflective literary non-fiction piece "Traduttore, Traditore: Translating How, Betraying What?" by Shushan Avagyan. Their film *Queering Yerevan's Collective Happenings in the Garden on Zarubyan Street 2008-2010* is a document composed out of video footage shot during the activities that took place in the garden.[2] Under the title "E-Mails 2007-2011", the documents from their listserv were included as an opened-up archive spanning four years of exchanges in their book *Queered: What's to be Done With ^{x}Centric Art*. In addition to the access provided by the documentary and the archival, I was afforded the opportunity to meet with members of the collective in person. I first met with lusine talalyan in the summer of 2012 when I visited Yerevan, and I met the three core members of the Queering Yerevan Collective when they came to visit Vienna. These personal encounters provided the foundation for continuing exchanges via e-mail and Skype.

Forming a Collective

Living as a queer woman in the context of the twenty-first century Yerevan remains challenging. "[F]rom 1936 till 2003 homosexuals were shamed, criminalized and imprisoned on account of Article 116 of the

[1] For social turn, see Bishop 2006; Dimitrakaki 2013; for documentary turn, see: Groys 2004; for archival turn, in particular queer archival turn, see: Cvetkovich 2003; Frantz and Locks 2011.

[2] The idea for this film first originated in conversations between Shushan Avagyan and myself on the occasion of the exhibition Suzanne Lacy's International Dinner Party in Feminist Curatorial Thought I curated at the gallery of Zurich University of the Arts in 2015.

Armenian Criminal Code" ("'Two Years in Correspondence' from the WOW Collective in Armenia"). Despite the fact that the "laws have become more tolerant towards the LGBT community since then . . . non-heteronormativity is still heavily condemned in most strata of Armenian society" ("'Two Years in Correspondence'"). Heteronormative culture and traditions are strongly upheld by lived patriarchy in Armenia. Against this backdrop, personal articulations of everyday queer experiences and expressions of queer orientations via artistic practice are met with strategic ignorance and violent hostility.

In 2007, Nancy Agabian, a bisexual American-Armenian writer, came to Yerevan as a Fulbright Scholar (see Agabian, *nancyagabian*). She gave a writing workshop for local women in Yerevan and encouraged them to "voice women's lives" (Sargsyan-Pitman 16). The experience of expressing "the personal realm of the family, and choice of romantic/sexual/life partners, and issues of the body" led to friendships between women who attended the workshop. Active in the arts, they were inspired by the workshop experience to form a collective for future activities. In 2007, they formed the Women-Oriented Women Collective—WOW—from which the Queering Yerevan Collective emerged.

A year later, in 2008, Armenia officially adopted the UN declaration against discrimination based on sexual orientation. This raised awareness for the rights of sexual minorities and gave rise to the increase of violent anti-queer rhetorics with politicians speaking out publicly against non-heteronormative sexual orientations and declaring them to be pathologies and diseases. Therefore, in January 2009, the WOW Collective authored an "Open Letter Against Intolerance" which they posted on their blog: 'queeringyerevan.blogspot.com' (28 Jan. 2009). The letter was also circulated for petition on PINK Armenia and on Unzipped: Gay Armenia (*pinkarmenia* 29 Jan. 2009; *gayarmenia.blogspot* 2 Feb. 2009). The "Open Letter Against Intolerance" was published simultaneously in English and in Armenian and referred to public anti-gay statements by Republican Party politician Eduard Sharmazanov. It also included the following quote by Karine Danielyan, head of the Sustainable Human Development agency in Armenia: "It's been always considered that 4-5% of humanity has such pathologies . . . these should be regarded as a disease" (28 Jan. 2009). The WOW Collective revealed the "violent rhetoric" that put at risk "the safety and well-being" of sexual minorities in Armenia (ibid.). In their *Open Letter Against Intolerance* the collective revealed the structural violence rooted in strategic ignorance as expressed via both mainstream and oppositional media alike and the cruel hostility voiced by individual politicians as their statements assume the guise of official state policy, rather than being perceived as what they are, individual beliefs held toward sexual orientation.

In her work on sexual orientation Sara Ahmed has argued that "the idea of 'sexual orientation' does not position the figures of the homosexual and heterosexual in a relation of equivalence. Rather, it is the homosexual who is constituted as having an 'orientation': the heterosexual would be proclaimed neutral" (69). Sexual orientation leads to "how one is placed" (ibid.). The public statements by Armenian politicians use sexual orientation in order to place sexual minorities as aberrant and deviant in relation to heteronormativity which is presented as "in line" with the public interest of the nation state (Ahmed 53). The hostile rhetoric is employed by Armenian politicians to rectify and even promote expressions of everyday violence against sexual minorities.

Within the discrimination against the sexual orientations of sexual minorities, there is a difference to be made out with regard to how male homosexuality and female homosexuality are considered. "[M]ale homosexuality in Armenia has been consistently described as a threat to national security, a result of accepting European decadent values or a pathology and disease, while homosexual women have been denied of existence altogether or condemned in not fitting into the image of a 'proper' Armenian woman" ("Open Letter Against Intolerance"). While male homosexuality is considered a national security threat, female homosexuality is rendered inexistent through silencing. These were the prevailing conditions under which the WOW Collective sought to collectivize personal experiences and to make lived and artistic female queer experiences visible, effectively counteracting queer women's dual oppression via "non-heteronormativity . . . predominantly associated with men" and "the burdens of women's traditional roles of marriage and motherhood" ("'Two Years in Correspondence'"). The group's orientation was informed by queer artists and intellectuals in Yerevan and from the Armenian diaspora as well as by women and feminist allies, both locally and from the transnational Armenian migrant community. The group's formation was motivated by the personal experiences of silenced queer orientations including their expressions in visual art and literature, and by the politically promoted violent homophobic oppression of queer sexualities.

What's in a Name?

"If you see us in the street we will not respond to being called WOW (Women-Oriented Women) any more" ("An Obituary to WOW"). With the publication of "An Obituary to WOW" they renounced their previous name and moved on to adopting their new name of Queering Yerevan Collective. It evolved from discussions between Melissa Boyajian, Arpi Adamyan, and Shushan Avagyan (Avagyan in an e-mail to the author, Oct. 1 2016). In 2010, Melissa Boyajian, a Boston-based American-Armenian artist, came to Yerevan to work with the WOW Collective. Melissa, Arpi and Shushan met in Arpi Adamyan's house to discuss a series of happenings they were planning for the summer. They decided to use Queering Translation as the umbrella title for their summer happenings. While Boyajian was more interested in the critical legacies and potentials to be found in the concept of "queer", Avagyan envisioned their collective as "doers" (ibid.). Also, Arpi Adamyan remembers that they took seriously Melissa Boyajian's criticism of the collective's name WOW. Melissa "viewed the notion of 'women-oriented women' as obsolete and limiting and suggested to rename the group" ("E-Mails 2007-2011 29). Following these discussions, they decided to renounce their old name Women-Oriented Women Collective, and "idea of 'doing' i.e. queering" was adopted as the central concept for choosing the collective's new name of Queering Yerevan (Avagyan in an e-mail to the author, Oct. 1 2016). This can also be understood as the intent of orientating queer via localizing it from a Yerevan perspective in order to differentiate it from previously established globalized Western concepts of queer. By queering queer from a politics of location in Yerevan, the collective joins other appropriations as witnessed in "cuir (in Spanish), kirik (in Turkish), kvar (in Serbian-Croatian) or kuir in Portuguese" (Schwärzler n.p.). They appropriated the existing Armenian adjective *tarorinak* which means strange or odd to extend it to queer including the reference to sexual orientations which *tarorinak* previously did not include in its meaning. From this adjective they derived a new Armenian verb for queering: *tarorinakel*. The Queering Yerevan Collective references queer traditions of translation and appropriation. At the same time it insists on defamiliarizing queer, thus resisting an import of visualities, aesthetic strategies, and concepts formed in Western art and theory. Their claim is that they in fact "de-queer the term" in order to fully engage with its "'estranging properties" (*In and Between the Republic* 25).

Yerevan is the direct object in the collective's name. Queering is directed at Yerevan. To direct means to turn in a particular direction. In her 2006 *Queer Phenonmenology. Orientations, Objects, Others*, Sara Ahmed has shown that direction is never casual:

> the body gets directed in some ways more than others. We might be used to thinking of direction as simply which way we turn. . . . Direction then would be a rather casual matter. But what if direction, as the way we face as well as move, is organized rather than casual? We might speak then of collective direction: of ways in which nations or other imagined communities might be 'going in a certain direction.' (Ahmed 15)

Queering Yerevan is very much a critical response to the lived and felt everyday urban experience that bodies are powerfully directed via heteronormativity. The oppressive traditions and normative conventions of lived patriarchy are strongly felt "in place" in Yerevan (Ahmed 11). As "bodies out of place" the Queering Yerevan Collective direct their actions at Yerevan and artistically exercise their right to be in place or out of place (37). Taking such directions other than toward the expected conformity with patriarchal gender norms remains challenging and might even provoke physical violence. On May 8, 2012, the gay-friendly DIY Club was firebombed and a week later "swastikas were sprayed on the bar's walls" ("Gay rights under attack in Armenia").

On May 21 the same year a demonstration held to celebrate the World Day of Cultural Diversity including "refugees and ethnic minorities as well as homosexuals" was met by opponents with an "'anti-parade'" leading to "skirmishes between the two groups" ("Gay rights under attack in Armenia"). Therefore, taking up dis/orientation and estranging directions in public, as the Queering Yerevan Collective does, is an act of artistic, and, by extension, political insistence that doing so is in fact not only possible but part of claiming their "right to the city" of Yerevan (Lefebvre).

Yerevan, the direct object of the collective's queering, needs more contextualization here. In what follows, I provide contextualizations to Yerevan's profound urban transformation resulting from oligarchic neoliberal capitalism, to Yerevan as a diasporic location, and finally to Yerevan as a location providing only scarce infrastructure for contemporary art. Yerevan's urban space as well as the city's memoryscape has changed dramatically in the twenty-first century. Deep urban transformation has taken place owing to the transition from Soviet communism into post-Soviet authoritarian oligarchic capitalism based in neoliberal economic policies. "Armenia, together with the other former Soviet republics and former socialist countries in Eastern Europe, was the site of neoliberal 'shock therapy' policies" (Ishkanian). Following the notion of "actually existing neoliberalism" as it orients how urban space assumes spatial form resulting increased social injustice and highly uneven access to space, we have to conceive of 'actually existing authoritarian oligarchic neoliberalism' and its impact on Yerevan's urban transformation since the dissolution of the Soviet Union (Brenner and Theodore 351). New constructions reorienting urban space include the Shangri La Yerevan Casino, the Harsnaqar Restaurant complex, the Elite Plaza, and thousands of empty apartments in so-called elite buildings or elite complexes. It is against the backdrop of such deep transformation in Yerevan with more and more space corrupted and made vulnerable that the Queering Yerevan Collective is active in the city.

Yerevan is a profoundly diasporic location marked by the historic trauma of the Armenian Genocide between 1915 and 1923. Today, "around 8-10 million people of Armenian descent [are] currently living outside Armenia (whose own population is currently estimated at around 2.9 million)" (Foreign and Commonwealth Office). While travel for Armenians remains restricted, with visas required in 80 countries around the world, Armenia became accessible for travel to the worldwide Armenian diaspora after the USSR came to an end. The formation of the Queering Yerevan Collective has to be located within these newly emerging links between members of the Armenian diaspora who express an interest in their country of origin from which they might have been separated for over four to five generations and might never have been to. Nancy Agabian, who was instrumental to the collective's formation, offers an example for this in her writing. "When the Soviet Union finally broke open, my friends and family trekked back to the homeland, returning on the emotional power of being in a place where your appearance and Armenianness was, for once, not unusual" (Agabian 149). Artists and intellectuals who are part of the queer diaspora within the Armenian diaspora were also particularly interested in connecting with locally lived queer experience in Armenia. Another example for such an interest can be found in the work of Melissa Boyajian, who crucially contributed to the collective's new name. Boyajian had come to Armenia in 2003 and then again in 2007 in order to do "video interviews of queer people in Yerevan who were willing to interview" (*Queered* 12). With regard to a politics of location and its orientations, the artistic practice of Queering Yerevan has to be as much understood in terms of localizing as in terms of diasporizing and in the complex dis/orientations resulting from a collective practice of joining together diasporizing and localizing.

The artmaking practiced by Queering Yerevan is solely self-supported and self-organized, and can therefore be understood as self-defined. This also has to be understood against the backdrop of very scarce additional infrastructure available for contemporary art. "Challenges for Art in Armenia" published online by Karine Aghajanyan in January 2015 points out some of the key problems. There are few galleries and hardly any public funding available. Apart from the Armenian Center for Contemporary Experimental Art which depends on EU money, international funds, and diaspora money, there are very few galleries. Yerevan-based curator Eva Khachatryan was interviewed on the occasion of this article. She diagnoses two main problems. Firstly she emphasizes the lack of paid work for artists. "The main problem for the contemporary artist is unemployment, because most of the artists will starve to death if they only choose to work as artists" (Aghajanyan). Secondly, she highlights how the lack of exhibition space leads to accepting any offer of showing one's work without distinguishing the context a given exhibition space represents (Aghajanyan). Lack of work and lack of exhibition space therefore define the conditions for artists in the local context of Yerevan. It is under these dire material conditions that Queering Yerevan developed their self-defined way of working. They formed a self-organized trans/local collective and chose to locate their work in the urbanscape and memoryscape of Yerevan without making use of its official public art infrastructure. This can also be understood as a rejection of the representational violence of traditional and patriarchal values expressed by official public institutions such as the National Gallery of Armenia or the Modern Art Museum of Yerevan. Apart from making use of Yerevan's urban space, Queering Yerevan locate their work in technologically enabled infrastructure such as a listserv, which they used from 2007 and 2011, and a blog that has been running continuously since 2007. Their blog (queeringyerevan. blogspot) communicates within their wider translocal network and provides outreach to the global art community that shares an interest in critical queer artistic practice in the post-Soviet and diasporic context of Yerevan.

Locating Queering in Yerevan

Queering as an artistic practice takes into account the societal, economic, and political conditions shaping twenty-first century Yerevan. Yet it does so in estranging and oblique ways adopting the form of slant and disorienting acts. Such involvement with Yerevan's urban space and with each other as a collective places queering firmly in the "social turn in art evident around 2000" which is characterized by "a new emphasis on collaborative artistic practice" and "a critical engagement with real life" (Dimitrakaki 5). Making use of spaces outside the designated art infrastructure of public institutions or galleries, their queering is at once urban intervention, experimental visual culture, and body-based performance art.

With regard to the two urban locations chosen for the account here—their act on Republic Square and their work in the garden at Zarubyan Street—there is a significant distinction to be made. While their New Year's act titled *Let there be im(war)ge* took place from within the dysfunctional inner workings of public space to be encountered by an accidental public and, even if obliquely, pointed out their demand for historical art by women, feminists, lesbians, and queers to be included in hegemonic public institutions such as the Museum of History or the National Gallery, their garden happenings with their experimental exhibition installations and collective readings form part of a history of sharing artistic practice on a much more intimate scale with an invited and involved audience in private or semi-private space. The garden belonged to the house rented jointly by tupiana and the Women's Resource Center. While it was not really a private garden as it was accessible to everyone who visited either of these two organizations, it was not a public space in the above sense of nation-/state-run museums or galleries. Therefore, the garden happenings have to be located in the emerging infrastructure of spaces established by civic society and NGOs characteristic to the period of post-Socialist transition in the territory of the former USSR and Eastern Europe.

On the one hand they raise awareness of the fact that art outside the hegemonic canon constitutive to the national memoryscapes in public space or museum institutions based upon representational violence and its gendered division of recognition discriminating against art made by women, feminists, and sexual minorities needs to be recognized. On the other hand, they protect their own work from the potential capture via national institutions or international funding agencies since they do not want to be turned into anyone's "ideological tokens" ("E-Mails 2007-2011" 204). lusine talalyan, one of the three core members, emphasizes that "we did everything through our own means and abilities" (ibid.). She expresses the fear that financial support via international organizations might turn the collective into "an instrument" providing the funders to present "themselves as advocates of progressivism" (ibid.). This presents the risk of "glamorizing and normalizing what is queer" (ibid.). Therefore, they take upon themselves the work of self-organization and self-funding to create a measure of protection shielding their artistic work of queering of the above-described mechanisms of capture via legitimization and normalization. The collective's work, protected from both the representational violence of official national culture and the normalizing effects of celebratory international art world progressivism, thrives in self-organized spaces involved with human rights, cultural activism, civic society, and the lived socio-economic conditions.

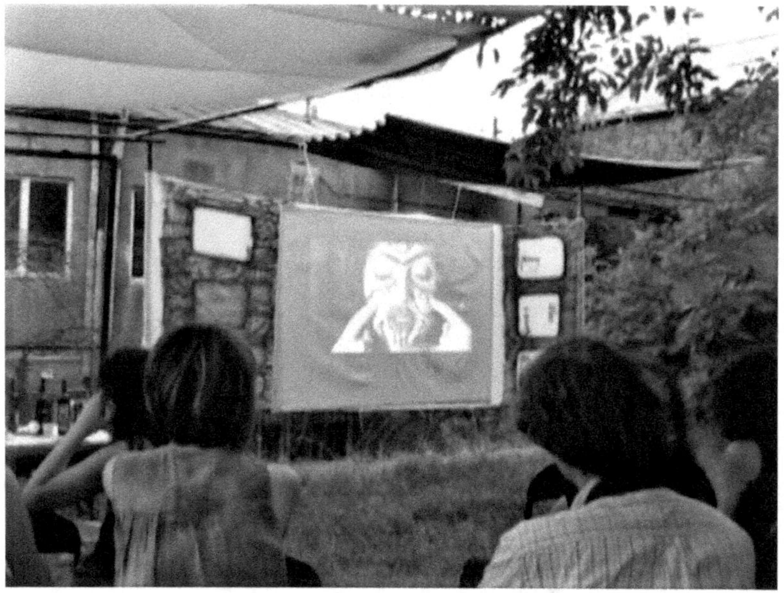

Film still from Queering Yerevan's Collective Happenings in the Garden on Zarubyan Street 2008-2010, 2015. Copyright: Queering Yerevan Collective.

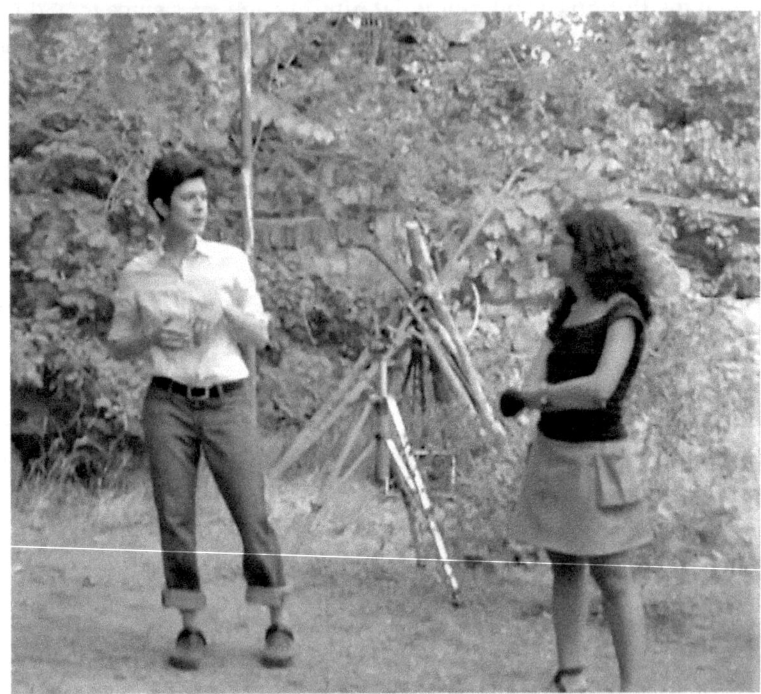

Film still from Queering Yerevan's Collective Happenings in the Garden on Zarubyan Street 2008-2010, 2015. Copyright: Queering Yerevan Collective.

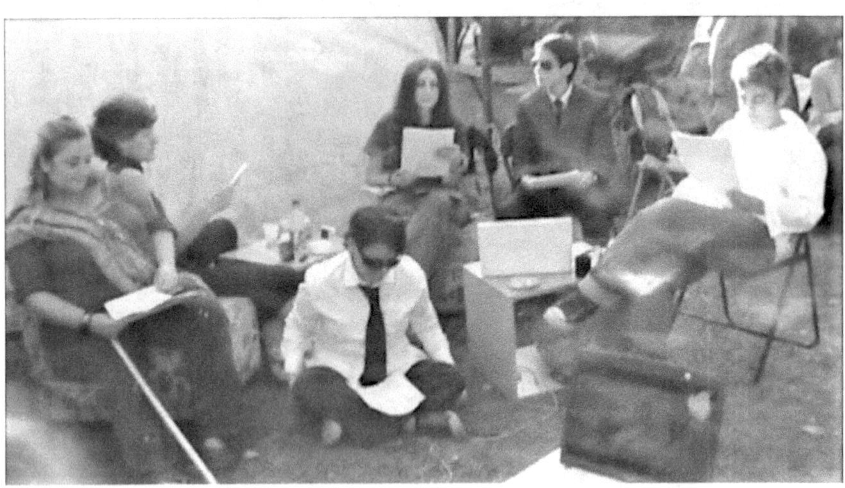

Film still from Queering Yerevan's Collective Happenings in the Garden on Zarubyan Street 2008-2010, 2015. Copyright: Queering Yerevan Collective.

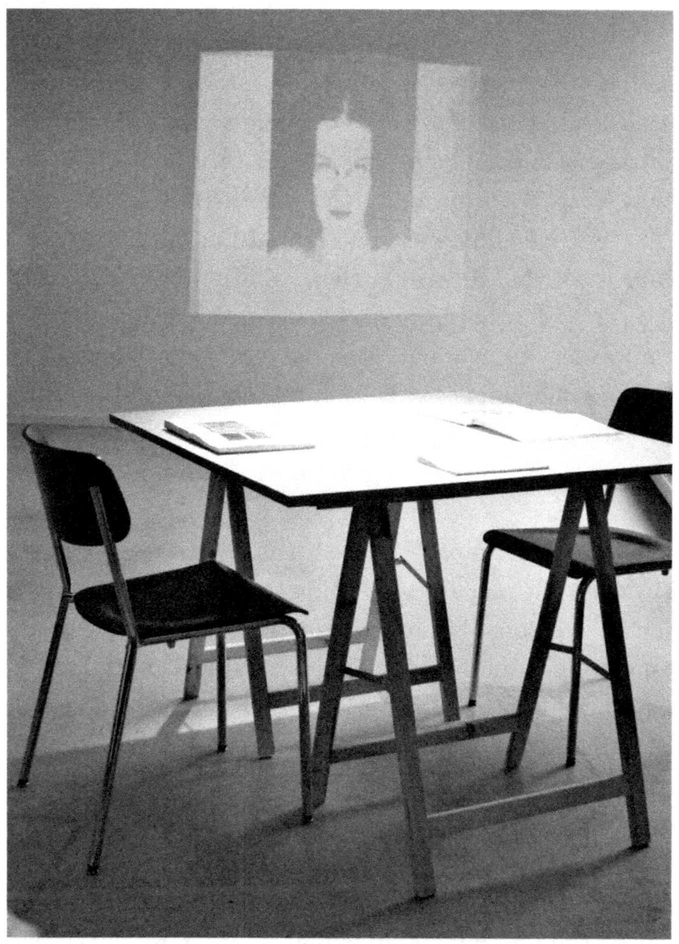

Queering Yerevan Collective, Installation View from the exhibition Suzanne Lacy's International Dinner Party in Feminist Curatorial Thought, curated by Elke Krasny, ZHdK Zurich University of the Arts, 2015. Photograph: Alexander Schuh.

Dis/Orientating Republic Square

"[O]n January 1, 2010, at 2:11 am" Arpi Adamyan, lusine talalyan, and Shushan Avagyan descended into the fountain basin of the monumental water fountain on Republic Square (*Queered* 55). With the

New Year's celebration going on at this early hour, the square "is still overcrowded with mostly young people celebrating" (Avagyan 57). Place and time are chosen with great care. Queering Yerevan, in a highly symbolic tactical move, chose to perform unannounced and uninvited at Yerevan's most prestigious public square marking the beginning of the New Year. They directed their queering act at the square, dis/orientating its hegemonic meaning, and at the same time, estranging its popular use. What follows is an account of their performative act mindful to the politics of location represented via Republican Square. My account places the act in its material location and traces it through the literary non-fiction piece "Traduttore, Traditore, Translating How, Betraying What?" by Shushan Avagyan. Her text presents the ephemeral act's lasting document. Queering Yerevan approaches documentation from an oblique angle. Conventionally, one expects performative acts to be captured via photographs or films in the context of performative and visual arts. Here, the document is not based primarily on visual media, even though two small photographs are included in the text, but on translating the embodied experience of spatiality and visuality into text. This is not owed to an artistic decision refusing visual documentation but much rather to the violent politics of location in this central public square in Yerevan. Shushan Avagyan explains that they "don't have many photographs from this act. The person who was there to take photographs was attacked by a group of young men and she was not able to take proper photographs" (Avagyan in an e-mail to the author, Oct. 6 2016). The few photographs that do exist are dark. "You can't really see anything" (ibid.). The documentary move that occurs here is that the "text replaces the images" (ibid.). The text also provides insights into their theoretical inspiration via Viktor Shklovsky's concept of *ostranenie* (defamiliarization), and the intentions motivating their choice of location. And it even includes the accidental public's reactions (Avagyan 54-61).

Republic Square needs further contextualization here. The centrally located Republic Square, previously named Lenin Square, is a lens through which the complexities of changing regimes in Armenia's political history are publicly magnified. Designed by neo-classical architect Alexander Tamanian, the square was included in the architect's 1924 general plan for the modern city of Yerevan and was to form the key part for Yerevan's move toward urban modernization. The "panopticon-like" square is surrounded by a host of buildings representing power, including the Government House, the History Museum, the Ministry of Finance, the Ministry of Foreign Affairs, and the National Gallery of Armenia (Avagyan 57). It occupies a central position in Yerevan's urban memoryscape as it was host to significant public manifestations characteristic of the different political and economic regimes governing twentieth and twenty-first century Armenia. During the Soviet period, Lenin Square provided the official stage for the spectacle of official power display with military parades taking place several times per year. From 1940 to 1991, a monumental Lenin statue was located in the southwestern corner of the square. The statue's pedestal doubled as a podium. During the Soviet period it was used "for Party leaders to address the nation" (Avagyan 56). After Armenia's declaration of independence from the Soviet Union in September 1991 and after the dissolution of the USSR in December of the same year, Lenin Square was renamed Republic Square. The square adopted a new meaning and was used for public civic action as "a site for protests and demonstrations against the political regime" (Avagyan 56). This remained a brief interlude in the square's uses. It was soon returned to its officially sanctioned representational functions, and today also serves as a major tourist attraction. "By the late 2000s, the Republic Square was reclaimed by the new government for holding its military parades" (*Queered* 56). In 2007, the water fountains were reopened after repair work and have now been incorporated into the urbanscape as it is reorientated toward tourism. Touristification is very much part of neoliberal urbanization processes. Therefore, Republic Square centrally embodies the changing regimes of politics, power, ideologies, and economies.

On New Year's Eve 2010, the "temporarily dysfunctional fountain in the Republic Square" made it possible for Queering Yerevan to use this prominent location for their 17-minute long act that addressed issues of time, memory, war, and sexuality. The fountain is located in front of the National Gallery and was built in 1953 by the architects Mark Grigoryan and Eduard Sarapyan. Queering Yerevan titled their performance "Togh lini pat(k)erazm [Let there be im(war)ge]" (Avagyan 55). Following Shklovsky's concept of defamiliarization, they relied on disorientation. With the fountain out of order and the water jets temporarily turned off, the circular water basin provides the ground for Queering Yerevan's performance.

At 2:11 a.m., the three artists slip into the basin. They render the inaccessible accessible.[3] They are in a highly controlled space. Police officers constantly patrol the space seeking to ensure that no trespassing takes place. The collective disorient time. They make use of estranging weapons. They perform a public reading that is silenced through the surrounding New Year's din. "Moving freely in the demarcated space of the basin and swinging a large yellow yarn ball filled with paper like a pendulum, Arpi Adamyan performs a movement that imitates the motion of timekeeping" (Avagyan 56). As Adamyan swings in the New Year, time no longer appears as a "straight line" toward the future (Ahmed 172). Much rather, time erupts via the "the irregular movement that often breaks from the oscillating back and forth pattern" (Avagyan 58). The strange and quirky movements of this pendulum time present a rupture of time conceived of as familial lineage guaranteed by "reproductive temporality" (Halberstam 4). Time appears from an oblique angle. The pendulum also serves to symbolize a "demolition weapon" aimed at the Museum of History and the National Gallery to attack their gatekeeper function of constructing and presenting tamed time rendered as official, exclusionary and hegemonic narrative of national art (history) and national history (Avagyan 58). Shushan Avagyan is "partially in drag with painted-on moustache, brandishing a blue dildo . . . and 'shooting' passersby" (Avagyan 59). Mimicking to shoot passersby, the dildo-weapon is defamiliarizing and disorienting (ibid.). As she reads a passage contemplating "mechanisms that automatize and disindivualize power" from her then unfinished novel *Zarubyan's Women in Armenia*, her voice is silenced by the surrounding

[3] Their act set a precedent that was followed by further acts of female bodies expressing resistance in public. On the occasion of this text, Shushan Avagyan shared the following information with me: "In May 2016 human rights activist Armine Arakelyan entered the same basin, this time with water in it. She sat there for a few minutes after which she was tackled and taken to a psychiatric hospital" (Avagyan, e-mail to the author, Oct. 6, 2016; http://www.epress.am/en/2016/06/03/human-rights-activist-alleges-torture-and-harassment-at-yerevan-psychiatric-clinic.html). A week later, Armine Arakelyan was commemorated in the same space by feminist activists who "repeated the same performance to question the actions of the police" (Avagyan in an e-mail to the author, Oct.6 2016; http://www.epress.am/en/2016/05/24/armenian-police-threaten-to-throw-citizens-into-psychiatric-wards-silent-action-in-central-yerevan.html). The fountain's water basin has now become a location for the repeated practice of such acts that make queering and its claim of queer feminist and feminist bodies to express their right to this hegemonic public space. The water basin is therefore both a location of performative commemoration and the expression of claims enacting the right of queering artists, feminists, and human rights activists to express their right to be present in public.

sounds of music, laughter, fireworks. While these activities go on, lusine talalyan lies on the ground. Her body is placed on a "keffiyeh" similar to the one worn by Yasser Arafat. She performs a silent ritual commemorating "the lives of Palestinian wo/men" (Avagyan 60). Toward the end of their 17-minute act, they are spotted by "a group of young men" (Avagyan 61). This incidental audience sees their "placard with the title 'Let there be im(war)ge" (ibid.). Yet, the young men immediately choose to reorient the disorientation. Instead of reading what is actually written on the placard, they read out loud "Let there be war" and immediately reestablish the militarized public sentiment in line with the then recent clashes at the Armenian-Azerbaijani border in August 2010 (ibid.). Queering Yerevan's disorienting words are straightened out and returned to the normalized conventions of "masculinity, national and military pride" (ibid.). Celebrating their New Year in the dysfunctional water basin they subversively make use of the material brokenness which they redirect to become legible as broken up histories, distorted lineages, and even the opening up toward different futures, including queering futures, on the ground in Yerevan. They perform what it means to be silenced. They perform what it means to expose oneself, to be seen as a body lying down on the ground, which could easily be misread as passively lying down as opposed to actively standing up. Moments of disorientating estrangement have taken place in Republic Square and are now inscribed in the square's memoryscape.

A Garden of Our Own at 34 Zarubyan Street

Queering Yerevan Collective's Happenings in the Garden on Zarubyan Street 2008-2010—bold white letters on black ground announce the title of this film entirely composed out of documentary video footage shot during three summers of exhibitions, readings, performances, and conversations held at the garden at 34 Zarubyan Street. In the opening sequence the camera hesitantly descends a staircase and leads into the garden. The vegetation is lush. Fig trees with their bent and twisted tree trunks fill the entire garden. Their branches reach over corrugated iron sheets, indication of informal building activities and structures added on incrementally over time. We see an artist at work. Astgik Melkonyan places a white cut-out silhouette on the ground. Then she folds the silhouette in half and picks it up again. The outline will soon be filled in with flour. Trees have been appropriated to hang art. The photo series

Fragmented Self by Adrineh Der-Boghossian dangles from branches, partially covered behind fig tree leaves. It is not easy to distinguish the invited audience from the contributing artists. They all mingle in the garden. They engage in conversation with each other. Some of them have gathered around a table and carefully open up books that had been placed on the table top. The leaves rustle. Wind chimes hung in the trees sound. Then the opening speech begins. Two women stand next to each other, Shushan Avagyan and Angela Harutunyan. In the background behind them there is a wall made out of stones piled up on top of each other. Before that wall, separating the garden from the neighbour's garden, there stands a tripod made out of freshly cut wooden poles bound together at the top. It provokes disorienting references. It resembles a haystack in the form of a wooden tripod used to keep the hay off the ground and let it dry better and a tipi used by indigenous populations in the Plains. Yet, here in the garden the wooden tripod marks a designated zone of display, a seemingly robust, yet quite fragile installation to shelter a laptop on which Oga Tsomak's video *Untitled* is screened. The disorientations are multiplied. Before this archaic wooden tripod that shelters a laptop, there is another tripod made out of aluminium. It holds a digital camera that almost entirely blocks the view of the video on the laptop. And, the angle at which the digital camera films behind the two speakers is clearly different from the footage used for what is now the beginning of the film *Queering Yerevan Collective's Happenings in the Garden on Zarubyan Street 2008-2010.* The opening speech alternates between English and Armenian. Both of them speak English. Both of them speak Armenian. The first one begins in Armenian and the second one translates into English. Then the second one continues in English and the first one translates into Armenian. There are moments of slippage in their opening speech. In a more subdued voice they explain to each other in front of the listening audience which direction their explanations will take and in which order they will continue to present the artists' contributions gathered together and installed throughout the garden. There is another visual slippage. While they speak about the works, while they stress presences and absences, the camera makes no effort to connect their words with the works that are actually present in the garden. The works remain invisible, they are made known via words. The opening speech also tells about the beginnings of the collective. Mention is made of issues of homosexuality, bisexuality, queer identity. My close reading of the opening minutes of the one hour and a half long video documentation serves to emphasize here the spatial and visual disorientations that occur when art installations, performances, and collective readings leave behind the normalizing art settings of twentieth-century white cubes or nineteenth-century museum galleries.

The location of *Queering Yerevan Collective's Happenings in the Garden on Zarubyan Street* needs contextualization. I will first locate the garden as part of the feminist women-specific and self-organized cultural infrastructure maintained by two different NGOs in Yerevan and then locate the garden in the history of self-organized and self-supported private spaces used for sharing art intimately with an invited audience.

The garden at 34 Zarubyan Street in downtown Yerevan was behind the house in which both the Women's Resource Center and the Utopiana Cultural Center had their spaces at the time. Though different in their goals, with one dedicated to women's rights and women's empowerment and the other on working against local artists' isolation and toward a different use of public space, they can both be considered translocal spaces in Yerevan dedicated to working on local concerns and part of the diasporic reach of transnational networks. Equally, they share an interest in civic and public engagement. Founded in 2003 by local women in Armenia and by women from the Armenian diaspora, the "Women's Resource Center is a feminist organisation working with and for women" (*humanrightshouse*). The Center belongs to the Human Rights House Network that is active in the Caucasus and eastern region of Europe, in the western Balkans, and in Western Europe. They are the "first resource centre created in the post-Soviet Armenia for young women, working in the area of women's human rights, reproductive and sexual rights, sexual violence and women's role in conflict resolution and peace building" (*humanrightshouse*). They are based upon democratic and participatory principles, run and governed by women, and seek to create safe environments for women. The Utopiana association was founded in 2001 by Anna Barseghian together with Stefan Kristensen, Isabelle Papaloïzos and the group Plantopic. Originally based in Geneva, Switzerland, and with artist and cultural activist Anna Barseghian involved in Yerevan, a sister organization under the same name was subsequently created in Yerevan as of 2003. "Utopiana aims to eliminate the isolation of the local scene and of local processes related to culture and civic/public thinking" (Pinther et al 109). Together, the two NGOs made it possible for the Queering Yerevan Collective to use their garden as a space to be opened up for sharing art with invited audience. There were close relations of collaboration between the Queering Yerevan Collective and the two NGOs. The founding members of the initial

WOW group worked for Utopiana. Sushan Avagyan was a founding member of the Women's Resource Center. Therefore, the members of the Queering Yerevan Collective knew very well the organizational structures of NGOs. Given this shared experience and knowledge of NGO culture, the collective desired both an unstructured organization and an unstructured space for their happenings. They desired "a garden/room of our own" and therefore located themselves in the history of the feminist claim to a room of one's own as expressed by Virginia Woolf (Avagyan in an e-mail to the author, Oct. 6 2016). At the same time they went beyond activating this claim and collectivized it. They turned the legacy of a room of one's own into a garden of our own.

The garden presented itself as an excellent space for such orientation, neither entirely public, nor entirely private. The garden was not the working space proper of the two NGOs, yet shared by them and made accessible and available through them. The garden was transformed into a temporary art space for installing photographs, video works, paintings, ephemeral sculptures and for staging performances, readings, and discursive events. Queering Yerevan thus created a space of their own for the viewing, sharing, and discussing of the art created by the collective. In art-world terms the space was estranging and disorienting, with large green fig leaves touching photographs, a laptop resting on patches of dried grass, wind chimes muting some of the opening speech, and a small cat nibbling on leftover corn on the cob served on the occasion of the opening. The collective demonstrated here that it was important to them to share their happenings on their own terms. They created their own temporary space, protected from the normalizing effects and legitimizing tokenism of state institutions dedicated to the representation of art and international funding bodies promoting cultural and civic progressivism.

With the garden Queering Yerevan created an intimately scaled space for exchanges between art, audience, and artists. The exhibitions installed in the garden and the readings performed collectively therefore differ radically from representations of art in designated public art institutions. In historical terms, as I want to suggest here, Queering Yerevan's garden can be located as part of a genealogy of two very different strands of sharing art(making) in private space with a group of invited guests or friends: firstly the women-led and lesbian-led nineteenth and early twentieth century Europe wide salon culture and secondly the late twentieth century avant-garde underground apartment exhibitions in the USSR and Eastern Europe. With their choice of the garden as an intimately-scaled space, Queering Yerevan manages to insert a space that slightly disorients the previous history of using the private space of homes, houses, and apartments for sharing art. The garden offers less of a protection for art works, yet affords more disorientating encounters with art. The Queering Yerevan Collective use the garden to gather together fragile, technology-dependent, screen-enabled, and ephemeral art works, installations, and acts. Invited guests have to move with great care. They are involved with the art works, be they installed or performative, closely and intimately. They need to watch out carefully. They look sideways. They look down onto the ground. They look up into the trees. They need to find out what is there to be seen. They have to orient themselves so as to avoid stepping on installations placed next to their feet. The garden is anything but a controlled environment. It is home to plants, animals, humans, and art works alike. It is exposed to the weather. And, the garden does not offer wall space for hanging or even floor space for placing. Quite the contrary, the garden offers branches, roots, grass, and stones. Creating wall space needed required hard physical labour. Over the course of several days, Alina Martiros, a Canadian-Armenian artist, built the surface she needed for her paintings. She made use of a dilapidated structure, maybe a garage or a garden shed, and flattened its rough walls with cement. The garden affords disorienting installations and defamiliarized constellations. Yet, the garden did not afford this easily. It was not a found art space ready for use. This included "cleaning of the garden with shovels and hoes during the hot summer" (Harutyunyan 208). The investment of physical labour was much needed to transform it into a garden of their own to be used temporarily for exchanging and meeting in art.

E-Mails 2007-2011: An Archive of Feelings/ A Collective Artistic Labour

> We were thinking with lusine (and a few others) that it would be great to do a weeklong multi-media project including a presentation of films, photography, performance art, text/ readings etc. lusine was suggesting to do it in the space of a functioning factory. . . . I was imagining a space in which we could feel more comfortable—certainly not a parade (I don't want to imitate the Western tradition of pride parades), instead I would like us to collaborate with each other to create something of our own. ("E-Mails 2007-2011" 246)

This is a quote from an e-mail written by Shushan Avagyan to Anna Barseghian, initiator and president of Utopiana, on August 23, 2007. It can be found in the collective's 2011 book *Queered: What's to be Done with ^{X}Centric Art* that includes their e-mail exchanges via a listserv between 2007 and 2011. The listserv provided their most important translocal location for building collective exchanges with some of the members of the "loose association" living in Yerevan and others belonging to the Armenian diaspora and to transnationally working artists and academics ("E-Mails 2007-2011" 254). The e-mails written in English, in Armenian and in Russian, using the Latin, the Armenian, and the Russian alphabets, present a radical archive of the artistic labour of forming a collective which conventionally remains hidden and invisibilized labour.

The archival turn has come to occupy an important position in contemporary artmaking. Following Gayatri Chakravorty Spivak's 1985 "The Rani of Sirmur: An Essay in Reading the Archives" and Jacques Derrida's 1996 publication of *Archive Fever: A Freudian Impression*, the archive has occupied an important position in postcolonial critique, cultural studies, artistic imagination, and innovative scholarly research. What is particularly of interest here is that, following Ann Cvetkovich, Queering Yerevan's published e-mail documents can be understood as "an archive of feelings", and following a materialist feminist art historical perspective as proposed in the work of Angela Dimitrakaki, the e-mail documents evidence the invisibilized and hidden labour needed both for working toward forming a collective and sustaining self-organized and self-supported artmaking collectively (Cvetkovich 2003; Dimitrakaki 2013).

In their archive I discern two key strands in their artistic labour: their search for a way of practicing queering as making art collectively and their continued efforts to secure funding and infrastructures necessary for this queering to happen. Forming a collective requires time and a lot of affective and intellectual labour. Strong feelings about decisions, orientations, and directions abound. Intellectual positions have to be assumed and fought for. Securing funding is not only a time-consuming and challenging work for self-organized artist-based projects per se, it is complicated by the perceived risk of capture and co-optation via the politics of funding bodies. It is important to emphasize here, that queering as artworking in the context of Yerevan is always unpaid labour. The three core members, Arpi Adamyan, Shushan Avagyan, and lusine talalyan, pursue income providing work other than their art.

Diasporic and transnational members have their individual academic and/or artistic practices and ways of generating income. Not only is queering unpaid labour, it also includes securing the resources for their production of books, exhibitions, screenings, or gatherings. Airfare has to be paid, materials have to be bought, books have to printed.

In taking seriously non-normative ways of working, they chose to remain a "loose association" rather than building a "rigid structure" ("E-Mails 2007-2011" 254). Therefore, they did neither become an NGO nor an association that can apply to funding bodies and then be held accountable. In the beginning, their artist-based project was supported by Utopiana and the Armenian Women's Resource Center in their efforts to find funding. The "E-Mails 2007-2011" include responses of rejection they received concerning their funding applications. Timothy D. Straight, Norwegian Honorary Consul in Armenia, responded to the request written by Utopiana on behalf of the project as follows: "While the issue of sexual minorities is an important one for Armenia, there were so many applications on so many pressing issues that all of the projects could not be chosen, unfortunately" ("E-Mails 2007-2011" 247). The Armenian Women's Resource Center applied for a grant for the project with the Astraea International Fund. They responded as follows: "Astraea receives many worthy proposals, more than we can possibly fund. We commend your efforts; however we were unable to fund Armenian Women's Resource Center at this time. . . . Our funding priority is to support groups with a clear social justice/human rights agenda, which are led by or have a history of working with and supporting the leadership of Lesbian, Gay, Bisexual, Transgender, and/or Intersex (LGTBTL) people" ("E-Mails 2007-2011" 248-249). Eventually, the book that includes "E-Mails 2007-2011" was funded via a kickstarter campaign and through the "generous support" of "individuals" ("'Two Years in Correspondence'"; *Queered* 334).

In 2008, they circulated the following list of contributors to their listserv: Nancy Agabyan, Arpi Adamyan, Lara Aharonian, Shushan Avagyan, Anna Barseghian, Sarah Chance, Lusine Chergehstyan, Adrineh Der-Boghossian, Angela Harutyunyan, Alina Martiros, Asthgik Melkonyan, Gohar Shahnazaryan, and lusine talalyan. The contributors reflect the local, translocal, and diasporic nature of the Queering Yerevan project. Their exchanges localize queering in Yerevan as much as in the Armenian "queer diaspora" (Fortier 183). I employ this term to speak about the queer identifications among the Armenian diaspora with many of the contributors to the Queering Yerevan Collective born and raised outside of Armenia. I use diaspora to refer to both the older layer in its meaning "once used to describe exiled and forced dispersal of Jews or Armenians" and the newer and wider layer in its meaning "used to describe transnational networks of immigrants, refugees, guest workers and so on" (Fortier 184). Their artistic labour includes as much "diasporizing the queer" as localizing queering in Yerevan. Together, they share thoughts on theoretical positions as developed by Michel Foucault and Judith Butler (see "E-Mails 2007-2011" 280, 302-303). As a group they work toward possible translations of sexual orientations into Armenian. "1. miaserakan (homosexual), 2. hamaserakan (bisexual), 3. andrerakan kam transserakan (transsexual), 4. taraserakan kam heteroserakan (heterosexual)" ("E-Mails 2007-2011" 270). A word for queer is chosen: "tarorinakogh" (277). They also express their thoughts, ideas, and mixed feelings about publishing their archive of e-mails. These include that such a decision to publish should take into account the needs and concerns of all (318). There are also strong feelings expressed that "archiving our conversations" amounts to being "totally dead as a group" (322). And there is the concern that "the publication of the correspondence . . . means risking our safety" (324). After much internal disagreements and debate, they arrived at publishing this open archive including the disagreements and debate.

In concluding, I return once more to the opening quote from Shushan Avagyan's e-mail. The following four points raised in her e-mail are of interest. The project firstly envisioned the creation of a space affording the collaborators to relate to each other comfortably. Secondly, there is a clear rejection of importing Western traditions of public queer mobilization such as parades. Thirdly, there is an expression of desire to 'collaborate with each other' to 'create something of our own'. And fourthly, a finite and defined artwork is not the expressed goal. "The final result could be the collaborative process itself" ("E-Mails 2007-2011" 246). Even though never outlined as a program, what is described here holds true for much of their collective queering.

"Something has been left unfinished..."

("E-Mails 2007-2011" 320)

The Queering Yerevan Collective use the present continuous for their name. The present continuous refers to a specific temporality. It is an indication that said activity has already begun. At the same time, it is indication that said activity has not been finished yet. Choosing the temporality of the present continuous establishes a long-term endeavour.

Their queering seeks to "put the normative out of action" and this necessarily involves "collective action" (Ahmed 184). Since Queering Yerevan is a fully artist-based project, the contributors to the collective have to come up with the time, the resources, and the infrastructures necessary to live up to the expectations and desires of the present continuous expressed in their name. Not only does it serve as a public announcement, it is also an expression of collective self-commitment. And, as of time of writing, they continue to work on location in Yerevan.

Works Cited

Agabian, Nancy. http://nancyagabian.com.

Aghajanyan, Karine. "Challenges for Art in Armenia: View from Three Contemporary Artists and an Art Curator." *Hetq*. http://hetq.am/eng/news/58285/challenges-for-art-in-armenia-view-from-three-contemporary-artists-and-an-art-curator.html.

Ahmed, Sara. *Queer Phenomenology: Orientations. Objects. Others.* Durham, NC: Duke University Press, 2006.

"Armenian Police Threaten to Throw Citizen into Psychiatric Ward: Action in Central Yerevan." *Epress*. 24 May 2016. http://www.epress.am/en/2016/05/24/armenian-police-threaten-to-throw-citizens-into-psychiatric-wards-silent-action-in-central-yerevan.html.

Avagyan, Shushan. "Traduttore, Traditore: Translating How, Betraying What." *Queered: What's to be Done With ^{X}Centric Art*. Eds. lusine talalyan, Arpi Adamyan, and Shushan Avagyan. Yerevan: QY collective, 2011. 54-61.

Avagyan, Shushan and Elke Krasny. E-Mail correspondence with the author. 1 Oct. and 6 Oct. 2016.

Bishop, Claire. "The Social Turn: Collaboration and Its Discontents." *Artforum* 44.6 (February 2006): 179-185.

Brenner, Neil and Nik Theodore. "Cities and Geographies of Actually Existing Neoliberalism." *Antipode* 34.3 (June 2002): 349-379.

Cvetkovich, Ann. *An Archive of Feelings: Trauma, Sexuality, and Lesbian Cultures*. Durham, NC: Duke University Press, 2003.

Derrida, Jacques. "Archive Fever: A Freudian Impression." *Diacritics* 25.2 (Summer 1995): 9-63.

Dimitrakaki, Angela. *Gender, artWork and the Global Imperative: A Materialist Feminist Critique*. Manchester: Manchester University Press, 2013.

Eder, Barbara. "From an Interview with Queering Yerevan." *In and Between the Republic*. Ed. QY Collective. Yerevan: QY Collective, 2014. 24-25.

Fortier, Ann-Marie. "Queer Diaspora." *Handbook of Lesbian and Gay Studies*. Eds. Diane Richardson and Steven Seidman. Thousand Oak, CA; London: Sage Publications, 2002. 183-198.

Frantz David, and Mia Locks, Eds. *Cruising the Archive: Queer Art and Culture in Los Angeles, 1945–1980*. Los Angeles: ONE National & Gay Lesbian Archives, 2011.

Foreign & Commonwealth Office. "Armenia's Diaspora—Its Role & Influence." *Refworld*. http://www.refworld.org/pdfid/55375ae94.pdf.

Groys, Boris. "Art in the Age of Biopolitics: From Artwork to Art Documentation." *Catalogue to Documenta 11*. Ostfildern-Ruit: Hatje Cantz, 2002. 108–114.

Halberstam, Judith. *In a Queer Time and Place: Transgender Bodies, Subcultural Lives*. New York: New York University Press, 2005.

Harutyunyan, Angela. "Live from Angela: Apart We Are Together." *Queered: What's to be Done With ^{X}Centric Art*. Eds. lusine talalyan, Arpi adamyan, and Shushan avagyan. Yerevan: QY collective, 2011. 200–209.

"Human Rights Activist Alleges Torture and Harassment at Yerevan Psychiatric Clinic." *Epress*. 3 June 2016. http://www.epress.am/en/2016/06/03/human-rights-activist-alleges-torture-and-harassment-at-yerevan-psychiatric-clinic.html.

Ionesyan, Karine. "Gay Rights under Attack in Armenia." Institute for War & Peace Reporting. CRS Issue 643. 25 May 2012. https://iwpr.net/global-voices/gay-rights-under-attack-armenia.

Ishkanian, Armine. "Civil Society and Development in Postsocialist Armenia." *Critical Postsocialisms*. postsocialisms.wordpress, https://postsocialisms.wordpress.com/presentations/neoliberalism-civil-society-and-development-in-postsocialist-armenia/

Jones, Amelia and Erin Silver, Eds. *Otherwise: Imagining Queer Feminist Art Histories*. Manchester: Manchester University Press, 2016.

Krasny, Elke. "The Salon Model: The Conversational Complex." *Feminism and Art History Now: Radical Critiques of Theory and Practice*. Eds. Victoria Horne and Lara Perry. New York: I. B. Tauris, 2017. 147-163.

Lefebvre, Henri. *Le droit à la ville.* Paris: Anthropos, 1968.

Pink Armenia. http://www.pinkarmenia.org.

Pinther, Kerstin, Berit Fischer, and Ugochukwu-Smooth C. Nzewi, Eds. *New Spaces for Negotiating Art and Histories in Africa.* Münster: LiT Verlag, 2015.

Queering Yerevan Collective. "E-Mails 2007-2011." *Queered: What's to be Done With ˣCentric Art.* Ed. lusine talalyan, Arpi Adamyan, and Shushan Avagyan. Yerevan: QY collective, 2011. 242–330.

________. *Queered: What's to be Done With ˣCentric Art.* Eds. lusine talalyan, Arpi Adamyan, and Shushan Avagyan. Yerevan: QY Collective, 2011.

________. *In and Between the Republic.* Yerevan: QY Collective, 2014.

Rich, Adrienne. "Notes Toward a Politics of Location (1984)." *Blood, Bread and Poetry: Selected Prose 1979-1985.* New York and London: W.W. Norton, 1986. 211-231.

Sargsyan, Pitman. "Interviews with Four Artists." *Queered: What's to be Done With ˣCentric Art.* Eds. lusine talalyan, Arpi Adamyan, and Shushan Avagyan. Yerevan: QY collective, 2011. 11–35.

Schwärzler, Dietmar. "Queer and Questioning." *Pink Labour on Golden Streets: Queer Art Practices.* Eds. Christiane Erharter, Dietmar Schwärzler, Ruby Sircar, and Hans Scheirl. Berlin: Sternberg Press, 2015. 18–27.

Spivak, Gayatri Chakravorty. "The Rani of Sirmur: An Essay in Reading the Archives." *History and Theory* 24.3 (October 1985): 247–272.

Unzipped: Gay Armenia. http://gayarmenia.blogspot.co.at.

Utopiana. utopiana, http://utopiana.ch/en/lassociation.

Women's Resource Center Armenia. *Humanrightshouse.* http://humanrightshouse.org/Articles/20651.html.

WOW Collective. "Open Letter Against Intolerance." *queeringyerevan.blogspot.* http://queeringyerevan.blogspot.co.at/2009/01/open-letter-against-intolerance.html.

________. "An Obituary to WOW." *queeringyerevan.blogspot.* http://queeringyerevan.blogspot.co.at/2010/07/obituary-to-wow.html.

________. "'Two Years in Correspondence' from the WOW Collective in Armenia." *Kickstarter.* https://www.kickstarter.com/projects/aglany/two-years-in-correspondence-from-the-wow-collect/description.

The Visual Representation of Queer Bollywood: Mistaken Identities and Misreadings in *Dostana*[1]

ROHIT K. DASGUPTA

Introduction

Indian cinema has attracted much attention globally and within a short space of time has moved from the "periphery to the centre of World Cinema" (Gokulsing and Dissanayake, "Introduction" 1). The reasons for this remarkable journey are many and quite complex; they include India's urbanisation, a growth of consumer economy, and the emergence of globalisation, which has firmly placed India as a significant global nation. Much of the Indian cinema that has proliferated and entered the global consciousness is the popular variety synonymous with 'Bollywood.'[2] Even as Bollywood devotes itself to the celebration of normative heterosexual desire, their passionate engagement with forbidden, transgressive, cross-religion, cross-national love stories such as *Devdas* (2002) and *Veer Zara* (2004), have held a particular significance for queer spectators. Alongside this has been Bollywood's preoccupation with 'dosti' (friendship between two men and sometimes women) such as in *Razia Sultana* (1983), *Sholay* (1975) and the more recent *Student of the Year* (2012) celebrating intense same sex love between two friends which according to Ghosh (2007) can be read as homoerotic texts.

Although gay themes and queer characters are relatively underrepresented in the output of the Hindi film industry, the rendering of queer is neither wholly unrecorded, nor is it a contemporary development. Cinema in India has repeatedly addressed queer representations through

[1] A version of this essay appeared in *JAWS: Journal of Arts Writing* 1.1 (January 2015): 91-101.

[2] The term Bollywood is a late invention and the emergence of this category can be traced back only to the latter half of the 1990s when it started being used profusely in trade magazines, newspapers, etc. Rajyadaksha (2003) designates it in broader terms as referring to the contemporary entertainment industry where film is just one element.

stereotyped depictions, such as the ambiguous gendered side characters in *Raja Hindustani* ('King India,' 1996), or the drag performances of Amitabh Bachchan in *Laawaaris* ('Orphan,' 1981) whose elemental function appeared to be limited to the provision of comic relief. Alternatively, a modest number of commercial films presenting queer narratives are also in existence, which in contrast emphasise the disconsolate or the tragic. *My Brother Nikhil* (2005) and *I Am* (2010)—which take HIV and gay bashing/blackmailing (in the latter) as their major themes—are perhaps the best known examples of this genre.

Tarun Mansukhani's *Dostana* ('Friendship,' 2008) is the first commercial popular feature film from India to exclusively engage in a queer dialogue using the devices of 'mistaken identity' and 'misreading' (Ghosh). This film provides a rich site for studying the traffic between discourses of sexuality, Indian-ness, diaspora and performativity. This article will analyse the concepts of 'dosti' and 'yaarana,' the trope of the homo-social triangle, and the queer representation of characters (or queer framing), in Hindi cinema. By acknowledging the slippages between 'real identity' and 'mistaken identity' these films usher in a new queer cinematic discourse within popular Bollywood. While *Dostana* (2008) cannot legitimately lay claim to the mantle of the first gay film in India,[3] it is one of the first mainstream commercial films from Bollywood to explicitly engage in a queer dialogue by means of rerouting traditional rituals and denaturalising family structures, thus reimagining Indian-ness through a queer lens.

'Dosti,' 'Yaarana,' Dostana

Bollywood cinema is saturated with rich images of intense love and friendship between men. According to Madhava Prasad, 'dosti' (friendship) in Bollywood takes precedence over heterosexual love; he argues that:

> The code of dosti takes precedence over that of heterosexual love and in the case of conflict, the latter must yield to the former. Thus, in a conflict over love between male friends, the woman remains out of the picture, while the two males decide

[3] Riyadh Wadia's *Bomgay* (1996), a short twelve-minute film has the distinction of being called India's first gay film. Similarly, Sridhar Rangayan's *Pink Mirror* (2003) is called India's first 'kothi' film. Both these short features have only been screened in film festivals with limited distribution. See: Shahani, 2008 and Wadia, 2000.

> between themselves who will have her. . . . The bond of 'dosti' is then a prototype of the compact among men that institutes the social contract. (83-84)

This space of homosocial male bonding within which 'dosti' and 'yaarana' is inscribed, then becomes a subversive space within which queer desires are referenced and articulated. It is significant to note that the concepts of 'yaarana' and 'dosti' have been central to much queer reading of Indian cinema (Ghosh, 2007; Kavi, 2000; Rao, 2000; Gopinath, 2005). An oft cited case of this key trope in the Hindi film repertoire is *Sholay* (Embers, 1975). Jai and Veeru's dosti is played out most tellingly in the song 'Yeh Dosti' ('This Friendship'). According to Kavi, this song "features lyrics plainly homosexual in content" (310). One verse, openly sexual, says: "I will take anything from you . . . Tere Liye Lelenge." "Lelenge" is Hindi street slang for the phrase "getting fucked."[4] The word 'yaar' (friend) is itself quite ambiguous. As R. Raj Rao (2000) has noted, it can be used to denote a male or female friend, one's spouse, or in a pejorative sense, that of a wife's lover. As such the representation of 'yaarana' in Hindi films is open to multiple interpretations, whilst 'dosti' is an honoured institution that triumphs over all other forms of love and emotion (including heterosexual love), and loyalty to one's 'yaar' or 'dost,' is an accepted virtue. For a queer community struggling for recognition in India (Narrain and Bhan, 2005), this playing out of male-male bonding and attachment becomes significant in the absence of a more deliberately articulated political position on sexuality.

I want to suggest extending the textual reading of these films beyond the materiality of the film alone, in terms of how we might think about the queer representation as being played out in related cultural geographies. For instance, the song 'Yeh Dosti' has long been an anthem for South Asian queer marches and events all over the world, the opening lines being utilised as expression of queer solidarity:

Yeh dosti hum nahin chodenge, Todenge dum agar, tera saath na chodenge.

('We will not give up this friendship. We may die but we will never part.')

Similarly, *Dostana*'s queer currency extends from its 'pseudo-queer' storyline and the numerous fan fictions written about it, to its public performance in queer South Asian Clubs in the diaspora. I want to recall

[4] The word 'le lenge' (which literally translates as 'take from you') was again translated as 'fuck you' in the recent song 'Tujhe Kehke lunga' ('I will tell you and then fuck you') from the film Gangs of Wasseypur (2012), unlike Sholay, where the word was left untranslated.

here a recreation of a particular song from *Dostana*, 'Maa Da Laadla Bigad Gaya' ('Mamma's boy has become a brat'), which is often played at South Asian queer spaces in the UK, and can be used to posit how queer sensibilities are recreated in urban geographies. In the film, the song shows a homophobic mother, terrified at her son's homosexuality, trying to 'cure' him with witch doctors, and keeping him and his partner apart. As this song is played in queer spaces, it can be understood as an acknowledged queer text, where the audiences identify as the 'spoilt son,' corrupted by the influence of homosexuality. Actual physical bodies in the club setting thus start recreating and articulating the queer tangent of the song. It would be useful to point out that despite the homophobic and stereotypical visual accompaniment to the song, it is a very popular song for its affirmation of the male queer identity within popular Indian cinema and this recognition (and celebration) is part of a larger reclamation process in the absence of too many popular queer signifiers within Indian Cinema.

Dostana starts in Miami and explores the story of two men who pretend to be gay, so that they can rent an apartment from an older lady and her niece. Two newly acquainted men on Miami Beach—Kunal (John Abraham) the fashion photographer, and Sameer (Abhishek Bachchan) the male nurse—find themselves in dire housing straits. They chance upon a gorgeous luxury apartment where Neha (Priyanka Chopra) needs two flat mates, but her aunt the landlady, will only allow female flat mates for her niece. At this point reminiscent of *Bosom Buddies* (1980-82) where Tom Hanks and Peter Scolari dress up as women to live in a girl's dorm, our heroes pretend to be a gay couple so that they can live in this house. However other circumstances force the two to dig deeper into the lie, which gets further complicated when they each fall in love with Neha. Their competition for her love strains the two men's friendship and adds another layer of narrative between the three, whilst the mistaken sexual identity drives the plot. The mistaken sexual identities of the two men, and the responses to them by others, account for much of the humour in the film. *Dostana* can be considered the first film in mainstream Hindi cinema with direct homosexual references as its main thread, which has achieved global box office success (Dudrah).

Whilst queer representation in mainstream Indian cinema still has some way to go, there are enough 'queer signifiers' (the hypermasculine imagery of Kunal, the depilated torso shots, the metrosexual patterned shirts) within the film for both non South Asian audiences and the gay spectator to identify with. I suggest that this appending of queer signifiers is often projected onto the actor, and is not necessarily initiated by him; as Waugh considers, 'Something queer is clearly going on in Bollywood. This is true certainly within the increasingly brazen and devious Mumbai studio subcultures' (297). Hence, the apportioning of a gay façade, seems to be instigated from a behind the scenes authority. In examining who wields control in the presentation of the star as spectacle, Richard Dyer (5) identifies the range of manufacturers who collaborate in film fabrication: the star actors/actresses, make-up artists, hairdressers, dress designers, dieticians, personal trainers, publicists, pin-up photographers and gossip columnists, not to mention the acting and dancing itself, crafted by teachers, choreographers, director and producers.

Where the actor is presented as spectacle for the queer gaze, the imagery clearly draws parallels with the homoerotic; Mansukhani establishes this early on through the representation of Kunal. Shown emerging from the water, the camera focuses on Kunal, cutting his body into parts through medium and close up shots: first his waist, then his midriff, chest, arms and biceps, culminating in a view of his full body; he is presented as an object of desire. This particular scene is unique through its presentation of the direct male gaze that Kunal delivers to the camera. Borrowing from Waugh's description of the homosocial axes (2001), I would like to place Kunal and Sameer on two different sides of the homoerotic axes; whilst Kunal has been characterised as the 'masculine' partner with his muscled torso and bared bodied visualisation, Sameer is seen through a more feminised lens in his floral print shirts and intricate scarves.

I consider these images important as they mark a transformation of masculinity and the desiring gaze, which is shifted from Neha to Kunal and Sameer. Kunal and Sameer's 'dosti' (friendship) is situated within a queer space, where they enact their friendship through physical intimacy inscribed into a pleasurable spectacle, offering multiple locations of identification, without raising any significant disruptions to the heteronormative order. The strong friendship bonds or 'yaarana' that exists between male characters is an important trope in Hindi film. Unsurprisingly, homoerotic readings of this relationship are continually speculated on by fans, critics and academics. Reading films through a queer eye and 'slash' readings 4 of male relationships in film are some of the methods in which queer elements are explored. It raises the question if the bodily gestures and performativity between the two men is for the straight audience who has come to see a comedy film about two men pretending to be gay, or for a subculture of queer audiences within a so-called mainstream straight audience, who are also present in watching this film (Dudrah).

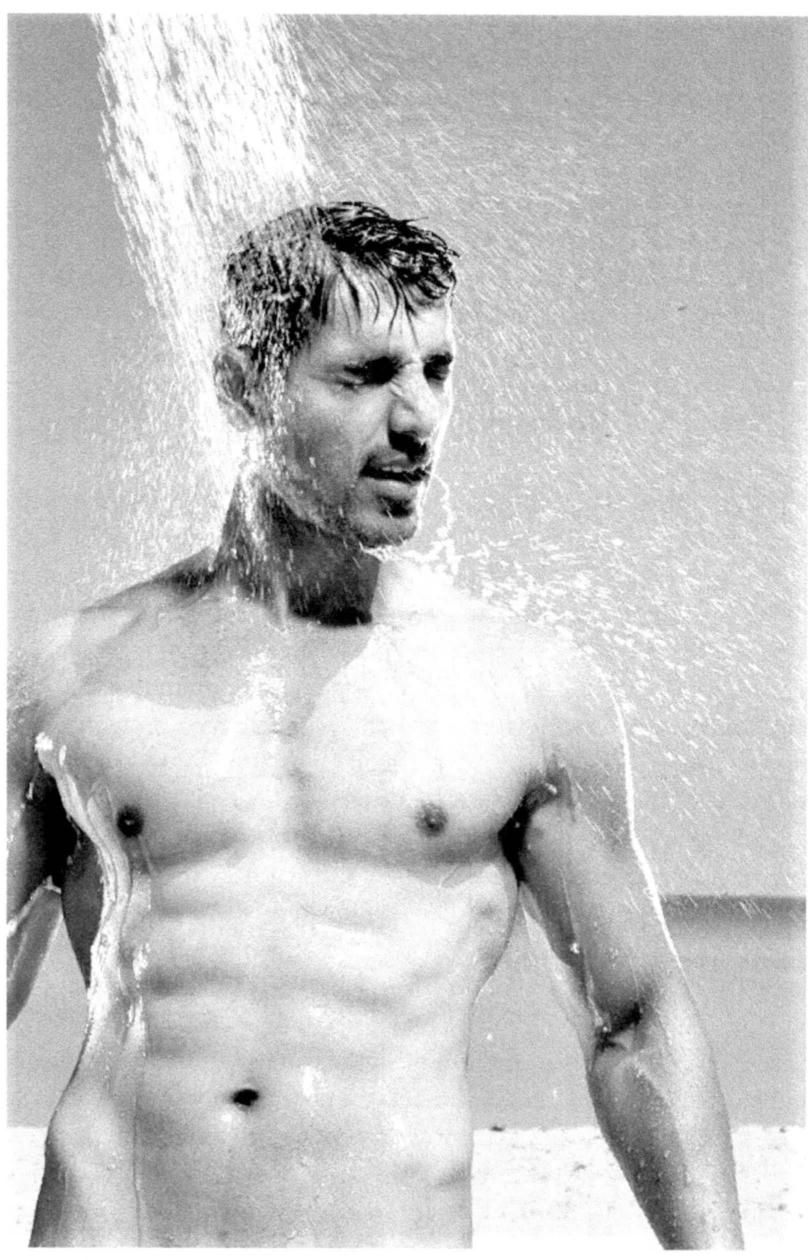

Image 1: Kunal in the opening sequence of *Dostana*.

My attempt here is to emphasise that the act of seeing and deriving pleasure needs to be seen as dialectic, with an ever-slipping trajectory of signification. According to Dudrah, the "display of Kunal's body and the dressing of Sam in highly metrosexual, and at times, effeminate way . . . make them available to both men and women" (49). The South Asian diaspora's queer community has taken on Bollywood icons independently of their context in films, and as a result of this they have been

> able to seize on the numerous ruptures, slippages, and inconsistencies produced by the cinematic text's heterogeneity in form and address to produce pleasures and identifications that may not necessarily be authorized or condoned within the ideological framework of the text itself. (Gopinath 98)

Item Boy and the Queer Gaze

The 'queer play' between the characters is also made available through the songs in the film. Songs are an integral element of the filmic experience, they serve to propel the story whilst underlining morality and catalyzing emotions. Dance sequences in particular are frequently deployed to intensify the spectacle (Gokulsing and Dissanayake). The title sequence which begins with the song and dance number 'Shut Up and Bounce' establishes Kunal and Sameer as the main protagonists of the film. It acts as a 'narrative accelerator' (Dudrah 48), introducing us to the bachelor lifestyle of the two characters—young, single and sexually promiscuous. However the pleasures of the opening credits are more than this, it suggests the possibility of queer 'misreadings.' The song 'Desi Girl' presents the triangular relationship between the three lead characters, as Sam and Kunal vie to get the attention of Neha, or, as it could be read, to get the attention of each other. Viewing a song promo[5] outside of the context of the film is an accepted practice by audiences; it can however give an inaccurate or misrepresentative portrayal of the plot and storyline. I would suggest that the initial promos, however, focus on scenes from the song that show the homo-social interplay between Sam and Kunal with a montage of images such as a comic portrayal of sadomasochism. Kunal is established as the sexualized 'item boy'

[5] By promo I mean the promotional song features which act as an advert for the film usually shown on television. It consists of both a montage of footage from the film played alongside the song or is just a snapshot advertisement for the song itself.

subverting the role of the 'item girl' in Indian cinema. The concept of the item song is unique in Indian cinema. The item song is usually a musical number that may have little to do with the actual film plotline. It usually features another established star in a guest appearance (for example *Dostana* had Shilpa Shetty for the opening song: 'Shut Up and Bounce'). It is often a sexualized routine and adds to the marketability of the film. The woman performing the song is called the 'item girl' whilst the song itself is called an 'item number' or simply 'item song.' According to Morcom (174), the use of film songs has become core to the large part of India's contemporary erotic entertainment traditions, adding new layers of ironic and non ironic referencing of the fictional and the real through their codes of eroticism, performance and morality.

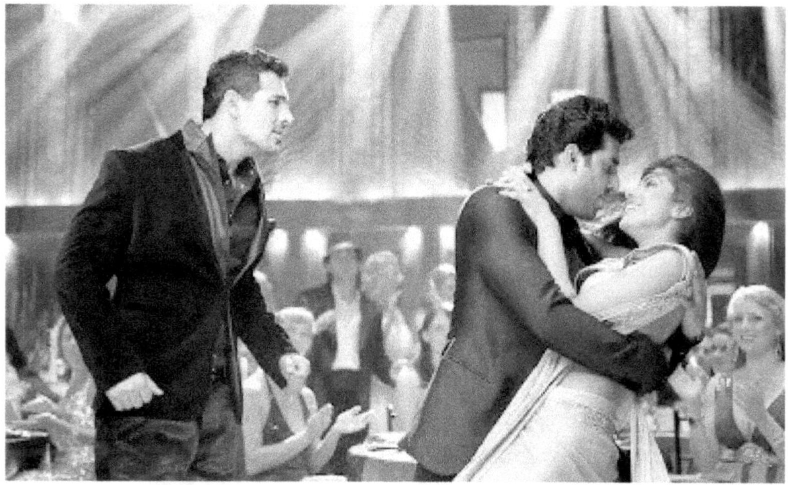

Image 2: 'Desi Girl'

Gabriel further suggests that 'Men cannot relate to each other without women's bodies' (145), which is evident in the song 'Desi Girl,' whereby the female is a necessary link for men to be able to connect with other males. Additionally, in the sequence for 'Jaane Kyon' ('Why/Who Knows'), Sam and Kunal (reminiscent of the Jai-Veeru sequence from *Sholay* mentioned earlier) celebrate their friendship by singing 'Jaane Kyon, dil jaanta hain, tu hain toh I'll be alright' ('My Heart knows, if you are there, everything will be alright'). In my opinion this song serves two purposes. It introduces the ambiguity in the film by placing all three characters—Sam, Kunal and Neha—within the same frame, yet the lyrics are not assigned to any characters in particular, allowing for a 'misreading' by queer spectators. Dwyer (2000) has previously argued that song sequences are the primary vehicle for the bulk of the erotic display of the female body in Hindi films, and that this allows for sensuous and erotic views of the heroine, not found in the main narrative. This is somewhat subverted in *Dostana*, as it is not Neha who is presented as the erotic figure but rather Sam and Kunal. In this song we are presented with a montage of images where the strongest link presented is the male friendship bond, at the exclusion of Neha.

Queer and Indian?

By situating a film (geographically and morally) outside of Hindi culture, and populating it with diasporic figures, an emphatic rejection of family-values-centric Hindi-film ideals is enabled. This is in contrast to earlier negative portrayals of the *desi in pardes* (the outside Indian), with the corrupted characters of *Purab aur Paschim* (1970), being perhaps the best-known example (Dudrah 67). Unlike *Purab aur Paschim, Dostana* presents diaspora in a positive light, whilst, akin to *Purab aur Paschim*, still provides audiences with a tableau outlined by Dwyer of 'the decadent pleasures of Western life' (189).

I would like to propose that the film minimalises any level of opposition or protest by presenting the narrative in a western context. This I suggest is a necessary step to avoid the controversy and effigy burning which can be a part of the Indian societal landscape. *Dostana* avoided such protest, most likely due to the overseas location in the film, combined with the use of humour to convey the story. Perhaps this was also due to the queer narrative being overshadowed (or at least made ambiguous) by heteronormative signifiers, which curtailed potential detractors. As the film was released, there were only minor demonstrations against some of the 'homosexual content,' and a ban in Pakistan, which is not uncommon for many Hindi film releases in that region.

Mansukhani has omitted questions of ethnography, by not connecting his characters to India. Other than the Venice backstory, a fabricated concoction made by Sameer to convince Neha's aunt, Ms Melwani, about his and Kunal's relationship, there is very little that the film reveals about the characters' backgrounds. An interesting observation can be made for situating Venice (or more widely Europe) for this 'gay' backstory. Europe is characterised as a queer utopia where the possibilities of living life openly as queer men and women is acknowledged. Also by not referencing India in the backstory, the film avoids the conservative and problematic link between sexuality and national identity within an Indian context. Mapping homoeroticism onto the national space is complex. The homeland is seen as the site of sexual oppression that must be left behind to realise queer subjectivity. Gopinath writes about the diasporic importance of these images, arguing that

> these images travel transnationally, [serving] to provide a common visual vocabulary for queer spectators in disparate diasporic locations, one that reconciles not only the contradiction between queer image and heterosexual narrative . . . but also the contradiction between the space of the nation as implicitly heterosexual and the space of diaspora as foreign, inauthentic, and indeed "queer." (113)

The cosmopolitan European setting allows Sam and Kunal (in their made-up story) to live openly as a gay couple. Similarly, although we are informed that Kunal has lived in the US for just three years, there is no reference to his geographical origin, social status or family in India. Likewise, the character of Sameer is described as previously residing in the UK. We are presented the image of his London home with a Miamiesque front garden and incongruous palm trees, utilizing a conventional Hindi film trope: the meaninglessness of the foreign space. Although it is not explicitly stated, we can infer that Sam is a first-generation Indian migrant, dislocated from the norms and conventions of India socially and geographically.

Neha (Priyanka Chopra) and her Aunt (Sushmita Mukherjee) define themselves at one point as Sindhi, but as an audience we are privy to nothing else of their provenance. Indeed, to an Indian spectator their lifestyles might seem distinctly American. The fact that Neha lives alone despite her aunt living in the same city may surprise Indian cinemagoers, as might the Aunt's patronage of strip clubs. The sole representative from the North Indian patriarchal family is the mother figure played by Kirron Kher. The mother's visual performance of 'aarti' (ritual of worship), and the auditory signifiers of 'dhol' (drum) and 'bale bale' (popular Punjabi way of expressing happiness), establish her as the stereotypical Punjabi mother from Hindi film. Although she may be deracinated from her homeland, the graduation photographs of Sam on her mantelpiece and gold bangles on her wrist, demarcate her as very much the Indian 'Maa' (mother) figure.

The notion of being gay is initially framed as something absurd. The overdramatic response from the mother, whose resounding slap and disapproval is framed as comical, brings to fore the realities associated with coming out:

Mother: "You went to Venice? It is all my fault. Had I not given you so much freedom, you would not have made these mistakes."

Neha: "But aunty, Love is not wrong, it is blind."

Mother: "Love should not be so blind that it can't tell the difference between a man and a woman."

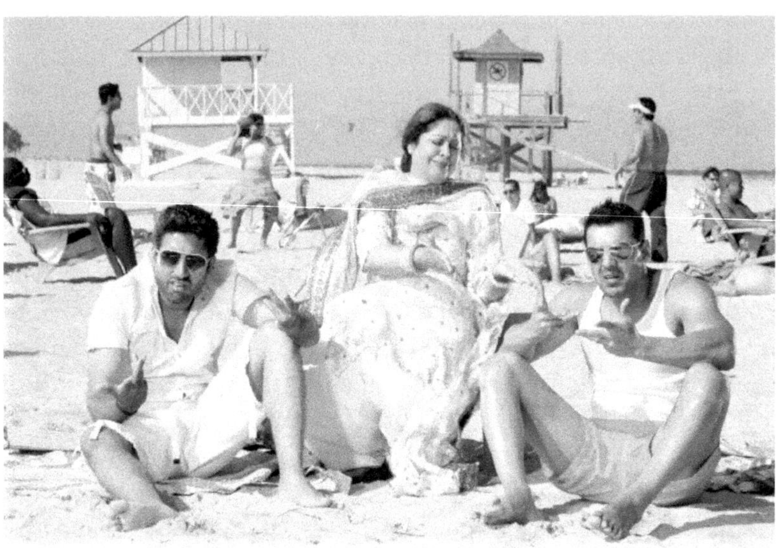

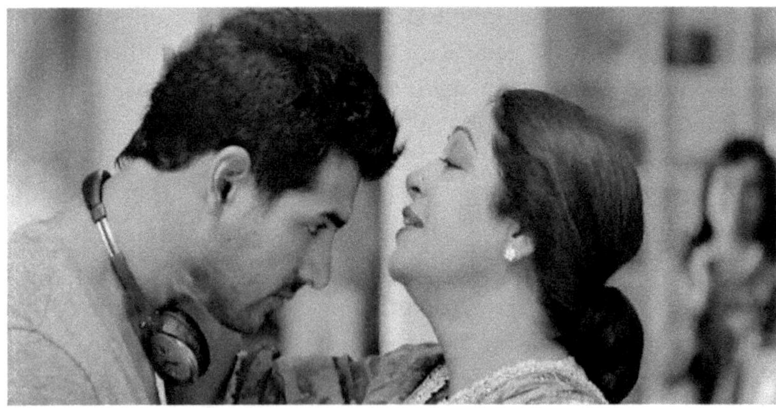

Images 3 and 4: Before and After: the mother accepting the 'sham' gay relationship of her son

Subsequently, as the idea becomes accepted, it is the mother who is then depicted in an absurd manner for not accepting the sexuality of her son. Finally, whilst surrounded by traditional Indian signifiers, the mother figure demonstrates her acceptance through a combination of Indianness and religion; she gives consent to the sham relationship of Sam and Kunal in a ceremony mirroring Hindi religious imagery, and states that "whatever God does is for the best." This feeling is magnified due to the appropriation of the title track from *Kabhi Kushi Kabhi Gham* ('Happiness and Sadness,' 2001), a popular film which espouses the value of family life in India; this song is played in the filmic reality, through an iPod, alluding to a collusion of the traditional and modern, Western and Indian.

Thus, the queer family is formed, in a kinship that exists outside of traditional family bonds. Yet, it is able to form a connected group, whereas the Indian figure of the mother here is isolated and not an accepted member of this microcosm, until her later acceptance of homosexuality. Queer kinship according to Butler (2002), is not the same as gay marriage, it can be read as a reworking and revision of the social organisation of friendship, sexual contacts, and community to produce non-state-centred forms of support and alliance (as Neha, Kunal, Sam and Ms Melwani portray). This collective bond is then acknowledged by Sam after Kunal receives his residency permit for the US—"Thanks for making me gay, because of you I found a family, I love you, dude"—and it is then cemented in the closing image after the end credits, with the caption 'And they lived happily ever after.' The final ambiguous image is of Sam and Kunal, whilst there is a conspicuous absence of Neha.

Whilst *Dostana* represents queer possibilities existing within the Indian culture and society, it also plays with the negative and positive attributes that we might associate with these characters. It is imperative to explore how Sam and Kunal self-identify and the means by which other characters within the film refer to their presumed relationship. Language and dialogue is one area where such labelling can be decoded, with the most indicative pattern being the feminising of the queer male. From the lead male characters self defining "We both are girls," to Sam advising Kunal "Think like a woman feel like a man," it is clear that queer men are viewed in contra-masculine terms. Equally, the Aunt figure projects the same notion, articulating the relationship of Sam and Kunal as, "They are boyfriend/girlfriend."

Conclusion

Dostana can be read as a 'queer hyper text' (Gehlawat 104), as it comes out of the closet, in the Sedgweckian sense so to speak and deals with queerness in a much more blatant manner. Sedgwick (1990) argues that the closet, representing a known secret, is a central trope structuring contemporary western thinking, and that sustaining heterosexual normativity requires some considerable effort. In other words it is hard work to keep the known secret of homosexuality safely hidden away. In light of such a struggle to maintain the illusion of normative heterosexuality, the closet is repositioned. Instead of always being a vulnerable site of shameful hiding, it can transform into a powerful site of deliberate subterfuge. *Dostana*, as this article has already established, is not about homosexuality, rather it represents and celebrates an alleged queer union through Butler's (1990) notion of 'gender parody' and 'performativity.'

Ellis Hansen notes that every film with a queer theme, notwithstanding the sexuality of its director or the origin of its funding, is still embattled in a highly moralistic debate over the correctness of its politics, "as though art were to be valued only as sexual propaganda" (11). My concern in this article is therefore not simply about good and bad politics of representation around sexuality, it is an attempt to understand how queer sexuality, since it can no longer be elided or silenced, begins to get acknowledged and understood in Bombay Cinema. The emergence of new sexualities and a diversity of desires in cinema are clearly a response to many years of feminist and queer rights movements (Ghosh 433). As I have discussed above, mainstream films register this acknowledgement of queer sexualities but at the same time display great anxiety. The horror and fascination with which queer sexualities are being regarded today, allow both radical ruptures and reactionary closures. The ambivalent narrative of *Dostana* registers the existence of queer desires but eventually establishes the inevitability of heterosexuality. This film is certainly not revolutionary or progressive in giving the queer identity a solidified voice; rather it is somewhat reactionary in its struggle to grapple with new sexual identities, as heterosexuality is thrown into predicament.

Gokulsing and Dissanayake have recently argued that "the discourse of Indian Popular Cinema has been evolving steadily over a century in response to newer social developments and historical conjunctures" (17). This film might be seen as one such response. The prominence of the overseas market, the transglobalisation of Hindi cinema, and the growth of the multiplex (catering for niche genres and urban audiences) should ensure that the number of queer themed films produced will continue to increase. In addition to significant regional releases such as *Memories in March* (2010) and *Not Another Love Story* (2011),which have central queer characters, it is vital to observe future trends in film releases on this theme. Thus Dostana is significant in opening closets in the Indian film industry, and more significantly, in the culture and society of India.

Works Cited

Butler, Judith. *Gender Trouble: Feminism and the Subversion of Identity*. New York: Routledge, 1990.

________. "Is Kinship Always Already Heterosexual?" *Differences: A Journal of Feminist Cultural Studies* 13.1 (2002): 14-44.

Dudrah, Rajinder. *Bollywood: Sociology Goes to the Movies*. New Delhi: Sage, 2006.

________. *Bollywood Travels: Culture, Diaspora and Border Crossings in Popular Hindi Cinema*. London: Routledge, 2012.

Dwyer, Rachel. "Shooting Stars: The Indian Film Magazine Stardust." *Pleasure and the Nation: The History, Politics and Consumption of Public Culture in India*. Eds. Rachel Dwyer and Christopher Pinney. New Delhi: Oxford University Press, 2000. 247-85.

________. *100 Bollywood Films*. New Delhi: Roli Books, 2006.

Dyer, Richard. *Heavenly Bodies*. London: Routledge, 2004.

Gabriel, Karen. *Imaging a Nation: The Sexual Economies of the Contemporary Mainstream Bombay Cinema (1970 – 2000)*. Maastricht: Shaker Publishing, 2005.

Ganti, Tejaswini. *Bollywood: A Guidebook to Popular Hindi Cinema*. London: Routledge, 2004.

Gehlawat, Ajay. *Reframing Bollywood: Theories of Popular Hindi Cinema*. London: Sage, 2010.

Ghosh, Shohini. "False Appearances and Mistaken Identities: The Phobic and the Erotic in Bombay Cinema's Queer Vision." *The Phobic and the Erotic: The Politics of Sexualities in Contemporary India*. Eds. Brinda Bose and Subhabrata Bhattacharya. Kolkata: Seagull, 2007. 417-436.

Gokulsing, K. Moti and Wimal Dissanayake. *From Aan to Lagaan and Beyond: A Guide to the Study of India Cinema.* Stoke-on-Trent: Trentham, 2012.

________. "Introduction." *Routledge Handbook of Indian Cinemas.* Eds. K. Moti Gokulsing and Wimal Dissanayake. London: Routledge, 2013. 1-3.

Gopinath, Gayatri. *Impossible Desires: Queer Diasporas and South Asian Public Cultures.* Durham, NC: Duke University Press, 2005.

Hansen, Ellis. *Out Takes: Essays on Queer Theory and Film.* Durham, NC: Duke University Press, 1999.

Kavi, Ashok Row. "Contract of Silence." *Yaarana: Gay Writing from India.* Ed. Hoshang Merchant. New Delhi: Penguin, 1999. 2-25.

Morcom, Anna. (2010). "Film Songs and the Cultural Synergies of Bollywood in and Beyond South Asia." *Beyond the Boundaries of Bollywood.* Eds. Rachel Dwyer and Jerry Pinto. Oxford: Oxford University Press, 2010. 156-187.

Narrain, Arvind and Gautam Bhan, Eds. *Because I Have a Voice: Queer Politics in India.* New Delhi: Yoda Press, 2005.

Penley, C. "Feminism, Psychoanalysis, and Popular Culture." *Visual Culture: Images and Interpretations.* Eds. Norman Bryson, Michael Ann Holly, and Keith Moxey. Middletown, CT: Wesleyan University Press, 1994. 302-324.

Prasad, Madhava M. *Ideology of the Hindi Film: A Historical Construction.* New Delhi: Oxford University Press, 1998.

Rajyadaksha, Ashish. "The Bollywoodisation of Indian Cinema: Cultural Nationalism in a Global Arena." *Inter Asian Cultural Studies* 4.1 (2003): 25-39.

Rao, R. Raj. "Memories Pierce the heart: Homoeroticism, Bollywood-Style." *Journal of Homosexuality* 39. 3-4 (2000): 299-306.

Sedgwick, Eve Kosofsky. *Epistemology of the Closet.* Berkeley: University of California Press, 1999.

Shahani, Parmesh. *Gay Bombay: Globalisation, Love and (Be)Longing in Contemporary India.* New Delhi: Sage, 2008.

Waugh, Thomas. "Queer Bollywood or 'I'm the Player, you're the naïve one': patterns of sexual subversion in recent Indian popular cinema." *Keyframes: Popular Cinema and Cultural Studies.* Eds. Matthew Tinkcom and Amy Villarejo. London: Routledge, 2001.

"Gross Indecency:" Depicting Oscar Wilde on the Stage

ARGHA BANERJEE

"The portrait of Wilde as homosexual martyr in the 1960s was brought into sharper focus in the 1980s by the rise of gender criticism and queer theory."—John Sloan

"One hundred years after the trials, it is time to re-evaluate the character that emerged from them. Because, like it or not, that character produced a distinctly queer identity for succeeding generations of gay men."—David Schultz

In the second trial scene of Moisés Kaufman's play *Gross Indecency: The Three Trials of Oscar Wilde*, Wilde makes a passionate plea for 'love that dare not speak its name'—a direct extension of the writer's historic proclamation in the courtroom. A little more than a century later, even today, Wilde's fervent courtroom entreaty remains perhaps as one of the classical instances of an ardent affirmation of same-sex love. Wilde's extraordinary assertion combines aesthetic tradition with contemporary reality to weave a brilliant dramatic narrative—magical in its impact—not only in the late Victorian catastrophic set up of an impending tragic doom but in the present-day situation as well; more particularly, in the context of modern visual representation of Wilde's misfortune on the stage:

> The 'Love that dare not speak its name' in this century is such a great affection of an elder for a younger man as there was between David and Jonathan, such as Plato made the very basis of his philosophy, and such as you find in the sonnets of Michelangelo and Shakespeare. It is that deep, spiritual affection that is as pure as it is perfect. . . . There is nothing unnatural about it. It is intellectual, and it repeatedly exists between an elder and a younger man when the elder man has intellect and the younger man has all the joy, hope, and glamour of life before him. That it should be so the world does not understand. The world mocks at it and sometimes puts one in the pillory for it. (Kaufman 111)

Today, perhaps, Oscar Wilde is more celebrated as a theatrical character than as a playwright, more particularly, as there are more scripts focusing on Wilde's personality than his composed plays. Focusing primarily on some of the dramatic representations of Wilde's character on the stage, this analysis intends to explore and examine various depictions of Wilde's historic on-stage personality since his extraordinary trial in 1895. By doing so, this analysis indirectly traces the cultural drifts and cross currents prevalent at large beyond such biographical representations. This analysis concludes focusing on Kaufman's play *Gross Indecency: The Three Trials of Oscar Wilde* as an illustrative dramatic representation on the stage. Interest in Wilde's personality as a stage character multiplied especially in the latter part of the twentieth century with several plays based on his life being produced in quick succession. A quick survey of some of these productions, spanning from the second half of the twentieth century to the present day, reveals the obsession of modern playwrights to visually represent the personality of Oscar Wilde on the stage. It is also interesting to note that even today the deep interest in Wilde's personality continues unabated as contemporary stage productions seek innovative means of representing his life on the stage.

Deeply influenced by the Brechtian theory, in 1960 the Irish actor Micheal MacLiammoir's one-man show entitled *The Importance of Being Oscar* emerged as a successful production leading to its subsequent publication three years later. In the next decade, Adrian Hall and Richard Cumming's play *Feasting with Panthers* set in the backdrop of the Reading Gaol was enacted at the Trinity Repertory Company in Providence, Rhode Island. Following a gap of five years, Vincent Price staged his solo performance of *Diversions and Delights* based on Wilde's biography. This play, written by John Gay and directed by Joseph Hardy, focussed on Oscar Wilde's later life, especially post incarceration in the infamous Reading Gaol. Staged as an autobiographical lecture delivered in a theatre in Paris on November 28, 1899, a year before Wilde's demise in 1900, this play was a grand success—an instant hit with the masses. With Donald Sinden in the lead, the play was again performed in London in 1990. In the late 1980s, interest in Wilde's life was again revived on the stage in a different light altogether through Terry Eagleton's play *Saint Oscar* (1989). This production, an imaginative adaptation of Wilde's life, based its dialogue purely on fiction. In his foreword to the play Terry Eagleton pointed out:

> I first thought of writing about Oscar Wilde when I discovered that hardly any of the Oxford students who asked to study him with me realized that he was Irish. Since Wilde himself realized this only fitfully, this is hardly a grievous crime, though it might be said to evidence of one. English students of literature would know of course that Yeats and Joyce were Irish, and probably—thinking of those tasty babies of A Modest Proposal—Jonathan Swift; but it is more doubtful that they could name the nationality of Sterne, Sheridan, Goldsmith and Burke, and they might even hesitate over Bernard Shaw. British cultural imperialism has long annexed these gifted offshore islanders to its own literary canon, and of course Wilde himself was in many ways glad enough to be recruited. Yet several of the characteristics which make him appear most typically upper-class English—the scorn for bourgeois normality, the flamboyant self-display, the verbal brio and iconoclasm—are also, interestingly enough, where one might claim he is most distinctively Irish; and pondering this odd paradox was one point of origin of this play. (Eagleton vii)

The interest generated by Terry Eagleton continued in the 1990s. Extensively using quotations and pastiche from Wilde's play *The Importance of Being Earnest*, Tom Holland's play *The Importance of Being Frank* (first professional performance in 1991, text published 1997) focused on Wilde's trials, sentence and exile. David Hare's play *The Judas Kiss* (first performed in 1998) also took a closer look at Wilde's relationship with Bosie (Lord Alfred Douglas), Wilde's fall from grace and subsequent humiliation. Focusing on Wilde's lectures in the US during the 1880s, Romulus Linney's *Oscar over Here* (first performed in 1995, published in 1999) also tried to explore Wilde's prison experience. Interestingly, the play included a dialogue between the author and a Jesus Christ figure. The four short plays together celebrate the remarkable wit of Wilde combining tragedy with humour. Not all stage adaptations though met with similar success. Mike Read's stage musical entitled *Oscar* had a truncated run due to adverse criticism in 2004. Elisabeth Mahoney in *The Guardian* (21 Oct 2004) lambasted the musical categorically stating that "the production suffers from a number of problems that could be fixed: cheapness is the main one." On a more successful note however, in the same year, *De Profundis*, an award-winning dramaturgical reworking of Wilde's work, was enacted by Don Anderson at the Segal Centre for the Arts in Montreal, Quebec.

More recently, Merlin Holland and John O'Connor's *The Trials of Oscar Wilde* was staged in 2014. The play was adapted from Holland's book *The Real Trial of Oscar Wilde* (2003)—which brought to light some of the transcripts of Wilde's trials from his grandson. Recounting the experience, Merlin Holland points out that "Oscar went into court in part to defend his art against accusations of immorality, which is often forgotten and is an aspect we've tried to emphasize on stage. There are many other elements to the trials other than just being about his sexuality" (Bosanquet).

Simultaneously with these various stage productions, the portrayals of Wilde's character on the television too did not lag far behind. *Lillie,* a television series produced on the life of Lillie Langtry by the London Weekend Television in 1978, witnessed Peter Egan cast in the role of Oscar. Most of its episodes concentrated on Wilde's close association including his tours to the US in 1882. The 1985 BBC series *Oscar* focused on Wilde's trial and prison term; Michael Gambon played the lead role with Robin Lermitte as Lord Alfred Douglas, Tim Hardy as Alfred Taylor, Emily Richard as Constance Wilde, and Norman Rodway as the Marquis of Queensberry. The play *Oscar Wilde* written by Leslie and Sewell Stokes was converted into a film in 1960 with Robert Morley in the lead role. In the same year, *The Trials of Oscar Wilde* (also known as *The Man with the Green Carnation* and *The Green Carnation*), a film directed by Ken Hughes, was released. Based on the play *The Stringed Lute* by John Furnell, the film starred Peter Finch as Wilde, Lionel Jeffries as Queensberry and John Fraser as Bosie. Finch's performance earned him the BAFTA and Moscow International Film Festival awards for the best actor that particular year. In a review of the movie, the critic Bosley Crowther observed: "Mr Wilde himself could not have expected his rare personality or his unfortunate encounters with British justice on a morals charge to have been more sympathetically or affectingly dramatized."

Most of these representations by and large have been inspired by Wilde's biography, yet as in the case of most aesthetic representations of biographical proceedings, the fictional element, much at the discretion of the writer or the director, intrudes in the script often riding on the wings of the director/playwright's imagination. Interestingly, the roots of such fictional transcendence can be traced in the context of Wilde's personal life as well. As Francesca Coppa rightly observes in the essay "The Artist as Protagonist: Wilde on Stage": "Wilde began his life as a fictional character early in his career, agreeing to become the real life cognate of the fictional aesthetic poet Reginald Bunthorne in Gilbert and Sullivan's *Patience* (1881)" (Coppa 261). Yet beyond the stage productions, Oscar Wilde's personality has been represented through other fictional characters as well, most notable among them being Lord Risley's portrayal in E.M. Forster's *Maurice*. However, the Merchant-Ivory film version of *Maurice* which appeared in 1987, displayed a marked departure in the portrayal of the character of Lord Risley, as Coppa points out: "the rewriting of Lord Risley between 1913 and 1987 demonstrates the rapid evolution of ideas about male homosexuality in general and the received significance of Oscar Wilde's life in particular" (260). Other so called Wildean characters in fiction, closely modelled on or inspired by the historic personality of Oscar Wilde, include Esme Amarinth's character in Robert Hichen's novel *The Green Carnation* (1894) and Wilde's very own Lord Henry Wotton in *The Picture of Dorian Gray* (1890, revised 1891).

A study of stage chronology interestingly reveals that immediately following Wilde's ignominious prosecution, subsequent incarceration and demise his character did not figure as a subject of representations on the stage for quite some time, "though his distinctive personality and mode of self-presentation filtered rapidly through the culture and formed the basis of the early twentieth century gay stereotype" (Coppa 261). The revival of interest in representation of Wilde's dramatic personality was spearheaded by several European countries and America, as these nations took the lead in portraying the character of Wilde on the stage. In the first half of the twentieth century, the character of Wilde was represented in at least four plays. The first was a Dutch tragedy by Adolphe Engers in the first decade of the twentieth century, followed by Carl Sternheim's *Oskar Wilde: Sein Drama* (1924), American writer Lester Cohen's version (1928), Maurice Rostand's *Le process d'Oscar Wilde* (1934) and finally Leslie Stokes and Sewell Stokes's *Oscar Wilde* (1936). *Oscar Wilde*, which contains a great deal of Wilde's writings, was not granted permission by the Lord Chamberlain, as a consequence of which it could only be staged in a theatre club. According to Coppa:

> The Stokeses' play lays out the template that many later biographical dramas would follow: a first act that shows Oscar living dangerously; the courtroom drama leading to his conviction as a second act climax; and a third act of drunkenness and decline. In hindsight, it is surprising how overt the play is about Wilde's homosexuality, giving Wilde an entourage of two effeminate men: Louis Dijon, who, being French, apparently

> takes Wilde's behaviour as matter of course; and Eustace, an Englishman who admits to using rouge and was one of the many crowding the boat-trains out of London when Wilde was arrested at the Cadogan Hotel on 5 April 1895. . . . Then again, perhaps the overt depiction of homosexuality is not surprising: in 1936, a play about Oscar Wilde would have been one of the few places where such representation could legitimately and openly occur. (262)

The authors' note to the book expresses their indebtedness to Lord Alfred Douglas "for his kindness in permitting them to portray him on the stage, and also for his help in checking the authenticity of several facts contained in the play" (Stokes and Stokes 7). The play borrowed from diverse sources: *Wilde: Three Times Tried, Letters to the Sphinx* by Ada Leverson (1930), *Oscar Wilde: His Life and Confessions* by Frank Harris and *Oscar Wilde* by Andre Gide. The three-act play was produced in America by Norman Marshall at the Fulton Theatre on October 10, 1938. Though historically Alfred Douglas's role in course of the trial had drawn a great deal of flak from diverse quarters, in sharp contrast, the preface to the play gave Lord Alfred Douglas an opportunity to vindicate his stand. As John Sloan has observed, "The Stokeses received advice and approval from Alfred Douglas, who in a travesty of the truth is portrayed as caring, hardworking young poet to Wilde's genial but irresponsible hedonist" (172). In his prefatory comment to the play, however, Lord Alfred Douglas condemns the 'cruel' and 'unjust' treatment meted out to Wilde:

> But as I have been asked to write a preface for the present publication, I can say that I regard the play as truthful and dramatic in a high degree, and I am glad to know from the evidence of numerous people who witnessed it that it aroused great sympathy for a man whom I consider to have been cruelly and unjustly treated and whose brilliant genius, if he had not been condemned by an ungrateful country to prison and resulting early death, would have enriched the English stage with many more masterpieces of dramatic art. Wilde was at his best fine poet and a master of prose, and he was also the author of what I consider to be, apart from Shakespeare, the finest comedy ever written in the English language. If his fellow countrymen had treated him in a more Christian spirit, he would have written half a dozen more comedies as good. Let England bear the responsibility for what she did to him. (Douglas qtd. in Stokes and Stokes 11-12)

Leslie and Sewell Stokes's biographical portrait *Oscar Wilde* opened as a club performance at the Gate Theatre London in 1936 and was staged in New York a couple of years later in 1938. Produced by Norman Marshall, the play starred actor Robert Morley as Wilde, who achieved considerable fame for his performance, with accolades being showered on both sides of the Atlantic. Commenting on the play, the critic John Sloan observes:

> Based closely on the court transcripts of Wilde's trials, *Oscar Wilde* provided the first frank, factual presentation of homosexuality on the stage. The Stokeses' Wilde was a challenging iconoclast, bent on offending social and moral convention. "I like people with no principles better than anyone else in the world" he announces. . . . This was again the homosexual as effete and effeminate, as the Victorians had seen him, a victim of his own flagrant egotism and weakness, reduced by the end to a pitiable drunkard, living in exile abroad. (Sloan 172)

David Hare's play *The Judas Kiss* (1998) focuses on Wilde's humiliation and disgrace in the hands of his young lover Bosie or Lord Alfred Douglas. The play concentrates on two significant phases in Wilde's late life—his decision to stay in England and go through the trial facing incarceration, and the night after his release when Lord Alfred Douglas abandons him. The play juxtaposes Wilde's quest for freedom through love with Alfred's betrayal. The play portrays Wilde as a character who defends his sexuality on the grounds of love and liberty. Act I, symbolically subtitled "Deciding to Stay," opens with a luxurious bed, a comfortable sofa and a table in an ornate room at the elegant Cadogan Hotel in London on the afternoon of Wilde's arrest. It is the day in which Wilde decides to reject exile and stay back in England, where he is arrested at the end of this act. Act II, significantly subtitled "Deciding to Leave," is set near Naples. It is the night when Lord Alfred Douglas decides to abandon Wilde, who remains alone after Douglas has left. Thus the play may be interpreted as a portrayal of Wilde's journey from a prosperous luminary existence to one of ignominy and shame. The stage in itself is emblematic of Wilde's journey into a world of deep sense of void, trauma and loss. In the Spanish version of the play, director Miguel Narros insists that "even nowadays society 'tolerates' but does not really accept homosexuality" (qtd. in Aransáez). As Cristina Pascual Aransáez points out in the review of the play:

> This leads him to stage an original version of *The Judas Kiss* which revolves exclusively around the different manifestations

> of homosexuality in the play: the love relationship between Wilde and Douglas, the passionate encounters between Douglas and Galileo, the intimate friendship between Wilde and his former lover Robert Ross. Hence the absence of heterosexual relationships in the Spanish version of the play is intended to prevent the public from seeing homosexuality as an alternative to heterosexual love to give it the category of LOVE in its own right, and it marks a radical departure from those productions of the play staged in New York and London.

The Judas Kiss offers a subtle exploration of the most critical situations in Wilde's later years which make the audience reflect over the problems derived from the hypocrisy and homophobia which are still present in the society:

> However, *The Judas Kiss* is far from presenting a mythologized portrait of Wilde as a modern gay icon and it lays emphasis on the image of Wilde as a man who defends his sexuality on the grounds of love and liberty. In fact, one of the main purposes of the play is to contribute to undermine many clichés about Wilde's personality and to show many stereotypical attitudes of Wilde under a proper light. (Aransáez)

Visual representations of history and biographical proceedings on the stage carry their own set of challenges. Yet, of all these challenges, the most significant one perhaps lies in the creation of theatrical impact without compromising on the accuracy and veracity of the biographical details. In that context, Moisés Kaufman's stage adaptation of Oscar Wilde's trials attempts and manages to strike a remarkable balance. As a case study, an analysis of this play reveals the various socio-cultural forces and challenges that come into play while portraying Wilde's trials on the stage. As Todd Barry argues, "through Kaufman's play, the sodomy trial is repeated in contemporary theatres for a new jury, the theatrical spectators/witnesses" (Barry 55). First produced on the stage by Tectonic Theatre Project at the Greenwich House Theatre in New York City on February 27, 1997, Moisés Kaufman's *Gross Indecency: The Three Trials of Oscar Wilde* makes an earnest effort to transform century-old transcripts, newspaper accounts, various letters and telegrams, to conjure up a riveting theatrical presentation of the 1895 arrest and trials that culminated in Oscar Wilde's two-year imprisonment for the 'gross indecency' of sodomy. The compelling narrative on the stage visually tries to re-capture the time, while brilliantly portraying the protagonist in his self-aggrandizing complexity and deep-rooted aesthetic convictions. In the author's introduction to the play, Moises Kaufman states:

> In making *Gross Indecency: The Three Trials of Oscar Wilde* I was interested in two things: First, I wanted to tell the story—a story—of these trials. And second, I was interested in using this story to continue to explore theatrical language and form. Specifically how can theatre reconstruct history? (Kaufman xiv)

The adaptation of Wilde's trial scenes for the stage had its own storehouse of problems. The difficulty of portrayal on the stage was further compounded by the existence of various versions of the same tortuous experience. Kaufman's effort to reconstruct the historical occurrence attempts to strike a balance between these diverse accounts of the trial. As he asserts, there were various factors to be balanced for the stage adaptation: the impact of the trial on Wilde's personal life, his association with Alfred Douglas, the reactions of the homophobic society, the hostility of the contemporary press and legal system and several others. Balancing all these issues was extremely difficult for Kaufman:

> Very early in the process of researching the play, I found that there were as many versions of what had occurred at the trials as there were people involved. . . . It seemed to me that any legitimate attempt to reconstruct this historical event had to incorporate, in one way or another, the diversity of accounts. This posed a fascinating problem: how to create a theatre piece that could encompass all the different stories, and yet have a coherent, dramatic through-line. (Kaufman xiv)

Directing such a challenging script inflated Kaufman's task of portraying biographical history on the stage. Perhaps some of these dominant issues were at the back of Kaufman's mind, as he mentions in his prefatory note:

> As soon as the actors began to personify historical characters, they brought to these portrayals their own histories, their own "versions" of who the characters were and what the conflict between them was about. I knew that the piece had to make that presence—the presence of the actor telling the story—visible. (Kaufman xiv-xv)

Kaufman's tryst with queer politics on the stage has been a continuous process. Besides *Gross Indecency,* his reputation also rests on *The Laramie Project*—a three-act play about the 1998 murder of gay college student Matthew Shepard from the University of Wyoming, Laramie. The play was premiered at the Ricketson Theatre by the Denver Centre Theatre Company in February 2000. Akin to *Gross Indecency,* a great deal of extensive research went into construction of this play. In association with other members of the Tectonic Theatre Project, of which Kaufman is founder and director, the members conducted interviews and drew on news reports as well as their own experiences in the local community to create a documentary-style drama that relates the story with a combination of good investigative journalism and deeply felt emotions. Yet the roots of this dramatic technique can be traced to *Gross Indecency: The Three Trials of Oscar Wilde*, which also strove to strike a balance between history and theatrics to weave a compelling piece of theatre. In the authorial note to the play, Moisés Kaufman delineates the basic premises:

> This play has been inspired by techniques used by Erwin Piscator and the young Bertolt Brecht. In this regard, the performers should portray the characters in the play without "disappearing" into the parts. (Kaufman 5)

Commenting on the source material Kaufman elaborates:

> When the text in the play comes from a historical account, the author and name of the book from which the text comes is stated by the narrators. There are two exceptions to this:
>
> One is when there are several texts that come from different books by the same author. When this is the case, only the first book is mentioned.
>
> Second, as the play progresses and Oscar Wilde's world collapses, so does this formal device. Therefore, in the second act not all sources are stated. (Kaufman 5)

The play opens with the first trial of Wilde. In the late nineteenth century, the trial had generated a huge amount of interest among the masses, the elite and the common alike. This aspect has been explored through the narrators' voices in the play. As narrator 4 articulates: "Several hours before the day's business opened at the Old Bailey this morning people were using every effort to gain admission to the old court. Never, perhaps, have so many prominent persons been disappointed to find their prominence would not serve them to gain entrance to a criminal court" (Kaufman 12).

However, Kaufman's play scores on other areas. His visual representation incorporates a miscellany of perspectives accumulated from other documentary and literary sources. Notable literary references include "Ballad of the Reading Gaol," *De Profundis*, *The Autobiography of Lord Alfred Douglas* among several others. In this context, Kaufman's incorporation of extracts from *The Autobiography of Lord Alfred Douglas*, which was written three decades after the trial, is worthy of mention. Enacted by Bill Dawes in the original cast, Kaufman puts the following words in his recollection of the 'astonishing' experience of first meeting with Wilde:

> I had never heard a man talking with such perfect sentences before, as if he had written them all overnight with labour and yet all spontaneous. He did succeed in weaving spells. It all appeared to be Wisdom and Power and Beauty and Enchantment. One sat and listened to him enthralled. (Kaufman 17)

Gross Indecency: The Three Trials of Oscar Wilde captures and masterfully recreates the gradual evolution of the relationship between Wilde and Douglas on the stage, by making both characters engage in a conversation, underlining the gradual evolution of the fatal relationship. As their conversation reveals, both Douglas and Wilde were besotted with each other, and visual representation on stage recreates it authentically:

> Douglas: From the moment we met he made up to me in every possible way. He was continually asking me to dine or lunch with him. He flattered me, gave me presents and made much of me in every way. He gave me copies of all his books, with inscriptions in them.
>
> Wilde: Your slim gilt soul walks between passion and poetry. I know Hyacinthus, whom Apollo loved so madly, was you in Greek days.
>
> Douglas: I was from the first flattered that a man as distinguished as he should pay me so much attention and attach so much importance to all my views and preferences and whims. . . .
>
> Douglas: I will say of him that even if he had never written a line of poetry, he would still be the most wonderful man I ever met. (Kaufman 17-18)

Kaufman's script takes the reader/audience straight into the tussle between the aesthetic enunciation of an artist on the one hand and the clinical pragmatic undermining of the legal phraseology on the other. Queer representation on the stage remarkably reproduces this scrimmage. The dramatic struggle clearly demarcates the two worlds, each oblivious of the goals and objectives of the other, though unrelentingly steadfast in pursuit of respective agenda. Through his aesthetic assertions, Wilde gives out evidences unwittingly, which pave the way for further grilling by lawyers like Carson in the court room:

Carson: Apart from art, Mr Wilde?

Wilde: I cannot answer apart from art.

Carson: Suppose a man who was not an artist had written this letter, would you say it was a proper letter?

Wilde: A man who was not an artist could not have written that letter.

Carson: Why?

Wilde: Because nobody but an artist could write it. He certainly could not write the language unless he were a man of letters.

Carson: I can suggest, for the sake of your reputation, that there is nothing very wonderful in this "red rose lips of yours"?

Wilde: A great deal depends on the way it is read.

Carson: "Your slim gilt soul walks between passion and poetry." Is that a beautiful phrase?

Wilde: Not as you read it, Mr Carson. You read it very badly.

Carson: I do not profess to be artist; and when I hear you give evidence, I am glad I am not. (Kaufman 34-35)

A good deal of Carson's attacks in the court was insinuatory by nature, exploring and focusing on Wilde's literary output. Besides asking general queries on Wilde's contributions to *The Chameleon*, an Oxford undergraduate publication, Carson focused on Douglas's poem "Two Loves," and asked Wilde: "Did you think that made any improper suggestion?" "None whatever," Wilde replied, and referred to it as a beautiful poem. On the assumption that Wilde had sanctioned and approved the contents of "The Priest and the Acolyte" for inclusion and publication in The Chameleon, Carson accosted Wilde with a barrage of further insinuations. Branding it as an 'improper story' where "a priest falls in love with a boy who serves him at the altar, and is discovered by the rector in the priest's room" (38). Carson's cross-examination of Wilde, as portrayed in Kaufman's play, renews the artist's quest to counter the clinical legal dissection:

Carson: Have you read "The Priest and the Acolyte"?

Wilde: Yes.

Carson: You have no doubt whatever that that was an improper story?

Wilde: From a literary point of view it was highly improper. It would be impossible for a man of literature to judge it otherwise; by literature I mean treatment, selection of subject, and the like. I thought the treatment rotten and the subject rotten.

Carson: You are of the opinion, I believe, that there is no such thing as an immoral book?

Wilde: That is correct.

Carson: May I take it you think "The Priest and the Acolyte" was not immoral?

Wilde: It was worse. It was badly written.

Carson: Did you think the story blasphemous?

Wilde: The story filled me with disgust. The end was wrong.

Carson: Answer the question, sir. Did you or did you not consider the story blasphemous?

Wilde: I thought it horrible. "Blasphemous" is not a word of mine. In writing a play or a book, I am concerned entirely with literature, that is, with art. I am not at doing good or evil, but at making a thing that will have some quality of beauty. (Kaufman 38-39)

The second act of Kaufman's play opens with an interview with Professor Marvin Taylor, the Wilde scholar at New York University, and co-editor of the book *Reading Wilde*. Taylor's perspective opens up several issues for the audience:

> You know ... there is this real nexus of issues that are on trial with Oscar Wilde and they have to do with the role of art, with effeminacy, with homosexuality, with the Irish in England, with class.... So it's not just the fact that Wilde was being tried for sodomy ... that's not the ... major point of what's going on. I truly believe that the sodomy charges are really the less important. Wilde was being tried for his subversive beliefs about art, about morality hum ... about Victorian Society. (Kaufman 75)

In addition to the court proceedings, Kaufman's play moves on to cite from *The English Renaissance of Art*, as Wilde reiterates that "the arts are the only civilising influences in the world, and without them people are barbarians" (Kaufman 85). As Gill tries to entangle the notions of 'moral' and 'immoral' with the concept of art, Wilde waxes eloquent on the creed of aesthetics. In course of the grilling, Gill yet again refers to Douglas's poem "Two Loves" which makes the observation: "I am the Love that dare not speak its name." Wilde's rebuttal makes the lofty proclamation alluding to Plato, Michelangelo and Shakespeare, insisting that there is "nothing unnatural about it." Kaufman's portrayal of the third trial scene at the Old Bailey Central Criminal Court saw the verdict being delivered. On the day when the jury was to deliver its verdict on Wilde and the judge his sentence, Wilde wrote to console his lover in the face of inevitable separation:

> be happy to have filled with an immortal love the soul of a man who now weeps in hell, and yet carries heaven in his heart. I love you, I love you, my heart is a rose which your love has brought to bloom, my life is a desert fanned by the delicious breeze of your breath, and whose cool springs are your eyes; the imprint of your little feet makes valleys of shade for me, the odour of your hair is like myrrh, and wherever you go you exhale the perfumes of the cassia tree. (qtd. in Varty 207)

The historic verdict saw the incarceration of Wilde for two years. The visual representation of the verdict recreates the atmosphere of tragic doom and finality. Wilde's retort: "And I? May I say nothing, my lord?" fails to evoke any show of clemency as he had to surrender himself to the warders:

> Judge: Oscar Wilde, the crime of which you have been convicted is so bad that one has to put a firm restraint upon oneself to prevent oneself from describing, in terms I would rather not use, the sentiments which must rise to the breast of every man of honour who has heard the details of these terrible three trials. It is no use for me to address you. People who can do these things are dead to all sense of shame, and one cannot hope to produce any effect upon them. This is the worst case I have ever tried. I shall, under such circumstances, be expected to pass the severest sentence allowed by the law. It is in my opinion, totally inadequate for such a case as this. (Kaufman 116)

The Epilogue of the play compiles the reactions of the press to the verdict, underlining the layers of deep-rooted homophobia omnipresent in the British Victorian society. Most notably, *The Daily Telegraph* proclaimed: "Open the windows! Let in the fresh air!" *The News of the World* announced: "The Aesthetic Cult is over!" while *The St James Gazette* observed: "A dash of wholesome bigotry is better than over toleration!" The "Epilogue" also informs the reader about the fate of Wilde following his two-year incarceration. Following his death, Oscar Wilde was buried at Bagneux Cemetery on December 3, 1900. Lord Alfred Douglas was one of the twelve people who attended the burial. After Wilde's demise Lord Alfred Douglas married and had two children. He became a Catholic, and eventually a Nazi sympathiser. The third narrator informs the audience that the Marquess of Queensberry died in 1899, a pathetic victim of persecution mania, convinced to the last that he was being harried to the tomb by 'Oscar Wilders' as he used to describe is imaginary tormentors. The Coda of the play imparts a symbolic spiritual dimension to the visual representation of the trials:

Narrator 8: Surely I will send thee into Hell. Even into Hell will I send thee.
Narrator 5: And the Man cried out:
Narrator 1: Thou canst not.
Narrator 5: And God said to the Man:
Narrator 2: Wherefore can I not send thee to Hell, and for what reason?
Narrator 1: Because in Hell I have always lived,
Narrator 5: Answered the Man.
And there was silence in the House of Judgement.
And after a space God spake, and said to the Man:
Narrator 7: Then surely I will send thee unto Heaven. Even unto Heaven will I send thee.
Narrator 5: And the Man cried out:
Narrator 1: Thou canst not.
Narrator 5: And God said to the Man:
Narrator 6: Wherefore can I not send thee unto Heaven, and for what reason?
Narrator 1: Because never, and in no place, have I been able to imagine it,
Narrator 5: Answered the Man.
And there was silence in the House of Judgement.
(Kaufman 132-134)

In the "Afterword" to the play, Tony Kushner lauds the "marvellous subtlety" of the play. As he points out,

> Wilde's anti-government anarchism meant something very different in the 1880s and '90s than it does in the 1980s and '90s. All anarchisms, even ego-anarchism, a hundred years ago were politically positioned to the left; this is no longer the case. Wilde shares with all anarchisms both an inescapable truth, that where there is law there is no freedom (in the absolute sense—and anarchism is always absolute), and an unavoidable silliness. (Kaufman 137)

Visual representations of Oscar Wilde's character, especially as one refracted through endurance of the trial, has been a recurrent subject of portrayal on the stage. In his work *The Wilde Century*, Alan Sinfield asserts that the Wilde trials had a great role to play in shaping the cultural image of the homosexual man: "the trials helped to produce a major shift in perceptions of the scope of same-sex passions" (3). Sinfield argues that "the vaguely disconcerting nexus of effeminacy, leisure, idleness, immorality, luxury, insouciance, decadence and aestheticism, which Wilde was perceived" was gradually "transformed into a brilliantly precise image" (ibid.). As a consequence of such a transformation, according to Sinfield, "the principal twentieth-century stereotype entered our cultures: not just the homosexual, as the lawyers and medics would have it, but the queer" (ibid.). The trials had a significant role to play in this transformation. As David Schultz points out, "the trials are often implicitly credited as the event where the Homosexual emerged as a social subject" (37). It is undeniable that his trial brought the issue of homosexuality to the forefront as crucial social issue: "That the homosexual in question was a brilliant and controversial society dramatist who satirically fetishized society, and who fostered his own popular fetishization, only added to the irony and insidiousness of his persona" (ibid.). Schultz further rightly asserts, "To many an appalling but titillating spectacle, the Wilde trials also represent an important moment in the history of modern male homosexuality, providing for historians a marker to locate the emergence of a distinct homosexual identity" (ibid.). In concurrence with Schultz's opinion, Todd Barry further asserts in *From Wilde to Obergefell: Gay Legal Theatre, 1895-2015* that "since the Wilde trials, gradually gay legal theatre's master narrative worked toward cultural acceptance of gay identity" (28). Recurrent successful staging of the Wilde trial paves the way for the audience to empathize with the wider cultural anxiety surrounding the emergence of queer identity. This anxiety alludes to the defiance and distinctive breach of conduct as endorsed by the patriarchy for all generations alike. As Schultz observes, "The juridical proceedings in the spring of 1895 began the marshalling of widespread cultural forces intent on mending the breach in the patriarchy caused by Wilde's public posturing" (39). Wilde's extolling and glorification of homosexual relationship during the trials, as Barry also rightly argues, could be interpreted as "indicative of the performative construction" of the "hetero-patriarchal claim to power" (59). In accordance with these critical observations, the recurrent focus on portrayal of Wilde's trial on the stage, much beyond a century of the actual trial, doesn't come as much of a surprise. In his work *Oscar Wilde Prefigured: Queer Fashioning and British Caricature 1750-1900*, Dominic Janes argues that in the historic trial the question that mattered was not the issue of Wilde being a sodomite or not, but whether people could appear to be sodomites. As Alan Sinfield asserts, "the point is not Wilde's true identity but the identity that the trials foisted on him" (145).

Individualisation of various characters of the play further compounded the queer mechanics of representation of trauma and memory on the stage. On the stage, the psycho-dynamics and the mechanics of enactment of the Wilde trials operate at multiple levels. In fact, for a reader of the play, or a member of the audience watching it, the roots of this dramatic conflict persist even today at various levels: a conflict between the realities of queer existence in different time periods of history, the deep-rooted engagement between contemporary reality and the one that persisted during the late Victorian period, the struggle between exposure to the world and being in the closet, the tussle to weave a unique distinctive queer narrative or to endorse and articulate same-sex love within the parameters and limitations of a heteronormative discourse, the conflict between private choice and public disgrace, the struggle to garb sexuality with aesthetics and finally the most significant issue of the quest for a decisive queer identity.

Works Cited

Aransáez, Pascual Cristina. "The Judas Kiss in Madrid." Review of the Spanish Version of David Hare's The Judas Kiss. *The OScholars* 4.10(42) (October-November 2007). "The Critic as Critic." www.oscholarship.com/TO/Archive/Forty-two/Critic/ THE%20 CRITIC%20AS%20CRITIC.htm#_The_Judas_Kiss.

Barry, Todd. "From Wilde to Obergefell: Gay Legal Theatre, 1895-2015." Dissertation, University of Connecticut, 2016. digitalcommons:uconn.edu/cgi/viewcontent.

Bosanquet, Theo. "Oscar Wilde's Grandson Merlin Holland: 'We've Got as Close as We Can to Hearing Him Speak." *WhatsOnStage*. 13 October 2014. https://www.whatsonstage.com/london-theatre/news/merlin-holland-oscar-wilde-trials-interview_36091.html.

Coppa, Francesca. "The Artist as Protagonist: Wilde on Stage." *Oscar Wilde and Modern Culture: The Making of a Legend*. Ed. Joseph Bristow. Athens, OH: Ohio University Press, 2008. 259-284.

Crowther, Bosley. "Wilde Absolved: Writer's Trials Get New Examination." *The New York Times* 28 June 1960. 26.

Eagleton, Terry. *Saint Oscar*. Derry: Field Day, 1989.

Ellman, Richard. *Oscar Wilde*. London: Penguin, 1988.

Hare, David. *The Judas Kiss*. New York: Grove Press, 1998.

Kaufman, Moises. *Gross Indecency: The Three Trials of Oscar Wilde*. New York: Vintage, 1998.

Mahoney, Elisabeth. Review of Oscar Wilde. *The Guardian* 21 October 2004.

MacLiammoir, Micheal. *The Importance of Being Oscar*. Gerrards Cross, Bucks.: Colin Smythe, 1995.

Schultz, David. "Redressing Oscar: Performance and the Trials of Oscar Wilde." *TDR* 40.2 (Summer 1996): 37-59.

Sinfield, Alan. *The Wilde Century: Oscar Wilde, Effeminacy and the 'Queer' Moment*. New York: Columbia University Press, 1994.

________. "I See It Is My Name that Terrified Wilde in the Twentieth Century." *The Wilde Legacy*. Ed. Eilean Ni Chuilleanain. Dublin: Four Courts, 2003. 136-152.

Sloan, John. *Oscar Wilde*. Oxford: Oxford University Press, 2003.

Stokes, Leslie, and Sewell Stokes. *Oscar Wilde*. London: Random House, 1938.

Varty, Anne. *A Preface to Oscar Wilde*. London: Pearson, 2003.

"Just Say Yes:" Queer Theatrical Portrayals of AIDS and the Rejection of Safer Sex[1]

LARA S. NARCISI

> There's always been a difficulty with the rhetoric of AIDS. You're trying to find positive things in a holocaust like this, so you say, 'Well, it has taught people certain things and it's made us a different kind of community,' and it actually has forged alliances between the lesbian community and the gay community that didn't exist. Those are good things, but still, wouldn't we all much rather never have had it.
>
> —Tony Kushner, qtd. in Vorlicky (201)

Scare Tactics to Care Tactics

AIDS, the most dreaded epidemic in the final decades of the 20th century, has become an afterthought in the 21st. The seemingly miraculous preventive drug Truvada is only the most recent of incredible medical advances; increased awareness and behavioral changes have also helped to transform a previous plague into an innocuous news item. Nevertheless, HIV remains incurable and still afflicts 1.2 million Americans, and almost thirty-seven million people worldwide (CDC). Popular media has contributed to this transition; AIDS appears less and less frequently in the news, in television, in film. The animated series *South Park* used a running pun on "AIDS" and "aides" in the 2002 episode, "Jared Has Aides," in which AIDS is touted as a weight-loss strategy and, in the end, is declared funny because a sufficient (and arbitrary) amount of time had passed: "22.3 years. That's how long it takes for something tragic to become funny" (Parker).[2] Perhaps in response to trivializations such as these, Louise Hogarth created a short documentary with the telling title, *Does Anyone Die of AIDS Anymore?*; in

[1] A version of this essay appeared in *The Apollonian: A Journal of Interdisciplinary Studies* 2.3 (December 2015): 84-102.

[2] Interestingly, this episode was banned—but because of its references to child abuse, not AIDS.

2003 she completed a longer film, *The Gift*, which details the horrifying practice of "bugchasing," or engaging in risky behavior to deliberately catch HIV. Both films suggest the danger of our current societal attitude; while the disease is still a killer, it is rarely presented as such, thus encouraging complacency rather than activism.

The queer theater community, struck particularly hard by the disease, was once at the forefront of AIDS representations, galvanizing the populace to combat an encroaching epidemic. As Steven Winn described earlier plays in the *San Francisco Chronicle*, "It was in the live theater, more than anywhere else in the arts, that AIDS found its most penetrating voice. The forms and immediacy of the medium; the centuries-old potency of agit-prop; the almost sacramental power of live actors enacting stories of death, defiance and endurance all preordained it." This, too, has changed, in our contemporary era. A 2004 *Village Voice* article describes the recent trend in AIDS plays, citing *Biro*, *The Long Christmas Ride Home*, and *Small Tragedy*, as plays in which "when AIDS appears, it's just another bombshell—a thematic layer that alerts the audience to something profound" (Goldstein). When, then, did the theater community begin to move from a strong activist position to one of peaceful coexistence between man and disease? In this article I examine three queer AIDS plays of the 1990s indicative of the transition from demonizing the virus to demonizing excessive anxiety over its proliferation. As Tony Kushner's epigraph here implies, this change likely stems from an understandable desire to mitigate some of the harsh stereotypes of AIDS victims by creating "a kind of community" and "forg[ing] alliances" (Vorlicky 201). In *Angels in America*, *Jeffrey*, and *Rent*, this sense of community appears so important as to outweigh concerns for safe sex practices; indeed, it is consistently the uninfected who appear outcast and alone. Decades after these plays, what are we to make of their impact? Fear, once a galvanizing force for prevention, becomes the thing to fear itself; safe sex practices become denials of connection and intimacy; the HIV-negative suffer from survivor guilt and exclusion for this sense of community. As the AIDS crisis continues, our response to it—in the media and in art—may well impact out attempts at prevention and an actual cure.

Looking Back: How Did We Get Here?

Immediately following the first official announcement of the retrovirus by the Center for Disease Control in 1981, AIDS appeared a gradually encroaching intruder, and the theater of the time portrayed it as an emerging and increasingly horrifying menace. Much has been written about Larry Kramer's 1985 *The Normal Heart*, now revived into an HBO original movie, which contrasts enraged activism and timid passivity. William Finn's less well-known *Falsettos*, a two-part musical premiering in 1981 and 1990, respectively, contains a similar if subtler message. The second part, *Falsettoland*, features a rather comedic and light-hearted beginning involving baseball and bar mitzvahs which quickly changes tone once Dr. Charlotte looks up from her newspaper and declares, to ominous musical accompaniment, "Something very bad is happening / and it's spreading, spreading, spreading" (Finn 152). Because the musical is set in the early 1980s, this new disease afflicting homosexual men proves mystifying to Dr. Charlotte and the others; but the early-1990s audience is painfully aware that the "something bad" is AIDS and its lethality is inevitable. The remainder of the play has an aura of Greek tragedy to it, presenting a homosexual community that has finally risen to a state of strength and happiness, only to be struck down by the mysterious plague. As in Euripides or Sophocles, *Falsettoland* provides an uncomfortable dramatic irony, stemming in this case from the viewer's knowledge that the innocent homosexual sex scenes are in fact permeated by the threat of a then-unknown illness. And as in Greek drama, one of the protagonists dies in the end, leaving his family (of sorts) bereft and possibly infected as well. Through a chain of transmission Whizzer's illness implicates his lover Marvin, and thus Marvin's wife, their son, her new lover. The endearing and unique community of the play becomes dangerous: all intimacy is potentially lethal.

By the mid-1990s, a very different view was emerging: the perils of intimacy gave way instead to the perils of its lack. AIDS had rapidly become a permanent part of society, and the *Falsettoland* form of tragedy gave way to a new theatrical trendless concerned with promoting disease prevention and more invested in enabling PWAs (People with AIDS) and their loved ones to live with it as effectively as possible. Many critics observed this trend. In 1996 Charles McNulty wrote of *Angels in America* that "activism has lulled, militancy has subsided into earnest concern. . . . AIDS, though still deadly, has been symbolically tamed" (90).[3] In AIDS plays of the 1990s the disease increasingly became just one more strand in the fabric of daily life.

In recent years American society's focus has shifted from preventing and combating the disease to enabling the nation and individuals to live most effectively with it. Most plagues throughout history share this progression; the desire to live "normally" is a characteristic human

[3] See also Monica Pearl and Sarah Schulman on this topic.

phenomenon, and can often lead us to overlook or ignore potential risks. Daniel Defoe writes of the most famous of epidemics, The Plague: "in the middle of all this Horror . . . [the townsfolk] behaved with all the Revelling and roaring extravagances, as is usual for such People to do at other Times" (82). Defoe describes the persistent desire for human contact even in the face of the Black Death, at a time when quarantine was a necessary precaution. We see similar resistance in Camus' *The Plague*, or in the ebullient revelers operatically defying tuberculosis in both *La Traviata* and *La Bohème*. A growing awareness of a disease's lethality often creates a need to celebrate life rather than death; and, paradoxically, serves to encourage unsafe practices. Just as Londoners refused to be shut up in their houses during Defoe's Plague, characters in the AIDS plays of the 1990s refuse to be confined by sanitary sexual practices.

The three plays I discuss below all discourage safe sex as antithetical to our basic humanity, a barrier which impedes natural relationships and excludes the uninfected from a crucial sense of community. David Román's 1997 article, "Negative Identifications: HIV-Negative Gay Men in Representation and Performance," discusses the fear of being left out of a community, noting how HIV-negative men shifted from a cultural feeling of superiority to a sense of exclusion. He cites the appalling assumption of the time that all homosexuals would eventually become HIV-positive as one of the contributing societal factors, noting that the "logic of inevitability" can sometimes cause HIV-negative homosexual men to "embark on fantasies of seroconversion. In a response to a culture that systematically denies their identity and experience, some HIV-negative men assume the seroconversion will bring meaning to their lives and attention and love" (167). The trend that Románo observed over a decade ago has, I would argue, only increased, as seen in the practice of "bugchasing," however rare (Aldridge). While this perspective offers a crucially victim-friendly, life-affirming perspective of the illness, it also potentially decreases the scare factor that could be significant in halting the progress of the disease as an inducement to safer sex practices.

Tony Kushner's Angels in America: HIV-Positive and Positive Change

In his 1993 essay "Fick Oder Kaputt!" ("Fuck or Die"), Tony Kushner raises this weighty question: in the age of AIDS, "*Is* sex or life more important?" (15) His answer is understandably conflicted, but he resolves in the end, "if they decide kissing isn't safe then fuck it, we'd all rather be dead" (14). Kushner goes on to consider what life is possible if we over-sanitize or completely abstain from this basic life process. When questioned about the topic in the same year by *Body Positive*, an HIV+ support group publication, he replied with similar hesitation: "I do think sex is incredibly important, part of what we are. And I don't think we should let a health issue dictate... Oh, it's so complicated" (Vorlicky 53). Unsurprisingly, *Angels in America* mirrors this ambivalence: in the context of the play the risk of AIDS is far less terrifying than the alternative threat of isolation, and by the end of the play it is the HIV-negative Louis and Joe who remain on the outside of society while dying Prior is welcomed into heaven and touched by an angel.

If the play condemns Louis to isolation, it is for his crime of leaving the man he has loved for four and a half years simply because he cannot handle the disease. From the beginning he seeks spiritual solvency from the rabbi at his grandmother's funeral, only to be spurned:

> Louis: Rabbi, what does the Holy Writ say about someone who abandons someone he loves at a time of great need? . . . [Because] maybe that person can't, um, incorporate sickness into his sense of how things are supposed to go. Maybe vomit... and sores and disease... really frighten him, maybe... he isn't so good with death.
>
> Rabbi Isidore: The Holy Scriptures have nothing to say about such a person. (I. 25)

Louis' fears seem understandable, but his choice to abandon his beloved is, in the context of the play, unforgivable. Indeed, Louis himself knows this, as after he leaves Prior he punishes himself by attempting to join the ranks of the diseased. Acknowledging the injustice of the fact that he was more promiscuous than Prior and yet has been spared, Louis can neither bear to stay and watch Prior die, nor to live his life alone. Consequently he goes bugchasing in Central Park, and seeks anonymous sex with a man who is, significantly, played by the same actor who plays Prior:

> Man: I think it broke. The rubber. You want me to keep going? (*Little pause*) Pull out? Should I...
>
> Louis: Keep going. Infect me. I don't care. I don't care. (I.57)

Louis' apparent recklessness is a masochistic attempt at absolution for his survivor's guilt. The greater scheme of the play condemns him as well, as Louis ends up alone as he feared. One of his few redeeming actions is to say the Kaddish over Roy Cohn, in essence forgiving a man he deems unforgivable because AIDS has rendered him in some way worthy of this final kindness. As Kushner stated in a 1993 interview with Charlie Rose, "In a certain sense, [Roy Cohn's] dying of this disease [AIDS] made him a part of the gay and lesbian community even if we don't really want him to be a part of our community." Because community is so significant in the play, the otherwise-sympathetic Louis' act of abandoning one in need appears to outweigh even Roy's rather staggering list of immoral and/or criminal acts.

Louis' rebound Mormon lover, Joe, is similarly guilty of deserting the sick that depend on him. He first abandons Roy, his AIDS-ridden father-figure, by refusing to accept the Washington position Roy begs him to accept. The play is more concerned, however, with his choice to abandon his valium-addicted wife for a quest of personal fulfillment and sexual discovery, and the dynamic between Joe and Harper often parallels that between Louis and Prior. After their ill-fated affair, neither Louis nor Joe is allowed to return to where they began; in a split scene, Prior and Harper simultaneously reject their former lovers' pleas for reconciliation. After these renunciations, Prior ascends to the angels, and Harper ascends to the heavens through more average means, delivering her final monologue from an airplane bound for San Francisco. As the play equates these two characters and their fates, Prior's disease becomes little more than Harper's valium addiction: a persistent problem, but one that pales in comparison to the moral sickness of those who reject connection for individualistic interests.

This is not to say that AIDS isn't a formidable opponent in the play, but rather that struggling against it makes the characters stronger in the end. Kushner forces the audience into growing awareness—just as Prior forces Louis, and just as the disease itself has forced its way into global consciousness—by showing AIDS in all its corporeal horror. Prior faints, moans, screams in pain, and defecates blood on stage. He spends much of the play bedridden, either in the hospital or in his own home. Roy, though a far less sympathetic character, also suffers visibly from the disease, even spraying Joe with the blood from his extracted I.V. and threatening, "I'll bite. And I got rabies" (II.54). AIDS, however, grants Prior and, to a lesser extent, Roy, a separate status. Villainous Roy dies of AIDS disbarred and despised; he has no revelations, only visions of the woman he killed. He has lived his life afraid of being "booted out of the parade" (II.189), and indeed ends up excluded from the final community at the end. Despite all his actions in life, however, the play does ambivalently forgive him, granting him at least the final Kaddish by Louis and the ghost of Ethel Rosenberg.[4] Prior, always good, becomes a prophet as a result of the disease, ascending to the heavens and receiving a gift from the angels: not a miraculous cure, but simply more time. With the benefit of these additional five years Prior learns to live with AIDS, as he graciously tells the audience in the uplifting epilogue: "This disease will be the end of many of us, but not nearly all. . . . We won't die secret deaths anymore. The world only spins forward. We will be citizens. The time has come" (II.146). As Prior speaks to the audience of survival and hope, his friends cluster around the statue of the healing angel Bethesda, immersed in a heated political discussion that has nothing to do with diseases or cures. Not only has AIDS become less terrifying, but it has in fact become a mechanism for positive change. The virus itself is frighteningly adaptive, using the body's own defenses against itself; our only human response, then, is to become equally adaptive. Monica Pearl concisely summarizes the play's final message: "If the angels herald stasis, AIDS heralds change, argument, politics, complexity, and, paradoxically, life" (775-6). Indeed, death is absent from the play's conclusion, and while AIDS remains, it appears a challenge to be confronted rather than a looming disaster with a foregone conclusion.

In the end Prior is neither pitiable nor the play's tragic hero, but rather becomes our narrator and guide. The play compares him explicitly to Jacob in his successful wrestling match against an angel; Ela Natu observes that he also bears some similarity to the Biblical prophet Elijah. Indeed, amidst all the corruption in the play—from Reaganite greed to homophobia to the destruction of the ozone layer—only the AIDS victim rises above the ashes to receive this prophet status. Because of his central role in the narrative, it is Prior and his disease that help the other characters grow and change as well. As Framji Minwalla describes, "AIDS makes Prior a prophet, Roy a human being; AIDS teaches Louis and Ethel to forgive and accept" (105). Minwalla sees hints in the play of the same attempts at optimism that Kushner conveys in the epigraph to this essay: there must be some positive outcome to this immense human suffering. The impact of AIDS diminishes as a result; compared to abandonment, isolation, and a loss of community, it is even the preferable outcome.

[4] For more on the complicated issue of Roy as AIDS victim, see Atsushi Fujita, "Queer Politics to Fabulous Politics in Angels in America: Pinklisting and Forgiving Roy Cohn."

Paul Rudnick's *Jeffrey*: AIDS for Everyman, AIDS for laughs

In Rudnick's 1993 play *Jeffrey*, like in *Angels*, homosexuality is the norm: all the major characters and most of the minor ones, from priest to waiter, are gay men. It is a single woman, Ann Marwood Bartle, who dances alone in the raucous group-number square dance ("she might hold a hobby horse or fire her pistols," the stage directions inform us); it is the T.V. reporter Chuck Farling, a straight white successful male, who is the visibly uncomfortable outsider in the midst of the Gay Pride parade. From his prototypically average-American perspective, Farling offers the apt description of Jeffrey as "a regular fellow—why he could be anyone, your son, your brother, the guy next door" (79). While Kushner's Prior is not only a typical, but a self-proclaimed "*stereo*typical" homosexual (II. 97), Jeffrey's sexuality is not apparent even at a parade where everyone else is presumed gay. His "Everyman" quality universalizes his love story and creates an easily relatable protagonist, but it also metaphorically represents "mainstream" America's deepest fears about AIDS: that it is not, in fact, limited to the homosexual population, but can strike anyone.[5] In *Disease and Representation* Sander Gilman suggests that in order to distance ourselves from disease "we must construct boundaries between ourselves and those categories of individuals whom we believe (or hope) to be more at risk than ourselves" (4). It may be easier to believe in some telltale sign that distinguishes gay from straight, healthy from sick, but in reality the world is full of Jeffreys who provide no clues at all and diseases that respect no boundaries. Even the audience is never certain of Jeffrey's serostatus; he is only "possibly negative" (59). In Chuck Farling's seemingly innocuous description—"he could be anyone"—the play may force the audience to confront a homophobic fear that both sexuality and serostatus are invisible and undetectable.

Jeffrey's "Everyman" image also universalizes his fear of sex and commitment; these are concerns applicable to anyone. The progression in the play is away from abstinence, towards sexual expression—the reverse of *Falsettoland* and other earlier AIDS plays. The first act begins with a consummately threatening image of the 1990s: in the middle of

[5] Consider the case of David Acer, the dentist who infected multiple patients with AIDS in the early 1990s. By 1993 the news reported that these infections might have been deliberate, and that Acer was attempting to prove that the disease attacked indiscriminately.

passionate sex, the condom breaks. Jeffrey consequently swears off sex forever, and the play persuades us that only once he agrees to initiate a relationship with his HIV+ admirer, Steve, can he begin to grow and progress. Like in *Angels*, then, it is not disease but human connection that lies at the center of the play; the disease becomes merely a catalyst for positive change.

As Jeffrey's various friends and relations advise, the denial of sexuality is the more insidious disease. The priest Father Dan, shocked by Jeffrey's refusal of his sexual favors, proclaims, "There is only one real blasphemy—the refusal of joy!" (69). There is little awareness in this work of the physical horrors of AIDS that appear so vividly in *Angels;* Jeffrey's friends even chide him for being overly macabre:

> Jeffrey: I can't see one more twenty-eight-year-old man with a cane.
>
> Sterling: Don't be ridiculous.
>
> Jeffrey: What are we doing? Cruising? Giggling? Pretending it's all some kind of a hoot? I can't keep passing hors d'oeuvres in a graveyard! I went out with Todd! I just saw him in the hospital and I don't recognize him! (41)

Sterling not only dismisses Jeffrey's concerns as "ridiculous," but shortly thereafter comments to his lover Darius that "Jeffrey is just having some sort of anxiety moment." Sterling's glib attitude stems in part from his own denial of Darius' illness and pending death. Sterling is, however, among the most articulate and clever characters in the play, giving his words, like his name, considerable value. Furthermore, the tone of the entire work seems to mock Jeffrey's anguish, as even during his obvious distress his lines (specifically about hors d'oeuvres in a graveyard) appear comical.

Rudnick himself sympathizes with Sterling and company. In a *New York Times* article defending *Jeffrey*'s brand of comedy, Rudnick identifies with the friends laughing at the funeral by noting that the funerals themselves have become pieces of theater:[6] "I have attended memorials where the deceased's phone messages were played, where a road company of *Starlight Express* was reunited, where the guests were handed song sheets for Sondheim's *Broadway Baby*" ("Laughing at AIDS"). Rudnick further suggests that when AIDS victims make themselves drama queens, and when the profusion of multicolored ribbons implies that "agony has become a festive corsage," laughter is the only sane response.

[6] Angels also raises this issue, as Belize defends a show-stopper queen's funeral that Prior finds depressing.

This is not to say that the play ignores tragedy completely; the sweet chorus boy Darius does die of AIDS. Rudnick, however, omits his actual death from the play, and he returns from the grave to provide sage advice to Jeffrey. His death in essence becomes part of a theatrical motif rather than a moment intended to evoke real pathos; as Rudnick observes in his introduction, this is, throughout, a comedy. Darius appears post-mortem in a dazzling white *Cats* costume, apparently prepared to dance his way into the afterlife with only a brief stop-over to counsel his earth-bound friend:

Darius: Jeffrey, I'm dead. You're not.
Jeffrey: I know that.
Darius: You do? Prove it.
Jeffrey: What do you mean?
Darius: Go dancing. Go to a show. Make trouble. Make out.
Hate AIDS, Jeffrey, not life. (84)

Even Sterling, devastated by Darius' death, tells Jeffrey that he prefers to have loved and lost. Convinced by the testimony of his friends, Jeffrey prepares to step back into the world of sex and risk. In the final scene, Jeffrey pleasantly tosses a red balloon to his seropositive lover atop the Empire State Building. This moment proffers the traditional satisfaction of the romantic "happy ending" for our hero, who is prepared to embrace love and life as though the virus never existed. The only suggestion of disease comes metaphorically, as the red balloon recalls the broken condom from the play's opening: a fragile barrier indeed between life and death. Ultimately, the threat of AIDS becomes reduced to a balloon, a child's toy.

Many critics were shocked by this conclusion. Daniel Mufson notes the widespread view that *Jeffrey* was "morally and artistically evasive and irresponsible," observing that many critics "focused not so much on *Jeffrey*'s structural flaws as on Rudnick's levity in the face of tragedy," and that, "nearly everyone raised an eyebrow at mining AIDS for laughs" (116). Mufson observes aptly that Rudnick uses humor to lessen the misery the epidemic spawned. Rudnick makes this intention clear in his writings, interview, and even in the play's introduction when he describes his attempt to "capture the insanity of the AIDS era" through "a blend of the highest farce and the most devastating tragedy, laced with the gay style that has allowed a ravaged community to survive with its wisecracks and wardrobes intact" (vii).

While the play is extremely successful in its intended goal, I would argue that the farce and style of the play do threaten to supersede and perhaps eclipse the tragedy. Rudnick does not use humor in the service of a larger message, except on its own behalf: humor is an important weapon in our attempt to cope with any tragedy. Frank Rich, in a glowing review, notes that this is specifically not a black comedy: "Instead of writing about the bleak absurdity of meaningless death, Mr. Rudnick, with wicked honesty, focuses on the far more manic, at times bizarrely festive absurdity of those who survive." This is an apt description, but it reveals that the play's project is primarily to entertain rather than to galvanize. In the "lightness" of both its final balloon scene and the consistently comedic dialogue, Rudnick's play presents AIDS as a simple fact we must accept and live with rather than as a pandemic we must desperately attempt to avoid.

Rent: The Broader Community

Angels and *Jeffrey* examine AIDS through its effects on the homosexual communities most immediately impacted; Jonathan Larson's 1996 rock-opera, *Rent,* shows how the plague has spread beyond the boundaries of one particular group and infects people of all genders, races, and sexual orientations.[7] *Rent* is based on Puccini's *La Bohème* and, like the opera, focuses on a community of friends and a lethal disease. Of its three principal couples—one gay (male), one straight, and one lesbian—the first two are living with AIDS.[8] Like *Angels* and *Jeffrey, Rent* presents gay men with AIDS,[9] but it also depicts the heterosexual couple, Mimi and Roger, as heroin users who have presumably become infected from shared needles. Part of Larson's explicit project in writing the play was to challenge the view of the disease as a "gay cancer"; he observed that "the aim is to quash the already clichéd 'AIDS victim' stereotypes and point out that . . . AIDS affects everyone" (Gillies).[10] This is a challenging prospect, even today. According to Sander Gilman, even the ever-increasing evidence about the rapid spread of AIDS among heterosexuals has failed to eliminate

[7] The 2004 film *Team America* mocks the omnipresence of the disease in this play with its *Rent* parody, *Lease*, featuring a song, "Everyone has AIDS! / My grandma and my old dog blue / The Pope has got it and so do you."
[8] In line with statistical probability, the lesbian couple is uninfected.
[9] Homosexuality is still cited by the CDC as the most common means of transmission in the United States, but this is not necessarily true worldwide.
[10] In this context it is noteworthy that this is the only AIDS play discussed here authored by a straight playwright.

"the initial stereotyping of the individual living with AIDS as a marginal member of society" (269). Larson deliberately expands the scope of the disease beyond homosexuals, beyond men, and also beyond specific racial groups. As David Savran observes in an astutely critical article, *Rent* "takes an almost promiscuous pleasure in mixing races, sexualities, and a rainbow of genders," and is "the epitome of multiculturalism, in all its deceptive charm" (3). He goes on to critique its hip appropriation of a popular pluralism and simplistic ideology. I would add that the musical's tone implies that this "promiscuous pleasure" and the close-knit AIDS community—as in the previously discussed plays—is so important and, indeed, life-giving as to minimize the impact of the disease.

By focusing on community above all else, *Rent* normalizes AIDS as part of the simple fabric of society. A 1996 review of *Rent* published in *POZ*, a journal for people with AIDS, observes, "In *Rent* AIDS isn't a metaphor for the end of the century, the end of the world, the end of anything. AIDS just is. It's not pitied, it's not pampered, and it's not ignored" (Román 272). While the musical does not necessarily elide the trauma of the disease, none of the characters appear physically devastated by it in the same way Prior is in *Angels*; very close to the time of her near-death, Mimi is still singing her heart out and gyrating gymnastically at her strip club. Even her eventual decline can be attributed to heroin use and homelessness in winter rather than to the disease itself. This is a departure from typical depictions of AIDS, which, as Judith Sebesta points out, "is often viewed by society as a transgression of the normative body, particularly in its 'excretions' and the fear of spread of the disease from them, be they blood, semen, or wrongly, saliva" (436). She concludes that "Larson's modus operandi in depicting the AIDS body is to demystify its processes and functions, making it more visible" (436). I would argue that Larson's depiction, unlike Kushner's, makes the disease less visible—more akin to heart disease than to typical, more graphic, representations of Kaposi's sarcoma, lesions, emaciation, etc. This normalization of the disease is an important gesture in advocating for tolerance of PWAs as human beings, but it also contributes to the play's message that the infected community is so supportive as to be preferable to isolated health.

Here, as in *Angels* and *Jeffrey*, close connection and community appear worth the risk of infection. In a refrain of the show, the last line of which became its tagline, Mimi urges a "carpe diem" ideology:

There is no future, There is no past
I live this moment as my last

There's only us, There's only this,
Forget regret, or life is yours to miss
No other road, no other way,
No day but today. (87)

Although Mimi's philosophy is life-embracing, her negations still contain the language of the disease that has already claimed her: regret, missing life, last moments, no other way. AIDS is unfortunately a flagrant denial of Mimi's ideal of hedonism without consequences, a forced recognition of the possible aftermath of sexual or drug-induced pleasure. In "AIDS and its Metaphors" Susan Sontag observes this same issue:

> The fear of AIDS imposes on an act whose ideal is an experience of pure presentness (and a creation of the future) a relation to the past to be ignored at one's peril. Sex no longer withdraws its partners, if only for a moment, from the social. It cannot be considered just a coupling; it is a chain, a chain of transmission, from the past. (161)[11]

Mimi refuses to reflect on previous behaviors as the cause of contagion ("There is no past"); yet it is the shared thread of their pasts which unites the characters and forms their common bond. Sontag remarks that AIDS, unlike syphilis, never became romanticized as a hallmark of sexual prowess. In *Rent*, however, it becomes romanticized as the metaphorical link that connects people to one another. The play takes Sontag's negative image of a "chain of transmission" and converts it to a positive one.

Rent consistently emphasizes the importance of the community that has formed, in part, around their shared disease. The group, all disconnected from their parents, toasts "to being an 'us' for once, instead of a 'them'!" and delights that "this family tree has deep roots / friendship is thicker than blood." All eventually join Mimi's refrain that "There's only us." Notably, the two HIV+ couples only find love once they recognize their shared serostatus. Angel raises the issue almost immediately after meeting Collins:

Angel: Yes, this body provides a comfortable home
For the Acquired Immune Deficiency Syndrome.
Collins: As does mine.
Angel: Well! We'll get along fine! (74)[12]

These lines contain the same blithe tone as much of Rudnick's play, with the addition of rhymes and upbeat music. Similarly, Mimi's chipper call for an "AZT break!" informs Roger that they, too, share a disease; up until this moment Roger had been struggling repeatedly to confess his

[11] Interestingly, Larson cites this book as one of his influences in writing *Rent* (see Gillies, "Every Eight Seconds").
[12] Perhaps unsurprisingly, this glib line was cut from the 2005 film script.

serostatus to Mimi. Acknowledging their mutual condition opens the possibility of a relationship, and eventually connects the couples to their friends as well.

Paralleling the normative homosexual community in *Jeffrey*, the marginalized community of *Rent* is in fact so all-encompassing that it is Mark, the straight white healthy male, who is perpetually an outsider. Mark appears a stand-in for Larson, an HIV-negative man watching the disease's devastating effects on many of his peers: "A number of my friends, men and women, were finding out they were HIV-positive. I was devastated, and needed to do something" (Istel 16). Mark, much like Louis and Jeffrey, suffers emotionally for his health; sympathetic but detached, he can only observe as his friends attend AIDS support groups, fall in love, suffer loss, and connect with one another. "Why am I the witness?" he muses, "And when I capture it on film, does it mean that it's the end, and I'm alone?" (119). Mark's status as witness derives both from his disengagement ("You pretend to create and observe when you really detach from feeling alive," Roger accuses), and from his freedom from disease ("Perhaps it's because I'm the one of us to survive," Mark retorts) (121).

Mark's physical health seems only to increase his sense of isolation. In his book, *HIV-Negative: How the Uninfected Are Affected by AIDS*, William I. Johnston discusses this type of survivor guilt and sense of ostracism common to the HIV-negative members of communities devastated by AIDS. He discusses psychotherapist Walt Odets' concept of "the silent epidemic," which he describes as "widespread community depression among the HIV-negative [that] will continue to damage our physical, emotional, and spiritual health." Mark's internal struggles appear clearly through his painful awkwardness as he attends a Life Support meeting with Angel and Collins. Attempting only to videotape the proceedings, he fumbles over the simple act of introducing himself: "Oh—I'm not—I'm just here to—I don't have—I'm here with—Um—Mark—Mark—I'm Mark! Well—this is quite an operation" (81). Mark, like Jeffrey, appears to suffer from his lack of willingness to accept physical risk in exchange for love and connection.

Detachment and health are inextricably linked in *Rent*. Here again safe sex is equated with a spiritual death. The erotic song "Contact" begins as a seductive orgy, but—like the broken condom scene in *Jeffrey*—concludes in awkwardness, resentment, and a lack of connection due to the attempts at safe sex: "Yes! No! latex rubber rubber fire latex rubber latex bummer" (102).[13] The song suggests the ambivalence of how sexual contact can equally give life or take it away. In a play that so firmly embraces an attitude of celebrating life, however, it appears that the very attempts at protection are what destroys the passion between

[13] This song was also cut from the 2005 film.

the couples, as they all say simultaneously: "It was bad for me—was it bad for you?," indicating a unanimity of dissatisfaction in the attempt at safe sex.

In opposition to this is Angel, an innocent transvestite musician reminiscent of Darius, who is universally beloved and likewise dies of AIDS. In the midst of the safe-sex critique of "Contact" Angel cries his dying words: "Take me, take me, I love you" (102). These lines and the play as a whole suggest that Angel's willingness to risk connection renders him more content than the isolated, healthy Mark. Unlike Jeffrey, Mark does not find love in the conclusion; and while he, like Kushner's Louis, still has the comfortable companionship of all his friends, he remains the only one uncoupled. Roger becomes the focus in the conclusion, as he has the potential to risk a painful love or remain safe in unfulfilling isolation. Ultimately he, like Jeffrey, chooses love, in spite of the advancing disease which has already infected both him and Mimi.

As far as the play is concerned, AIDS never wins. *Rent* ends with Mimi's magical return to life, paralleling the reincarnations of Prior and, metaphorically, Jeffrey. This conclusion—the play's most obvious departure from its operatic source material[14]—is a controversial one. Unlike Angels, Rent does not gesture towards compromise or a temporary lease on life, but instead presents a complete and miraculous cure. Mimi even "moos" as she revitalizes, comically echoing her friend Maureen's earlier performance art piece and thus rendering both death and rebirth likewise performative acts. These reincarnations suggest of course that AIDS doesn't need to be the end of life; the human connection is of transcendent importance. Alternatively, however, these endings run the risk of descending into escapism, a denial of the plague's very real lethality.

Anti-Safe Sex Messages and Impacts

Does the fact that none of these plays ends in tragedy serve an artistic purpose, giving meaning to this dreaded disease? Earlier AIDS works contained a sense of hopelessness, but these later ones offer theatricality and magic in the face of growing fear and despair. In his essay "Heavenquake: Queer Anagogies in Kushner's America," James Miller calls this "their religious function as antidotes to the poisonous gloom on the medical front" (71). Miller also questions whether *Angels* fails to properly depict the horror of the AIDS crisis, observing that the play might in fact be demonstrating "the comic death of the aestheticism-

[14] *La Bohème* famously concludes with Mimi's tragic death from tuberculosis.

activism debate sparked in the late 1980's by the AIDS Coalition to Unleash Power (ACT-UP)" (56). The same can be said of *Jeffrey* and its preference for "wardrobes and wisecracks." Dying of AIDS, Darius admires the normal joy his friends are taking at a funeral: "I mean, cute guys, and Liza, and dish—it's not a cure for AIDS, Jeffrey. But it's the opposite of AIDS, right?" (57). Although Darius' words are hopeful, they are also among his last. His allusion to the fact that there is no cure is deemphasized but it is equally significant, and his weakening body serves as a constant reminder of that fact. His perspective, echoed in *Rent*'s "No day but today" and *Angels*' blessing of "more life," suggests a hopeful attitude for those with little hope. As political theater, however, it also runs the risk of counteracting an activist response by suggesting that we can combat the disease with parties and picnics; festive fundraisers can then replace the need to demand a stronger nationwide investment in finding not only preventions and palliatives, which we have, but a cure.

Indeed, national advertising campaigns support the idea that America's efforts in the AIDS battle have become increasingly more victim-centered and less prevention-centered. Early advertisements urged safe sex and abstinence, while the ones concurrent with these plays push for support groups and programs assisting those living with AIDS. A 1983 poster for an AIDS vigil stated simply and forcefully, "Fighting for our Lives: an AIDS candlelight march" (Kenrick); a 1987 ad features a simple, bold call for prevention tactics: "You can't see AIDS. Use condoms!" (SFAF). As the years and the disease progressed, the ads have adapted to the changing attitudes in our country. A 1993 ad features a young, attractive, and apparently healthy woman asserting her determination to live with AIDS: "Living with the virus, I can't get stressed out," the ad proclaims (SFAF). But perhaps most striking is a 1997 ad promoting support groups for the HIV-*negative*, beginning with the capitalized word "ISOLATION" (SFAF). The changing political attitudes of the AIDS plays are echoed in the real-world implications of such ads, as it is again the uninfected who are seen to be suffering from isolation.

Is offering people with AIDS a chance of hope and inspiration sufficient, or should both media and theater attempt to inspire political movements towards prevention and cures through the scare tactics of the early 1980s? By romanticizing the AIDS community and denigrating safe sex, these works generate several questions about the social responsibility of theater. Is it significant that after their works discussed here, Kushner's next play focused on tensions between Jews and blacks in 1960s Louisiana, and Rudnick's on a nineteenth-century Bavarian king, neither of which mentions AIDS?[15] Does theater that actively engages the topic of an epidemic incur a social responsibility? These questions lack clear answers, but suggest the significance of such an interrogation of the role of art in the new millennium.

Works Cited

Aldridge, Gemma. "Bug Chasing: Men Deliberately Trying to Catch HIV for Sexual Thrill in Astonishing Craze." *The Mirror* 7 July 2013. https://www.mirror.co.uk/news/uk-news/bug-chasing-men-deliberately-trying-2033433.

CDC. "HIV in the United States: At A Glance." http://www.cdc.gov/hiv/statistics/basics/ataglance.html.

Defoe, Daniel. *Journal of a Plague Year* [1722]. London: Penguin, 2003.

Finn, William. *Falsettos: Three One-Act Musicals*. New York: Plume, 1993.

Fujita, Atsushi. "Queer Politics to Fabulous Politics in Angels in America: Pinklisting and Forgiving Roy Cohn." *Tony Kushner: New Essays on the Art and Politics of the Plays*. Ed. James Fisher. Jefferson, NC: McFarland & Co, 2006. 112-126.

Gillies, Malcolm. "Every Eight Seconds: AIDS Revisited." 29-30 November 2000. http://essaydocs.org/every-eight-seconds-aids-revisited-29-30-november-2000.html.

Gilman, Sander L. *Disease and Representation: Images of Illness from Madness to AIDS*. Ithaca, NY: Cornell University Press, 1988.

Goldstein, Richard. "The Normalizing Heart." *The Village Voice* 13 April 2004. https://www.villagevoice.com/2004/04/13/the-normalizing-heart/

Istel, John. "I Have Something to Say." An Interview with Jonathan Larson. *American Theatre* (July-August 1996): 13-17.

Johnston, William I. *HIV-Negative: How the Uninfected Are Affected by AIDS*. New York: Insight Books-Plenum Press, 1995.

Kenrick, John. "Our Love Is Here To Stay VIII: AIDS and Beyond." *Musicals101.com*. The Cyber Enclopedia of Musical Theatre, Film & Television. 1996 [revised 2008]. http://www.musicals101.com/gay8.htm

Kushner, Tony. *Angels in America, Part I: Millennium Approaches and Part II: Perestroika*. New York: Theater Communications Group, 1993.

________. "Fick Oder Kaputt!" *Thinking about the Longstanding Problems of Virtue and Happiness: Essays, a Play, Two Poems, and a Prayer*. New York: Theater Communications Group, 1995.

[15] These plays are Kushner's *Caroline, or Change* and Rudnick's *Valhalla*. *Rent* was Larson's last work; he died of an aneurism at the age of thirty-five, shortly before opening night.

Larson, Jonathan. *Rent.* New York: William Morrow, 1997.

McNulty, Charles. "Angels in America: Tony Kushner's Theses on the Philosophy of History." *Modern Drama* 39.1 (Spring 1996): 84-96.

Miller, James. "Heavenquake: Queer Anagogies in Kushner's America." *Approaching the Millennium: Essays on Angels in America.* Eds. Deborah R. Geis and Steven F. Kruger. Ann Arbor: University of Michigan Press, 1997. 56-77.

Minwalla, Framji. "When Girls Collide: Considering Race in Angels in America."*Approaching the Millennium: Essays on Angels in America.* Eds. Deborah R. Geis and Steven F. Kruger. Ann Arbor: University of Michigan Press, 1997. 103-117.

Mufson, Daniel. "Quipping Boy." *Theater* 24.2 (1983): 116-119.

Pearl, Monica. "Epic AIDS: Angels in America from Stage to Screen." *Textual Practice* 21.4 (December 2007): 761-779.

Parker, Trey. "Jared Has Aides." Written and directed by Trey Parker. *South Park.* Comedy Central. 6 March 2002.

Rich, Frank. "Critic's Notebook; Laughing at AIDS Is First Line of Defense." *The New York Times* 3 February, 1993. https://www.nytimes.com/1993/02/03/theater/critic-s-notebook-laughing-at-aids-is-first-line-of-defense.html.

Román, David. *Acts of Intervention: Performance, Gay Culture, and AIDS.* Bloomington: Indiana University Press, 1998.

________. "Negative Identifications: HIV-Negative Gay Men in Representation and Performance." *Queer Representations: Reading Lives, Reading Cultures.* Ed. Martin Duberman. New York: New York University Press, 1997. 162-180.

Rudnick, Paul. *Jeffrey.* New York: Plume, 1994.

________. "Laughing at AIDS." *The New York Times* 23 January 1993. https://www.nytimes.com/1993/01/23/opinion/laughing-at-aids.html.

Savran, David. "Rent's Due: Multiculturalism and the Spectacle of Difference." *The Journal of American Drama and Theatre* 14.1 (Winter 2002). 1-14.

Sebesta, Judith. "Of Fire, Death, and Desire: Transgression and Carnival in Jonathan Larson's Rent." *Contemporary Theatre Review* 16.4 (November 2006): 419-438.

SFAF (San Francisco AIDS Foundation). www.sfaf.org.

Sontag, Susan. *AIDS and its Metaphors.* New York: Anchor, 1989.

Vorlicky, Robert, Ed. *Tony Kushner in Conversation.* Ann Arbor: University of Michigan Press, 1998.

Winn, Steven. "AIDS AT 25: How to respond to the devastating disease?" *San Francisco Chronicle* 7 June 2006. https://www.sfgate.com/health/article/AIDS-AT-25-How-to-respond-to-the-devastating-2495289.php

Mobbing, Bullying and the Queer Victim in Slasher Films of the 1980s

Fernando Gabriel Pagnoni Berns
Canela Ailen Rodriguez Fontao
Mariana Zárate

Introduction

In queer theory, schools are "cultural arenas where masculinity has become an important concept" (Mac an Ghaill and Haywood 69) to investigate formation of identity. Schools are also scenarios that symbolize immaturity configured through the interplay of definitions of childhood and gender. In turn, the slasher film is a conduit to illustrate problems associated with adolescence since it is the only horror subgenre that has teenagers as main characters. Thus, as noted by Brigid Cherry (2009), the slasher film is the perfect vehicle to speak of "teen sexuality" (185).

Despite the classic slasher film being considered formulaic and superficial, there are some notable and overlooked examples which present complex queer characters as the main heroes or villains. This essay will work with three classic slashers from the 1980s as exemplification of the 'deviant' male student that attracts the attention of bullies. This concept emerges from the social and scientific discourse about the phenomenon of bullying prevailing in the late seventies and early eighties (during the peak era of the slasher film). In this conception, the bullied kid is a 'passive' subject born from bad parenting who, because of his inability to socialize, is the perfect target for cruelty. This 'passivity' links these male teenagers with homosexuality; it should be noted that male adolescent homosexuality was a recurrent issue in critical and medical studies in the 1980s since, as was roughly stated in 1987, "homosexual activity is prevalent among US teenagers" (Remafedi 326).

Queer characters can either reinforce or resist dominant ideology and patriarchal values. *Sleepaway Camp* (Robert Hiltzik, 1983) seems to cement the equation queer character as monster since the killer, Angela (Felissa Rose), is a (motherly) creation of ambiguous sex. Meanwhile, in the overlooked slasher *The Burning* (Tony Maylam, 1981) the queer teenager suffering from harassment replaces, within the narrative, the female heroine. Since historically the female heroine embodies the traditional values of "goodness" (Robinson 21), the film offers an ideal disruption of heteronormative narrative. Lastly, *Terror Train* (Roger Spottiswoode, 1980) has both queer antagonists and a queer female protagonist. Using as framework notions of the deviant male, the "provocative" (Schott 30) victim typical of the first studies of bullying in the "macho 1980s" (Anderson 130), we argue that queerness pervades some classic slashers of the eighties as a response, within a queer sensibility, to the ideas that permeate adolescence in those years and bullying in particular.

Slasher, Bullying and the Deviant Victim

Slasher films are ideal for the analysis of adolescent queerness and 'deviant' subjects since this very successful genre was the first to introduce (even in a limited way) the problematic of bullying. Almost every slasher film has at least one scene of bullying, sometimes because the plot asks for it, sometimes just for shock value. It should be noted that slasher films were the first horror subgenre featuring exclusively teenagers (or, at least, the characters were teenagers: the actors were close to their thirties) and with an eye to an audience composed mostly by young people (Jerslev 188); so it is not surprising that issues typical of the adolescent stage make their appearance.

The slasher film took over the horror genre in the eighties and the theaters were flooded with masked serial killers who mutilated promiscuous teenagers (Prince 351) to the point that very few horror movies released in the eighties were not part of this cycle (Shary 182). Coincidentally, the first studies of the phenomenon of bullying begin at the end of the 1970s and in the first years of the 1980s in Britain and Scandinavia (Sanders 2). In these first studies, the phenomenon was not yet called bullying, but rather 'mobbing,' and, not coincidentally, bullying was configured following the matrices of mobbing when seen in the slasher films from the eighties.

In order to discuss mobbing, we will use Schott and Søndergaard's (2014) two paradigms of bullying: mobbing and bullying properly speaking (2). Peter-Paul Heinemann first introduced the term mobbing in 1969 (Schott and Søndergaard 2) and it was subsequently developed by the Norwegian psychologist Dan Olweus. Mobbing refers to group violence "which occurs and stops suddenly" (Schott 22) against a deviant individual. From the perspective of "paradigm one," bullying is understood as an act of violence by an individual with marked personality issues, such as aggressiveness, impulsivity and little empathy with the other. His victim is usually insecure, passive and weak (28), thus a perfect target to suffer from repetition of abuse (27). In brief, these two—'bully' and 'victim'— are fixed and antagonistic positions. Here, bullying would be understood as a phenomenon that depends on the personality traits of the involved participants. This first paradigm explores the aggressor's abusive family history, and 'mobbing' is a result of individual problems rather than a social phenomenon (as 'bullying' is in paradigm two). The aggressor is born of aggressive or dysfunctional families, while the passive victims are born into households with overprotective parents, especially mothers (Schott 28). In the definition of mobbing, the group violence is exerted upon some 'deviant' subject. The boy—since the concept of mobbing "was based chiefly on research with boys" (Taki 152)—is a deviant male, a weak, queer subject who in his own passivity calls the attention of aggressive males. In this way the boy/victim is 'provocative' because of his lack of manliness.

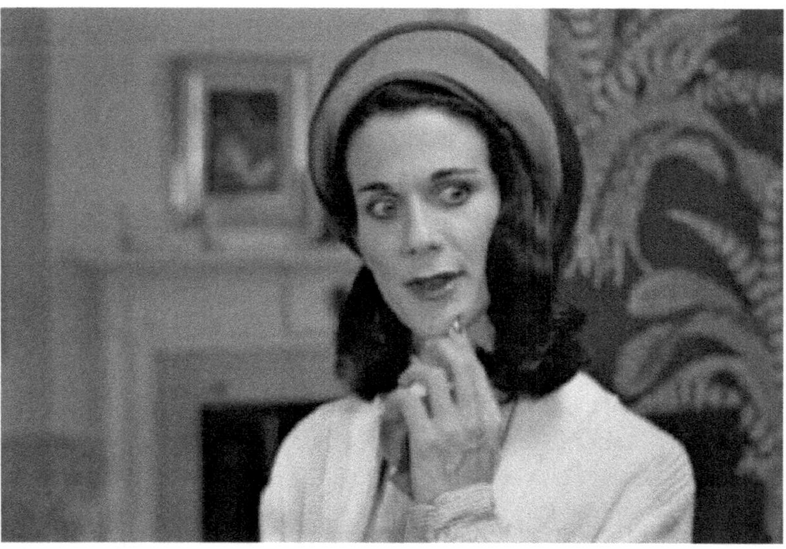

Aunt Martha (Desiree Gould) as the overprotective mother who creates effeminate boys in *Sleepaway Camp.*

The deviant masculinity of the victim of bullying can be understood not only as queerness, but also as an exploration of a masculinity that refuses to, or cannot achieve, to fit into the patterns of behaviors considered as 'essential' in the male subject. Among them, one of the most striking is aggressiveness, especially in the school arena. A male boy 'must' be street-smart and aggressive as part of his persona. If not, he is a queer subject who fails to fully embrace his masculine role. Thus, he is feminized. As Kevin Kumashiro argues, downplaying masculinity in school age is a form of deviant heterosexual masculinity (64). Then, queerness does not include only homosexuality but also any heterosexuality that could be considered as 'deviant' of the politics of masculinity.

None of the boys, victims or perpetrators, in the slashers that will be analyzed in the following sections, is presented as explicitly homosexual. Rather, our queer reading works against the grain as a way to disarm these films and show how the (presumed) heterosexuality of the bullied kids is linked with the issues that characterize the boy victim of bullying (rather, mobbing) who did not meet the 'adequate' levels of heterosexuality. However, these films have a (now obvious) homoerotic narrative/aesthetic frame that probably went unnoticed in those years.

The Burning: The Queer Boy as the Final Girl

Slasher films are a good example of how this first definition of bullying as mobbing interacts with popular culture since this subgenre is replete with aggressive males and weak, deviant boys. The slasher is repeatedly based on the story of a group of teenagers who are serially murdered by a masked psychopath, who usually is guided by a desire for revenge against those who caused him some kind of humiliation in the past. In her book *Men, Women and Chainsaws: Gender in the Modern Horror Film* (1992), Carol Clover has identified the presence of the "Final Girl" (35) as essential within the genre. The "Final Girl" is the female hero who in many slashers takes on and defeats the killer figure at the climax. Unlike her friends, she is virginal and conservative. The "Final Girl" in the slasher film survives the attack of the (male) monster by becoming male in some way (35). She is the massacre's only survivor and she represents moral values. Those teenagers who choose to engage in sex or excesses bound up dead, but the Final Girl prevails. This cycle of films is based on a system of punishments on those who do not respect traditional moral rules. One of the most intriguing issues of *The Burning* is that the Final Girl proposed by Clover will no longer be played by some young female embodying the positive moral values that American society in the 1980s expected (and desired) of adolescents, but by an introverted and marginalized queer boy suffering harassment.

The Burning begins with a flashback that establishes the reasons behind the killer's madness. At Camp Blackfoot, some teenagers plan to play a practical joke on a (allegedly cruel) janitor called Cropsy (Lou David), but the joke gets out of control and ends up causing a fire. Cropsy is horribly burned and scarred. Many years later, Cropsy returns to exact revenge upon his (now adults) tormentors, who are working in another sleepaway camp, Stonewater, populated with teenagers in their sexual awakening and led by one of the students who took part in the initial joke, Todd (Brian Matthews).

The Burning presents a very interesting character, Alfred (Brian Backer), a boy with a distinct role in the film. If at first his role as the passive kid suffering aggression at the hands of the bully Glazer (Larry Joshua) seems marginal, he will progressively take center stage until he becomes the film's Final Girl (or Final Queer Boy). From an analysis of the different characters, it is possible to see the construction of dichotomous pairs framed in the categories of abuser/abused typical of paradigm one: Cropsy versus Todd, and Alfred versus Glazer. The first relationship is what prompts the killing. Cropsy is, allegedly, an abuser—a violent and impulsive subject, while Todd was an insecure and weak boy who only by joining forces with other victims of abuse can then face his abuser. But the flashback is not that clear about the relationship between Cropsy and the young boys. Reading it otherwise: could Cropsy be the true victim of mobbing, a sudden burst of cruelty by Todd and his companions? Needless to say Todd, in the present time, no longer has the characteristics that he had as a teenager. Now he is a confident group leader, able to make adult decisions, and the object of female desire.

The relationship between Alfred and Glazer is pivotal in the film and is significant for this essay. Glazer is the main bully, a young sexually active boy with hyper-masculine characteristics (he is strong, womanizing, violent and uncaring), while Alfred is antisocial, extremely shy, a boy who enjoys voyeurism (i.e. passivity) rather than action. We state again that mobbing—or bullying in the first few years of the 1980s—was considered as a relationship between an aggressive kid and a deviant victim. It was a relationship, in other words, between two guys, one active and one passive. Within paradigm one, there are no other roles ascribed to this phenomenon. *The Burning* is constructed around this relationship between the rude guy (hyper-masculine Glazer) and the shy (i.e., effeminate) Alfred. Even if other characters call Alfred "perverse," it is Glazer who seems particularly disturbed by the presence of the bullied kid.

Consistently, Glazer feels threatened by Alfred's presence and gaze. Alfred is thus similar to many bullied kids, who are scapegoats (Macklem 62) for all the frustrations that the bully could carry within himself. Some of these anxieties can have a sexual manifestation. The question that arises is, why does Glazer feels so threatened by Alfred's gaze? Since Alfred is 'deviant' in his masculinity, because of his lack of male aggressiveness and confidence, he is effeminate. Thus, Glazer seems disturbed by Alfred's sexuality, which perhaps threatens the bully's masculinity. In fact, Glazer does not appear to be a good lover (at least, with girls). After a sexual encounter, Glazer's girlfriend Sally (Carrick Glenn) complains about "the lack of warmth" in her boyfriend.

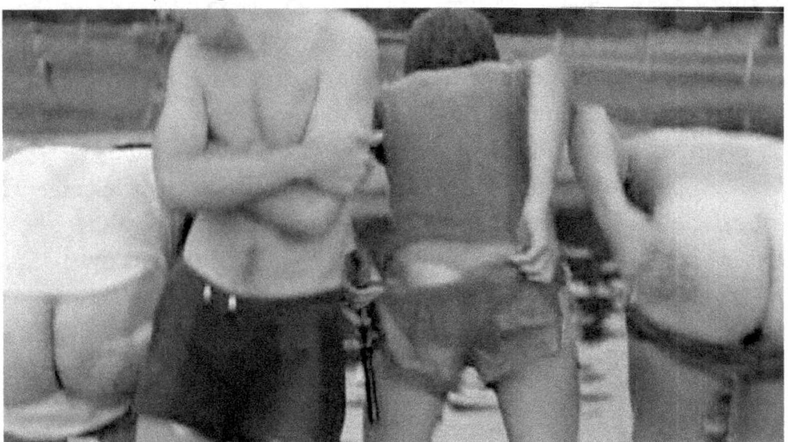

Male nakedness in *The Burning*

But if Glazer's masculinity can be placed under the microscope, Alfred's sexuality is clearly queer. On the one hand he undergoes continuous abuse by Glazer, but even so, Alfred systematically stalks his bully, exposing a homoerotic desire for him. Every time Glazer furtively leaves the sleepaway camp, Alfred surreptitiously follows him, presumably to see him making love with girls. But if it is girls that Alfred wants to watch, he could follow his female companions rather than his bully. In fact, Alfred is captured watching Glazer's girlfriend when she is taking a bath. But Alfred answers to the sleepaway camp's authorities that he does so to "scare her away." The interrogation now could turn to whether he is trying to scare the girl away to remain alone with Glazer within the camp. Alfred encounters the killer while following (as always)

Glazer to the woods. Alfred, in this scenario, is highly 'provocative' since he is always following the man who is abusing him.

For some time, the film insinuates that, quite possibly, Alfred is the killer. This is sustained by the fact that Alfred is always stalking or furtively watching others. His gaze and that of Cropsy's (a verified deviant subject) are comparable. At first, Alfred answers the Hollywood stereotype of gay men as serial killers (Crimp 310). But, as mentioned, the abused Alfred will take the role of the Final Girl, the character who represents socially accepted moral values. He is a victim of bullying, and, therefore, seen through the prism of weakness and insecurity that frames the concept of mobbing; but, at the same time, he is not seen as entirely 'innocent.' He is continuously seeking trouble, spying girls to scare them or following his tormentor with no discernible purpose other than a likely homoerotic attachment. This way, Alfred sustains the thesis of mobbing: in some way, much of the blame of the harassment falls on the victim (Olweus 10).

While he is a survivor and has the role of the Final Girl, a homosexual inclination is also insinuated, which was clearly not morally acceptable or desirable in the 1980s. The Final Girl embodies positive values, and while Alfred does not have sex or use drugs, all the characters from the film brand him as queer and sinister. But although he is classified as 'perverse' by his companions, the film presents him as the Final Girl, the real hero. He is the one who, together with Todd, faces Cropsy in the film's climax. While they do this, Todd's girlfriend is nowhere to be seen within the scene. In fact, she is far from this final confrontation and her role is only marginal. It is Alfred who uses the phallic weapon, a typical motif of appropriation of the Final Girl (Clover 32), to wound the killer. The film ends with Todd and Alfred walking away from the defeated Cropsy.

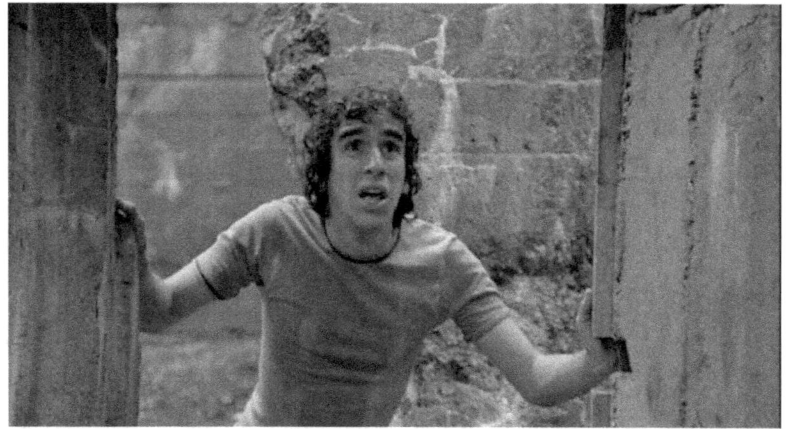

Alfred (Brian Backer) as the bloodied Final Girl/Boy

Alfred as Final Girl represents a change from the stereotypical representation of the queer. Despite maintaining certain characteristics in common with young survivors of slashers, his gender causes a profound disruption. The young 'passive' boy (both in terms of sexuality and as a victim of abuse) breaks into action becoming the only one able to stop Cropsy's onslaught. It is Alfred who saves Todd, becoming the most unlikely hero of the tale, thus establishing that the Final Girl can be a boy, but only via queering. Yet, *The Burning* is far from being a rarity and the only slasher with a queer Final Girl.

Terror Train and the Blurring of Genders

Terror Train begins with a group of teenagers playing (yet again) a practical joke on a shy classmate named Kenny (Derek McKinnon). They make Kenny believe that Alana (Jamie Lee Curtis), a popular girl, wants to have an intimate encounter with him. Alana reluctantly participates without knowing that the results of the joke will be terrible; Kenny loses his sanity by touching a corpse that the boys had put on a bed to replace Alana (since they are all students of medicine, corpses seem to be something easy to obtain). Years later, during a fraternity's costume ball held on a moving train, Kenny returns to exact revenge from all those involved in the prank.

Following the line of thought advanced by paradigm one, it is possible to notice that Kenny is the typical case of 'deviant' male, the weak guy characterized as less manly than his classmates, all of them hyper-masculinized in their (hetero)sexual appetite for sex. The audience sees very little of Kenny. His presence before the opening credits is very brief. Kenny does not speak (except for one word: "Alana") and it seems that his classmates decide everything for him. In fact, he does not seem to be interested in Alana at all: rather his companions have decided for him that he should be attracted to her. Also, it is clearly stated that Kenny is still a virgin, an issue that puts more pressure on him. Furthermore, Kenny is extremely skinny in contrast with his broad-shouldered male classmates, and his looks, especially his face, is androgynous, to the point that in some shots he looks almost like a woman passing for a man.

To (homo)erotize Kenny even more, he is seen undressing down to his underwear. In our visual culture, the male body is supposed to be kept to the shadows while the female body is represented as an erotic spectacle (Clover 43). Women are objects of the male gaze, spectacles to be looked at. Men, in turn, are the owners of the objectifying gaze.

Therefore, when Kenny undresses for the camera's eye, his almost naked and skinny, androgynous body is feminized, turning the character into a true queer persona. The act of men getting undressed for the camera has the effect of "dephallicizing" them (Thomas 15). Kenny is abused by his peers because of his shyness and his virginity, but also due to his questionable masculinity. It is no coincidence that the actor who plays Kenny, Derek McKinnon, had previously acted in the 70s as a drag queen in stage shows in Canada and, therefore, maintained very feminine features (delineated eyebrows, delicate movements, etc.).

Kenny is 'deviant' because he is not manly enough and, for that, he is the victim of mobbing. Here the definition of mobbing as an act of violence that starts and ends suddenly (rather than abuse maintained through time as in bullying) fits perfectly. There are no signs that Kenny is harassed on a daily basis. Rather, the joke seems a sudden burst of cruelty invented and practiced by aggressive boys on a very passive victim. But Kenny is also deviant because he is the film's killer, the one who is murdering his old classmates aboard the "terror train" of the title. Even at this stage, Kenny's sexuality is of importance within the narrative. He strives to go unnoticed among his peers, transvesting into a woman, the female helper of the magician in charge of leading the year-end party on the train (David Copperfield). In the end, Kenny seems to have embraced his identity as a woman, thus gaining the confidence that he had previously lacked as a man. This seems a crystallization of what is only suggested in the film's beginning. Kenny exacerbates the female component that made him so unbearable in the eyes of his peers and only then he unleashes his vengeance. The changing into the female gender is hugely significant in this scenario.

Also noteworthy is that during the prologue, and after discovering the corpse, Kenny's nervous breakdown is represented as the mocked kid turns around over and over, wrapping himself with the delicate white gauze hanging as decoration from the bed's posts, creating the perfect symbolic moment in which the kid starts to embrace a female's identity, as a man covered in soft veils. In that scene, Kenny enters a larval state to later fully blossom as a killer female butterfly.

As already mentioned, in the slashers, due to the presence of teenagers, with latent sexualities, and within the frame of the permissions granted by the genre, it is possible to find evidence of an alternative sexual discourse. Keeping this in mind, it is possible to point the queerness present in Doc (Hart Bochner), the best friend of Alana's boyfriend Mo (Timothy Webber). His exaggerated masculinity makes him the leader of the pack, even when, in a close reading, he has a strong homoerotic bond with his best friend, Mo. After a fight between Mo and Alana, the boy complains about the whole situation with Doc, who responds: "If she leaves you, you still have me. I mean it," while looking intently into Mo's eyes and keeping a straight face. Throughout the film, Doc will try a myriad of ways to separate the couple Alana-Mo, inducing his friend to perform activities that would certainly disgust the girl. Doc even pushes Mo to be unfaithful to Alana with the hope that the girl will find him in the act. Upon a closer look, then, it is possible to find another queer character in the film.

There is possibly a third queer character within *Terror Train*. Following Clover's thesis, Alana is the film's Final Girl. Alana has high moral values, has participated in the practical joke of the prologue only reluctantly (and without knowing the real extent of the joke) and, as mentioned, she is the only one who remembers Kenny with sorrow. As the Final Girl, she fights the killer alone and survives the whole ordeal. But as mentioned by Clover (48), there exists a masculinization of the final girl (and perhaps only this way can she be functional in a sexist/ patriarchal society), and in the character played by Jamie Lee Curtis this is clearly spelled out. Alana is not only strikingly less 'feminine,' from the point of view of fashion (she uses little make-up and shorter hair than her female classmates), she also shows up at the party wearing a male costume: that of a pirate. The costume not only links her with a figure popularly related to manliness, but also, with these clothes on, she hardly shows any skin, thus avoiding the eroticization of the female body. Meanwhile, Alana's best friend, Mitchy (Sandee Currie), comes to the party disguised as a 'sexy' witch, a common costume that responds to male fantasies. A masculinized Alana is the one who carries out the plot of the film since it is she, and not a male character, who gets suspicious of what is taking place on the train and it is she who will confront and defeat the killer.

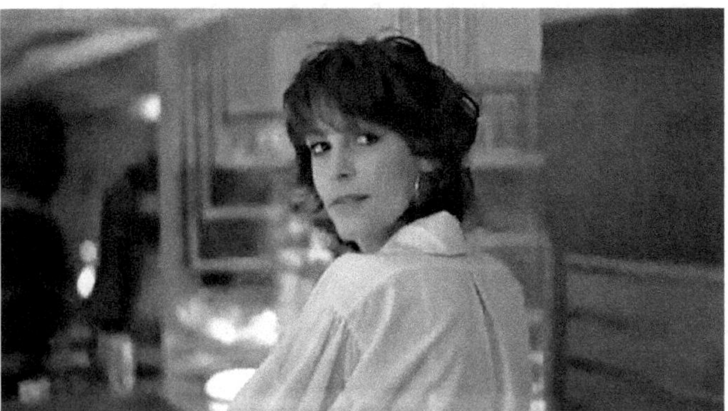

Alana (Jamie Lee Curtis) as an androgynous pirate in *Terror Train*

The final confrontation between Kenny and Alana is significant. The two characters face each other in the confines of a wagon. Kenny holds Alana's hands forcefully while attempting to kiss her, a form of sexual aggression (Kenny, now as a female, seems to have found the voice lacking in the prologue. He is more autonomous as a transvestite/ killer than as a man). She repeatedly apologizes for what happened in the past, but Kenny continues to coerce a kiss. When Alana finally conceives of a way to gain time, the image created is framed within queerness. One part of the couple is a feminized man (Kenny has just taken off his wig but he is still wearing blurred make-up), while the other is a masculinized woman (Alana in her pirate costume), sweaty and wearing no make-up. In other words, the sexes of the couple are blurred, producing a queer scene far from any simple reading of female passiveness and male aggression. The final kiss unleashes yet another crisis in Kenny, who turns around wrapping himself, this time in a heavy black fabric, foreshadowing his terrible and inevitable end. The realization of that kiss, the same that he was forced to seek at the beginning of the film, now raises Kenny's madness, concretized by contradiction and denial of what is expected of him, as a man now stripped of the female clothes that gave him a sense of security. After the kiss of a woman, he is just another bullied kid.

Queer readings therefore emerge at various levels in *Terror Train*. Sustained by the idea that the bullied kids are 'deviant' males, the film showcases the anxieties about gender and bullying. Queerness appears here as a reflection of the fictional nature of the sexualised gender.

Sleepaway Camp and the Monstrous Mother

As mentioned, the kid suffering mobbing in the early eighties was characterized as a boy suffering from bad parenting, especially from an excess of motherly presence. This issue is clearly connected with the common belief that domineering mothers and weak father figures lead to homosexual orientation in boys (Golombok 436). Even as late as 2002, books and manuals about ways to prevent 'sexual distortions' in children blame, in part, "narcissist mothers" (Nicolosi 72), i.e., delusional mothers, for their boys' sexual orientation. In this line of thought, the longer and closer the attachment the mother has with the son, the more effeminate he will be (ibid.). Statistically, effeminate boys form a high percentage of children suffering from bullying. In paradigm one, the mobbing occurs only between two elements: the abuser and the abused. No further external social forces complicate this simple equation. Both the abusers and the abused are the result of bad parenting and dysfunctional households. Thus, overprotective, narcissistic mothers create perfect victims for abuse at school. *Sleepaway Camp* is the only film here analyzed that displays this female construction of a victim of bullying. The film begins with a flashback that establishes the roots of the disturbing mental state of the main killer. Here, John (Dan Tursi) is taking a boat trip on a summer's day with his little son and daughter. John suffers a horrible boat accident that kills him and one of his children. The surviving child, Angela (Felissa Rose), is deeply traumatized. She moves with her eccentric Aunt Martha (Desiree Gould), and her overprotective cousin Ricky (Jonathan Tiersten). One summer, Martha sends the kids to Camp Arawak. Soon after their arrival, a series of horrible accidents begins to claim the lives of various campers.

The film's climax is now considered a classic among slasher films, because it is "legitimately shocking" (Muir 353). Angela is, indeed, the psychopathic killer in the movie, but more surprising is the final scene that reveals that the girl is, in fact, a boy. The truth is that in the boating accident in which John died, the child who survived (left ambiguous in the flashback) is actually little Peter (Maximo Sorrentino), not his sister. But Peter's nurturance is left in charge of Aunt Martha and she had always wanted a girl to care for, so gradually and over the years, Peter was transformed into a girl, erasing any trace of the boy's 'manhood' until Angela fully bloomed. In the film, Aunt Martha replaces the motherly figure since Peter/Angela has no mother. She is the 'narcissist' mother that creates effeminate boys; in this case, in a literal way. In her filmic representation, Martha is extravagant, has a syrupy voice, dresses in a campy way and sometimes is caught staring vacantly. Clearly, she is not quite sane. This characterization is not innocent. Martha embodies all the 'bad mothers' who, through overprotection, create bullied boys. Of course, Angela will be the victim of mobbing within the camp. The other girls look with disfavor upon the girl's antisocial attitudes. She refuses to talk to the other girls and also refuses to bathe with her companions. She prefers to spend time alone in a corner or talking to her cousin.

The notion of 'deviant' implies that the persona framed by it deviates from some norm or law. Angela deviates from heterosexuality. Also, in a clear relation with mobbing, she deviates from norms of socialization. In the concept of mobbing, the subject who suffers it almost 'deserves' aggression because of his or her lack of social skills. Angela, similarly to Kenny and Alfred, is in some way 'looking for trouble.' Not only does she make any attempt to socialize within the camp, but also when some mean girl comes to her looking for trouble, she does nothing to avoid her. Angela responds to harassment by looking intently in complete silence at the ones who are bullying her, several times with a slightly mocking smile. This attitude, far from quenching the desire of confrontation, fuels it. In this sense, she mirrors Alfred from *The Burning* since both bullied kids are always deepening their deviance: rather than avoiding the bullies, they engage with them.

Angela is erotically attached to her bullies, and in this aspect she too resembles Alfred. If we keep in mind that Angela is in fact a boy, then his attachment to the mean girls is a complex issue. As already mentioned, she looks at them intently and maybe this is not because she wants to mock them but because, deep down, she is still a boy fascinated with pretty girls, especially with the main bully Judy (Karen Fields), one of the prettiest girls in the camp. In this way, Angela is a metaphor for the confusion about sexual orientation that can take place during adolescence. Angela does not know if it is right to like boys or girls since she, as many real teenagers, does not know her own sexuality that well. Here, the issue of queerness is further complicated since the audience first must characterize Angela as a boy or a girl before deciding that her/his object of desire is truly homosexual.

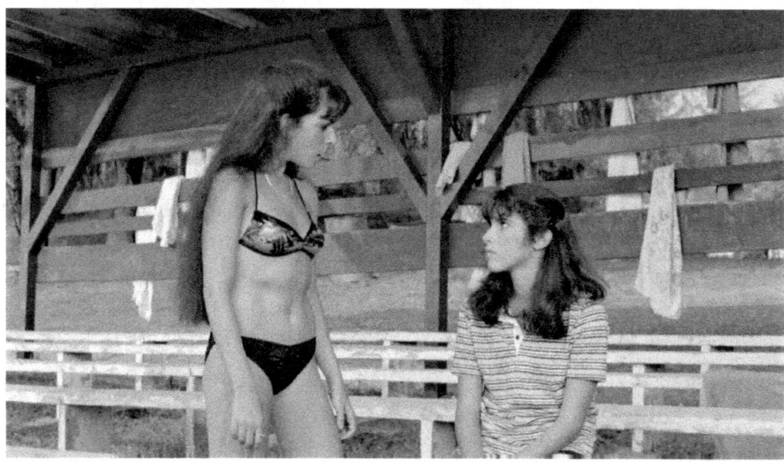

Queer Angela (Felissa Rose) and her bully Judy (Karen Fields)

The idea that Angela inadvertently provokes her bullies because of her sexual desire is sustained in one of the most brutal murder scenes. Angela sneaks inside Judy's cabin and rapes and kills her with a hot flat iron. This scene takes place close to the film's end, when Angela, apparently, cannot continue keeping down her illegible sexuality. The flat iron is a phallic element that replaces the penis that Angela has been forbidden the use of. Angela will use many phallic weapons beside the flat iron, but it is only with women that some sort of sexual aggression takes place: she kills boys by decapitating or drowning them, while a seedy chef is almost killed when she gets him scalded in burning water. But she, quite literally, penetrates only the girls: besides Judy, Angela kills the camp guard Meg (Katherine Kamhi) stabbing her from behind in the shower. Meg was also one of Angela's objects of desire and it is no coincidence that the guard dies while she is stark naked. All Angela's female victims die in a sexualized manner.

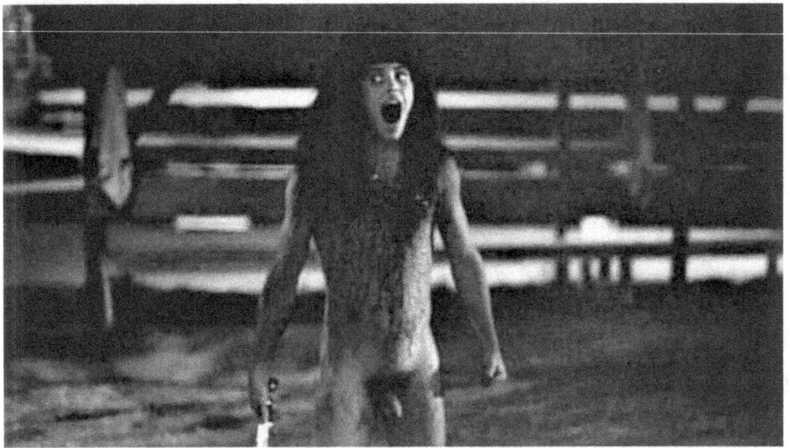

Felissa Rose as the queer boy/girl

It may be argued that *Sleepaway Camp*, with its transvestite monster, showcases a very negative image of the queer subject. Angela, as a 'queered' kid, only understands sex as murder. Her threatening nature is born from her deviant sexuality. Also, she is a monster constructed by deficient motherhood. Therefore, the film seemingly punishes any queerness and asks for normative ways of life. *Sleepaway Camp* sustains and helps to legitimize the idea that queer, bullied boys are a result of overprotective mothers. But even as a conservative text, the film's display of male flesh is somehow disturbing and engages in contradictory ways with the main thesis of the film. Even considering that male clothes in the first years of the 1980s were rather tight in appearance, the film displays a very sharp homoerotic aesthetic, firstly, because the film carefully denies even the briefest glimpse of female nakedness. Even during Judy's murder in the shower, the naked body of the girl is framed in such a way that her private parts are not exhibited. In a subgenre very well known for its profusion of T&A ('tits and ass'), this complete lack of female nudity is striking. But homoeroticism makes its appearance in the profusion of young hunks in different stages of undressing. The only nudity in the film is that of a male ass; but leaving aside this brief moment, all the young males in the cast are displayed as objects to-be-looked-at. The shorts pants that the boys wear are very revealing, especially those worn by Ronnie (Paul DeAngelo), the chief guardian. His tight shorts show the outline of his penis and his t-shirt displays his muscular torso with aplomb. A key homoerotically charged scene takes place when a group of boys invites a group of girls to swim in the lake at night. The male group starts to undress, while the girls, who rejected the invitation, remain fully clothed. The scene ends with the boys walking on the beach wearing only their underwear, while talking about sex and touching their crotches.

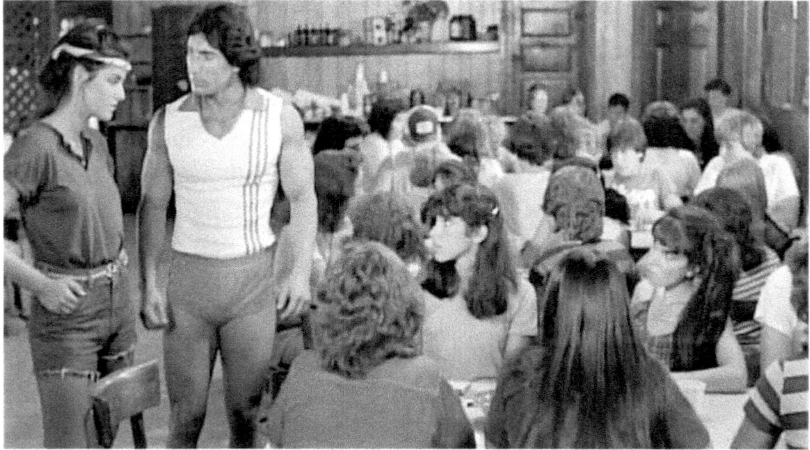

Ronnie (Paul DeAngelo) wearing tight clothes in *Sleepaway Camp* (above)
Homoerotic fashion in *Sleepaway Camp* (below)

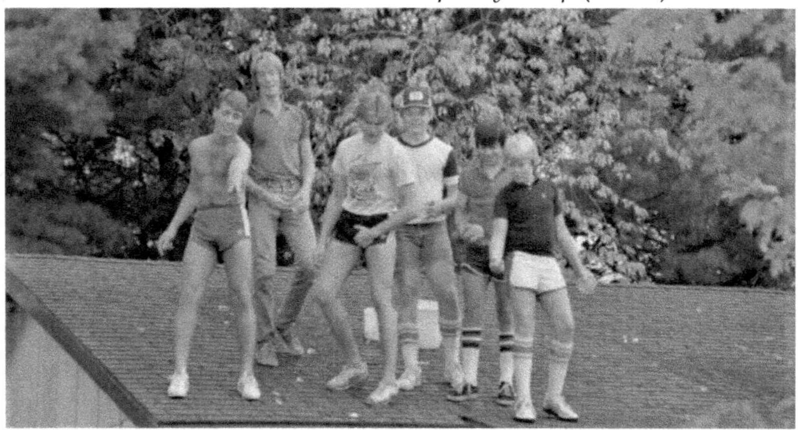

In *Sleepaway Camp*, the politics of homophobia concretized in Angela as the queer monster is further complicated by a strong homoerotic aesthetic which works in conjunction with the ambiguous sexual nature of the main character. In this scenario, the normative text is revealed as a fully queer one. Maybe the presentation of Angela as the bullied kid made monster because of her mother answers more to the notions of bullying leading the field in those years than to a conservative agenda. Ironically, Robert Hiltzik, the director, dedicated the film to his "mom," revealing a strong sentimental attachment to her. The deviant kid as a monster within the film can be read as a parody of this social cliché rather than as a support to theories of homosexuality and bullying. Even so, *Sleepaway Camp* will be a complex construction made with a conservative or a progressive mind, depending on the viewer for interpretation.

Conclusions

The second paradigm supposes a shift in the understanding of the problem of bullying. In this sense, it is necessary to include in studies of bullying not only the analysis of the personality of those involved (bully-victim), but also the social environment and cultural, technological and psychological forces involved in the act. If the first paradigm starts from the question of what characteristics of the family create an aggressive boy, the seconds paradigm emphasizes the social dynamics that not only include the binomial victimizer/victim (understanding the phenomenon in terms of individual violence), but other subjects in the school and social environment (teachers, principals, media) as well.

It is the second paradigm that is properly referred to as 'bullying.' But this phenomenon was understood, in the first years of the 1980s, as a relationship between a masculine boy and a kid whose lack of 'manliness' makes him queer. The slasher films analyzed here had taken this then widely known concept and created films in which the presence of a deviant bullied kid turns a classic narrative (that of a serial killer stalking teenagers) into a queer scenario. In this respect, *The Burning* is highly disruptive since the character who embodies the moral values that permeated the 1980s, the Final Girl, is embodied by a guy, one having a clear homoerotic desire towards his aggressive bully. Even so, Alfred holds the most important role within the slasher film formula, displacing the real girl. But it is apparent that only a queer boy can supplant a Final Girl, not a heterosexual man. *The Burning* is interesting for the fact that a gay male teenager is the real hero. Far from being the only example, *Terror Train* presents three queer characters. If it is true that the most queer character is the killer, it is also true that the (now properly woman) Final Girl is a masculine heroine. Her presence complements a slasher in which the main bully, Doc, clearly presents queer traits.

Of the three slashers here analyzed, only one seems apparently regressive: *Sleepaway Camp,* with its bullied kid made monster by motherly intervention, equalling psychopathy with deviant sexuality. Even so, the film presents a very clear queer narrative-aesthetic that legitimizes and complements the idea of Angela as a mirror to sexually confused teenagers rather than a simplistic equation of queerness as monstrous. Maybe the first paradigm is now legitimately considered simplistic, but at the time it tried to respond to social demands about adolescence, notions of masculinity and teen behavior. The passive, bullied, in brief queer, teenager was a clear source of anxieties that were deposited within the text of horror films.

Even if considered by some as regressive in the presentation of a monster, horror films of the 1980s also presented an alternative to the status quo. There is some difference, and that difference from the mainstream also has a voice. If queer, bullied kids can be considered as 'Others,' some slasher films of the era give space and voice to, otherwise, silenced characters. It is time to continue exploring the possibilities of queer representation in other slasher films, in horror films in general, and in popular culture worldwide as a source of information about the representation of what was being kept invisible. In the history of popular culture it is possible to find valuable sources of how the thinking of a certain time and culture was understood and developed. For example, how bullying and queerness was conceptualized not so long ago.

Works Cited

Anderson, Eric. "Masculinity and Homophobia in High School and College Sports." *Bullying: Experiences and Discourses of Sexuality and Gender.* Eds. Ian Rivers and Neil Duncan. London and New York: Routledge, 2013. 120-131.

Cherry, Brigid. *Horror.* London and New York: Routledge, 2009.

Clover, Carol J. *Men, Women, and Chainsaws: Gender in the Modern Horror Film.* Princeton, N.J.: Princeton University Press, 1992.

Crimp, Douglas. "Right On, Girlfriend!" *Fear of a Queer Planet: Queer Politics and Social Theory.* Ed. Michael Warner. Minneapolis: University of Minnesota Press, 1993. 300-320.

Golombok, Susan. "New Family Forms: Children Raised in Solo Mother Families, Lesbian Mother Families, and in Families Created by Assisted Reproduction." *Child Psychology: A Handbook of Contemporary Issues*. Eds. Lawrence Balter and Catherine Tamis-LeMonda. New York: Psychology Press, 2003. 429-446.

Jerslev, Anne. "Youth Films: Transforming Genre, Performing Audiences." *International Handbook of Children, Media and Culture*. Eds. Kirsten Drotner and Sonia Livingstone. London: SAGE, 2008. 183-195.

Kumashiro, Kevin. "Reading Queer Asian American Masculinities and Sexualities in Elementary School." *Queering Elementary Education: Advancing the Dialogue about Sexualities and Schooling*. Eds. William J. Letts IV and James T. Sears. Lanham, MD: Rowman & Littlefield, 1999. 61-70.

Mac an Ghaill, Máirtín, and Chris Haywood. "The Queer in Masculinity: Schooling, Boys, and Identity Formation." *Queer Masculinities: A Critical Reader in Education*. Eds. John C. Landreau and Nelson M. Rodriguez. Dordrecht: Springer, 2012. 69-84.

Macklem, Gayle L. *Bullying and Teasing: Social Power in Children's Groups*. New York: Kluwer Academic, 2003.

Muir, John Kenneth. *Horror Films of the 1980s*. Jefferson, NC: McFarland, 2007.

Nicolosi, Joseph, and Linda Ames Nicolosi. *A Parent's Guide to Preventing Homosexuality*. Downers Grove, IL: IVP Books, 2002.

Olweus, Dan. "Understanding and Researching Bullying: Some Critical Issues." *Handbook of School Bullying: An International Perspective*. Eds. Shane R. Jimerson, Susan M. Swearer, and Dorothy L. Espelage. London and New York: Routledge, 2010. 9-34.

Prince, Stephen. *A New Pot of Gold: Hollywood Under the Electronic Rainbow 1980-1989*. Berkeley: University of California Press, 2000.

Remafedi, Gary. "Male Homosexuality: The Adolescent's Perspective." *Pediatrics* 79.3 (March 1987): 326-330.

Robinson, Jessica. *Life Lessons from Slasher Films*. Lanham, MD: Scarecrow Press, 2012.

Sanders, Cheryl E. "What Is Bullying?" *Bullying: Implications for the Classroom*. Eds. Cheryl E. Sanders and Gary D. Phye. San Diego: Elsevier Academic Press, 2004. 2-18.

Schott, Robin May. "The Social Concept of Bullying: Philosophical Reflections on Definitions." *School Bullying: New Theories in Context*. Eds. Robin May Schott and Dorte Marie Søndergaard. New York: Cambridge University Press, 2014. 21-46.

Schott, Robin May, and Dorte Marie Søndergaard. "Introduction: New Approaches to School Bullying." *School Bullying: New Theories in Context*. Eds. Robin May Schott and Dorte Marie Søndergaard. New York: Cambridge University Press, 2014. 1-18.

Shary, Timothy. *Generation Multiplex: The Image of Youth in American Cinema since 1980*. Rev. ed. Austin: University of Texas Press, 2014.

Søndergaard, Dorte. "Social Exclusion Anxiety: Bullying and the Forces That Contribute to Bullying amongst Children at School." *School Bullying: New Theories in Context.* Eds. Robin May Schott and Dorte Marie Søndergaard. New York: Cambridge University Press, 2014. 47-80.

Taki, Mitsuru. "Relations among Bullying, Stresses, and Stressors: A Longitudinal and Comparative Survey among Countries." *Handbook of School Bullying: An International Perspective.* Eds. Shane R. Jimerson, Susan M. Swearer, and Dorothy L. Espelage. London and New York: Routledge, 2010. 151-162.

Thomas, Calvin. *Masculinity, Psychoanalysis, Straight Queer Theory.* New York: Palgrave Macmillan, 2008.

Performing Queer Identities and Mainstreaming Gay Culture in *Glee*[1]

FANNY BEURÉ

The hit musical television show *Glee* (Fox, 2009-2015) recounts the day-to-day life of a high school Glee Club in the fictional town of Lima, Ohio. While scripted musical series have been attempted on television before, none has experienced the success of *Glee*. The series rapidly grew from critical acclaim to a pop-culture phenomenon. The show's multi-modal expansion strategies included commercial release of the songs covered in the show just after the episodes were aired, as well as a concert tour during the summer break and a spin-off reality show *The Glee Project*.[2] The emergence of communities of self-identified 'gleeks' reenacting the show's performances all over the world is, in itself, proof of the strong impact the show had on youth worldwide—for some commentators, to the extent of even changing the reputation of show choirs (see Chenn). All in all, even if the positive reviews of the first three seasons were not quite matched later on, *Glee* remained one of Fox's strongest assets until its final cancellation after declining audience ratings in its fourth and fifth season (see O'Connell).

Glee has been noted for its depiction of minorities, and particularly of members of the LGBTQ community. Not only do several characters embody various figures of gay and queer teenagers, but the plots also explore the difficulty of being a gay/queer during adolescence: the bullying, the difficulty of coming out of the closet, and the question of being comfortable with one's self. This message of tolerance has been widely acknowledged by the critics: from the GLAAD Media awards, which hailed *Glee* as an Outstanding Comedy, to conservative media critic Dan Gainor accusing Ryan Murphy of promoting a "gay agenda" (see Fisher). Plenty of scholarly interest has already been elicited by the

[1] A version of this essay appeared first in French as "'So, you like show tunes?': Jouer la gamme des masculinités dans *Glee* (Fox, 2009-2015)" in *Genre en séries: Cinéma, télévision, médias* 5 (Printemps 2017): 159-184.
[2] *Glee Live! In Concert!* had two runs: May 2010 and May-June 2011. *The Glee Project* was a reality show broadcasted on Oxygen and served as audition for *Glee* (the prize for the winner was a minimum seven-episode arc in the following season); it ran for two seasons (2011 and 2012).

queer problematics of the show (Johnson and Faill; Parke). Most of the existing research focuses on the contradictory ideologies conveyed by a show that targets family audiences while also addressing queer topics. For some commentators, the show deeply challenges heterosexual norms (Brown), but for most it conveys simplistic, and therefore, problematic representations (Rosenberg; Santori).

Curiously enough, despite *Glee* being a musical, few papers have questioned the role played by music and dance with regard to the queer problematics of the series. Some pieces are notable exceptions, such as Allison McCracken's insights into the show's use of young male voices ("Glee: The Countertenor and The Crooner") or Katie Buckley's analysis of the way some of *Glee*'s female characters challenge hegemonic femininity through musical performances ("Identity and Solidarity in Online Communities: Queer Identities and *Glee*"). However, *Glee*'s musical performances appear to be especially valuable to an analysis of the queer issues raised by the show for at least two reasons. First, the songs and dances in *Glee* are explicitly designed to advance the plot and to develop characters: they often are moments of self-discovery for the ones singing (it is frequently by singing about their differences that students overcome them), or they are a means to redefine the power balance between the characters. In addition, although the songs featured in *Glee* belong to a wide range of musical styles, the show allows a predominant space for two styles with long-lasting associations to gay culture: musical show tunes and pop diva hits.

This essay seeks to analyze the various ways in which queerness is embodied in *Glee*'s music and dance: would it be possible for those musical numbers to counterbalance the sometimes one-dimensional aspects of the narrative? This essay also aims at questioning *Glee*'s relationship to gay musical culture: how should these references be understood when they take place on a show targeted at a broad young audience? It will focus on two characters: gay teen Kurt Hummel (Chris Colfer) and cheerleading coach Sue Sylvester (Jane Lynch). Both characters have a triple advantage for analysis: they are quite consistent through the six seasons (which is not true of all *Glee* protagonists), they perform solo songs which are quite definitional of their personality and they openly struggle with their femininity and masculinity. First, this article will analyze the depiction of gay youth proposed by Kurt Hummel; then it will demonstrate how Sue Sylvester's character can be read as camp.

"Ladies and Gentlemen, Your 2011 Prom Queen: Kurt Hummel" — *Prom Queen* [S2: E20]

Kurt Hummel, portrayed as a flamboyant gay teenager, is one of the starring characters for the six seasons of the show. He comes out to his friends as early as the third episode of season one (*Acafellas*), and to his dad during the fourth episode (*Preggers*). Even if his masculinity evolves slightly during the show's development (he toughens up as he gets older) the character's overall embodiment is the 'sissy' stereotype: he is obsessed by interests that are supposedly those of a woman (fashion, interior decoration, weddings, etc.) and this 'feminine side' is why he is bullied (insulting nicknames from cheerleading coach Sue Sylvester include "Gay Kid" as well as "Lady," "Lady Face" and "Porcelain").

Kurt's homosexuality is linked very early on with his ability and desire to sing: Kurt is the first boy to join glee club, and the only one to do so spontaneously. This highlights a negative association between performing in a show choir and being a 'sissy,' an association that is emboldened by the school bullies. During the first two seasons, being in the glee club is indeed repeatedly described as a threat to their virility and grounds for suspecting them of homosexuality. While *Glee* may seem progressive in showing that it is acceptable for a boy to perform, nevertheless Kurt's singing and repertoire remain clearly distinct from those of his fellow male glee club members. First of all, Colfer has an unusually high-pitched voice for a man—a countertenor—and can achieve the same notes as mezzos or sopranos. His ability to sing high is regularly put to use, especially when he performs with other boys and sings the 'female' voice—for example, in his duet with Blaine (Darren Criss) on "Baby, It's Cold Outside" [*A Very Glee Christmas* S2: E10]. As Allison McCracken convincingly demonstrates, while young male vocalizing in high-pitch voices was popular in the 1920s, the Great Depression brought fear of emasculation and cast a long-lasting stigma on that kind of singing. Kurt singing in a high-pitch voice is, thus, a departure from this taboo that makes him stand apart from the other male singers.

Secondly, Kurt's position is explicitly designed as ambivalent through his peculiar musical choices which are expressly coded as 'gay.' First of all, this 'musical gayness' comes from the importance of musical theater show tunes, as musicals have been, for long, closely associated with gay culture.[3] Of the 80 songs that involve Kurt (solo, in a duo, or

[3] On the relationship between gay men and musicals, see Clum (2001 [1999] or Miller (2000 [1998]).

as part of an ensemble), 36 are from musicals (45%). Moreover, out of his nine solo songs, all are from musicals, as are the songs from his 13 duets. The number of musicals in solo and duo songs highlights how this repertoire is particularly significant in shaping Kurt's identity. Musicals are not exclusively associated to Kurt: Rachel also has a strong relationship to musical theater.[4] Incidentally, they share a great deal of obsessions (they both are huge *Wicked* fans)[5] and often sing in duo (seven times, always songs from musicals). However, she is less systematically associated with the Broadway musical: 37 solos and only 12 from musicals (32%). Thus, there are proportionally fewer musicals solos for Rachel than for Kurt, as if musicals were less essential to Rachel's identity than they are to Kurt's. In addition, those songs might express more a devotion to one special singer, Barbra Streisand—Rachel's acknowledged idol—than a tribute to musicals as a genre: five of her songs are from *Funny Girl* and two are from Streisand's other musicals.[6] On the contrary, Kurt's repertoire includes a broader spectrum of shows, from Golden Age classics[7] to Broadway mega-musicals.[8] This diversity indicates that Kurt is closely inclined and associated to the musical as a genre, never mind the individual songs. The 'gayness' conveyed by this association with musical theater might also have to do with the fact that not only is Kurt associated with show

[4] During the six seasons of the show, there are 108 songs from musicals: Kurt sings 36 of them (i.e., a third of the total) but Rachel beats him by two songs, as she sings 38 of those songs.

[5] Kurt confesses that "[he's] got an iPod shuffle entirely dedicated to selections from *Wicked*" and Rachel goes further: "['Defying Gravity'] is my go-to-shower song. It's also my ring tone" (*Wheels* [S1: E4]).

[6] "Papa, Can You Hear Me?" from *Yentl* (*Grilled Cheesus* [S2: E3]) and "Being Good Isn't Good Enough" from *Hallelujah, Baby!* (*Swan Song* [S4: E9]).

[7] Kurt's corpus of solos and duos includes tunes from *Gypsy* ("Rose's Turn" in *Laryngitis* [S1: E18] and "Some People" in *Funeral* [S2: E21]) as well as Sondheim's *Company* ("Being Alive" in *Swan Song*) and *Follies* ("I'm Still Here" in *Bash* [S5: E15]). His repertoire also includes tunes from Hollywood classics: in *Duets* [S2: E4], the medley "Happy Days Are Here Again/Get Happy" (originally performed by Hollywood icons Judy Garland and Barbara Streisand) and "Le Jazz Hot!" from *Victor/Victoria*; in *A Very Glee Christmas*, "Baby, It's Cold Outside" (a pop standard sold to MGM and featured in the 1949 motion picture *Neptune's Daughter*).

[8] Kurt performs three songs from *Wicked*: "Defying Gravity," "For Good" and "Popular" (respectively in *Wheels* [S01: E9], *New York* [S2: E22], and *2009* [S6: E12]). His repertoire also includes a large share of Andrew Lloyd Webber's hits such as *The Phantom of the Opera* ("The Music of the Night," in *Choke* [S3: E18]), *Evita* ("Don't Cry For Me Argentina," in *Special Education* [S2: E9]), *Sunset Boulevard* ("As If We Never Said Goodbye" in *Born This Way* [S2: E18]).

tunes; he is specifically linked with its most flamboyant side. Indeed the parts he sings are typically 'Diva' numbers, from *Gypsy*'s Mama Rose to *Sunset Boulevard*'s Norma.

Not only does *Glee* embrace the long-lasting tradition linking male homosexuality and musical theater, it also calls upon the roster of female pop singers recognized as 'gay icons,' such as Lady Gaga, Madonna and Beyoncé.[9] Like in musical theater, Kurt's devotion to those singers serves to describe him in musical terms by strengthening his gayness. In *Theatricality* [S1: E20], nobody is surprised to learn that he is a huge Gaga fan, and he is, at first, the only boy taking part in the Gaga tribute while other male members of the glee club prefer to dress up as Kiss. In *Preggers*, Kurt's enjoyment at performing Beyoncé's "Single Ladies" is likewise explicitly linked to his being gay. His bravery to make the jocks, icons of hegemonic masculinity, also dance to the tune is symbol of the final overcoming of his prejudice about his own queerness, as this article's later analysis of the performance will demonstrate.

This reference game played by *Glee*, in which specific musical tunes are associated with the gay male population, can be interpreted in different ways. Is it merely a one-dimensional (and therefore problematic) stereotype? Or is it, as suggested by Allison McCracken, that the torch is being passed to a new generation? Three reasons favour the second option. Firstly (and most evidently) of all, Kurt is not the only option for self-identification by gay viewers. As mentioned earlier, there are many LGBTQ characters: the musical theater-diva-worshipping nerd is only one of many.

Secondly, it is not only through song choices that the show suggests that some musical genres particularly appeal to gay men: this idea is also discussed in the narrative. When Kurt suspects Sam of being gay, he suggests they perform together (in *Duets* [S2: E4]). When Sam wonders if a duet isn't supposed to be between a guy and a girl, Kurt replies that "Gene Kelly and Donald O'Connor would protest." Faced with Sam's puzzled silence, Kurt quickly adds: "'Make'em Laugh'? *Singin' in the Rain*? 1952?" As Sam shows an even more clueless face, Kurt sighs: "Nothing? Okay, maybe you are straight." Referencing

[9] The corpus is here much smaller because those songs call up for large groups rather than solos. Nevertheless, in duos or as a lead in a group, Kurt performs three Madonna songs ("4 Minutes" in *The Power of Madonna* [S1: E15], "I'll Remember" in *Goodbye* [S3: E22] and "Lucky Star" in *Old Dog, New Tricks* [S5: E19]) and two Lady Gaga songs ("Bad Romance" in *Theatricality* [S1: E20] and "Born This Way" in *Born This Way* [S2: E18]), as well as Beyoncé's "Single Ladies" (in *Preggers*).

musicals seems to be the badge of gayness, and its lack thereof, the badge of straightness.[10] This example is only one of the many times the show openly acknowledges the gay investment in some musical styles or stars. The recognition of these investments allows gays to place gay culture in historical perspective; it has nearly a pedagogical function for today's young queers. Making these associations explicit is typical of the postmodern position adopted by *Glee*: the show introduces a distance with the stereotypes depicted while relying upon them.

Thirdly (and probably most importantly), *Glee* explicitly places 'gay' songs at the heart of gendered issues. In doing so, the show provides, consciously or not, an unraveling of the potential for queer interpretations of many 'straight' texts. The fact that Kurt/Colfer's vocal ability blurs traditional gender assignments is particularly highlighted when he competes with Rachel for the privilege to sing the show-stopping number "Defying Gravity" from the hit musical *Wicked* (*Wheels* [S1: E9]). As Stacy Wolf has pointed out, "Defying Gravity" is female-empowering, asserting Elphaba's independence and determination (Wolf 15-16). In *Glee,* the song embodies Kurt's queer relation to music and dance. The lyrics here are in remarkable conjunction with the narrative challenge: to defy the laws of gravity means for Kurt to go against gender stereotypes and to fight for the right to interpret a song traditionally sung by a woman. The dramatic tension increases around his ability to hit the final note, all the more difficult to attain as it must be held strongly. The alternating montage sequence shows how Kurt controls the song as well as Rachel, each doubling in intensity. In the end however, he fails to sing it because he fears that his victory would show disorder in gender norms (his father having received an insulting phone call). As is usual in *Glee,* music serves as a metaphor for the problems faced by characters: to sing would be for Kurt the opportunity to fully compete and assume his identity. Later in the series, he gets a new chance to sing "Defying Gravity" (*100* [S5: E12]) and doesn't miss any notes, highlighting the progress made in embracing his gay identity.

Likewise, in the episode *Preggers,* performing "Single Ladies" is a metaphor for embracing his gay identity. "Single Ladies," like "Defying Gravity," is a female-empowering song which, here, is sung by a young gay man. When Kurt's father walks in on him rehearsing Beyoncé's choreography in his basement, the first thing Kurt can think of is to try to make the queer situation more 'masculine': he explains he is training for

[10] Little does it matter that the reference is incorrect and that "Make'em Laugh" is technically not a duet, but a solo by O'Connor.

football and that Tina is his girlfriend. This concession to the heterosexist stereotype is only a façade. Later on, when he makes the very masculine football team perform the dance with him, it is a way of asserting his difference and to gain acceptance without compromise: he plays football, in his own way, and is very good at it! Moreover, his presence is a vehicle to queering the very straight football team and leading them to victory. Kurt's feat opens a new perspective, full of possibilities: it is thanks to him that McKinley's football team is for once victorious. Even if it is just for a moment, he is no longer the one who 'plays for the other team.' Once again, the musical choices express gender problematics, and the musical performances signify gender performativity as defined by Judith Butler (gender as constructed through a set of acts complying with dominant societal norms—performance of said acts produces the individual; Butler 185-193). Here again, a reprise of the musical number later in the series serves to underline even more its symbolic value and the progress made by the characters through the series. Another performance of "Single Ladies" occurs during *Goodbye* [S3: E22], and this time it is Burt Hummel (Mike O'Malley) who assumes the role of Beyoncé, along with Brittany and Tina. This is a direct reference to Kurt's performance in his room; some images of Kurt's previous basement performance are also interspersed with the performance of Burt. As for the performance of "Defying Gravity," the citation from a previous episode aims at highlighting the evolution of the characters. By performing this dance, Burt shows how he now fully accepts the personality of his son, sexuality and musical tastes included.

If Kurt's characterization heavily relies on existing stereotypes about gay men and their musical culture, *Glee* roughly succeeds in going a little further from the one-dimensional stereotypes. Indeed, the show purposely exposes the ways in which those tunes are relevant to an exploration of gender problematics, thus explaining to mainstream TV audience what has, for long, only been a vague but commonly known cultural association. Let's now study another character that pushes this move even further: cheerleading coach Sue Sylvester.

Camp Cheerleading: That's How Sue C's It

While the number of LGBTQ characters in *Glee* has been widely celebrated, very few have pointed out the gender trouble introduced by Sue Sylvester's character. Sue doesn't perform as many musical numbers as Kurt; however, like Kurt, Sue's musical repertoire is coded as 'gay.' Out of the twelve songs performed by Sue either in solo or in duet, six are from musicals[11] and three are songs made famous by pop divas.[12]

It would seem that Sue is less clearly connected to LGBTQ issues than Kurt, as she identifies as a cisgender heterosexual woman. However, Sue's gender status is far from clear. The second part of this article seeks to underline how she is a unique example of a camp character in mainstream primetime TV. This analysis will rely upon Jack Babuscio's article "Camp and the Gay Sensibility," in which he identifies four basic features of camp: irony, aestheticism, theatricality and humour (41-47), as well as incongruous elements and outrageous interpretation. All those elements perfectly apply to Sue's performances, both in terms of narrative and of spectacle.

First of all, irony is defined by Babuscio as "any highly incongruous contrast between an individual or thing and its context or association" (41), such as masculine and feminine, youth and age, sacred and profane. In the series narrative, the depiction of Sue's character as a 'mannish woman' is a recurring joke: because of her short hair and track suit, she is regularly mistaken for a man.[13] Also, she regularly alludes to the fact that she takes hormones and repeatedly refutes any biological attributes of femininity: she claims not to menstruate and explains she doesn't want kids because she has "neither the time, nor the uterus."[14]

Her gender inconsistency is also shown in dance: in "Sing with a swing," Will Schuester teaches her some dance movements to prepare her for a date. Not only is Sue much taller and bulkier than Schuester, but her clumsy dance style is also anything but feminine. She completely lacks grace; she makes wide and abrupt movements, and she stretches her arms and legs wide open. In contrast, Schuester bounces and dances

[11] Two songs from *Annie* ("Little Girls" in *Lights Out* [S4: E20] and "NYC" in *Opening Night* [S5: E17]), one from *Funny Girl* ("Who Are You Now?," also in *Opening Night*), one from *Wonderful Town* ("Ohio" in *Furt* [S2:E8]), one from the musical film *Meet Me in Saint Louis* ("The Trolley Song" in *The Rise and Fall of Sue Sylvester* [S6: E10]) and another from *Top Hat* ("Cheek to Cheek" in *Puppet Master*). To this list can be added Abba's "The Winner Takes It All" (in *Dreams Come True* [S6: E13]), that has been reprised in the stage and film musical *Mamma Mia.*

[12] "Vogue" by Madonna in *The Power of Madonna* [S1: E15), "Physical" by Olivia Newton-John in *Bad Reputation* [S1: E17] and "Bitch" by Meredith Brooks in *The Hurt Locker* [S6: E5].

[13] This is the case in *Opening Night* [S05: E17] and in *Puppet Master* [S5: E7].

[14] "Sue: Iron tablet? Keeps your strength up when you're menstruating./ Will: I don't menstruate./ Sue: Yeah? Neither do I" (*Showmance* [S1: E2).

around, ending the dance in her arms. If not downright mannish, her dancing style might be reminiscent of the vaudeville tradition of 'eccentric dancing.' In the heyday of Hollywood musicals, supporting actors like Charlotte Greenwood or Buddy Ebsen were famous for their atypical dancing abilities.[15] Their incongruous style challenged the heteronormative model, as their dance associated them with values not traditionally assigned to their gender—Greenwood's high kicks evoked strength whereas Ebsen's rubber legs connoted softness. But because of the spectacular value of their performances, such gender-troubling was allowed. They were, thus, placed "aside" the heteronormative scope of Hollywood romance, apart from rarely a couple of times, or when not, completely desexualized.[16] Linking Sue to this vaudevillian tradition serves to underline how she is, likewise, kept 'above' gender.

But if Sue seems completely unaware of gender differentiation, this might be above all because she is, more generally, oblivious to standard social behaviours. Indeed, Sue's ironic incongruity also lies in her character being depicted as a kind of 'super-villain,' whose actions are so over-the-top they seem almost inhuman. She's overtly violent with students (both mentally and physically) and advocates for school decisions which cannot be judged as appropriate, such as enforcing a "caning policy" to prevent absences (*Puppet Master* [S5: E7]). Always wearing the same clothes, she is often likened to the figure of the 'super-villain,' as her emblematic tracksuit comes in various colours and variations (even her wedding dress is made in the track suit style). In *Puppet Master*, she explains her motivations for wearing the tracksuit: to get respect. In a flashback sequence she is shown wearing blown-out hair and a typical 1980s pink lace skirt; cordial with students, she has to put up with their insolence and mockery. That is when she decides to metamorphose. She cuts her hair and puts on a tracksuit; the effect is immediate: students flee as soon as they see her. The music of *Carmina Burana* is heard, a recurring musical motif designed to highlight the disproportionate terror Sue inspires. The tracksuit has provided her with superpowers.

This over-the-top-ness is also expressed in her musical performances. A fondness for excess can be spotted in the peculiar way Sue's performances are 'integrated' into the narrative. *Glee* generally favours

[15] Greenwood was popular for her high kicks, Ebsen for his rubber legs.
[16] A middle-aged woman when she starred in the Fox musicals, Greenwood was allowed to behave in a not-sexualized way. Likewise, Ebsen was often used as a comic sidekick, thus being exempted from the imperative to act as a male romantic lead.

the model made popular by the backstage musical, in which the songs are set in a performance or rehearsal context. However, half of Sue's songs (and two of her three solos) are non-diegetic performances in which her singing is out of place in the fictional world.[17] Even when she is not the only one singing non-diegetically, she does it quite often, taking into account her relatively few songs. The non-integration of performance reinforces the excess and incongruity associated with her character in that she is shown in a common context behaving in extraordinary ways. Whereas "Little Girls" and "Bitch" are very different, both songs are affirmative tunes, conveying the character's strong ego. The two sequences use direct address to the camera: with a long close-up at the beginning of "Bitch" as well as through "Little Girls." They insist on the character's ability to brutally take the space over: long tracking shots follow her all the way through the high school corridors, clearly making her the driving force of the number. She displays an expression of rage which is as disproportionate and unjustified: she pushes a student away using a fire extinguisher, destroys a planetarium with a baseball bat (in "Bitch") and pushes cheerleaders over a railing (in "Little Girls"). Sue's brutality is a spectacle: in both songs, the epic storm she carries is amplified by cinematic effect, such as slow motion in "Bitch" and crane back travelling as she belts the final note of "Little Girls." The excess of Sue's character is also encapsulated by her apparitions in disturbing locations and context: in "Bitch," she fits into Rachel's drawer and in Jane's locker. In "Little Girls," she sneaks out by the bathroom door to spy on a student's intimacy. These manifestations of excess somehow make her character so unrealistic that she can't be seen anything else but campy.

Besides irony, the second feature underlined by Babuscio as typical of camp is "aestheticism." More precisely, camp arises when the emphasis on style is "too much": because of its love of incongruities, camp is often exaggerated and outrageous. Sue's camp aesthetic taste can be witnessed in her love for drag and outrageous costume. In *Mash-up* [S1: E8], not only does she dance in her own unusual way (as stated above), she also puts on a Zoot suit to show Rod what she intends to wear on their swing-contest date. When learning that only men wear those outfits, she soberly comments: "Further embarrassed." Similar clothing incongruity can also be found in *Rumours* [S2: E19], when she dresses up as David Bowie, then as Ann Coulter, in order to be "incognito" in

[17] Those songs are "Vogue," "Little Girls," "Cheek to Cheek," "NYC," "Who Are You Now?" and "Bitch." Among them, "Little Girls" and "Bitch" are performed in solo.

the school café—whereas those outfits make her, on the contrary, much more noticeable. Camp then lies as much in the incongruous context (being costumed in the school premises) as in the way a stone-faced Sue pretends not to acknowledge the absurdity of the situation.

Out of all the performances re-created in *Glee*, two of the most stylish are starring Sue: "Vogue" (from Madonna's movie clip of the same name) and "Cheek to Cheek" (from Mark Sandrich's 1935 film *Top Hat* starring Fred Astaire and Gingers Rogers). Both numbers are very close to their respective lavish original, in settings, costumes and photography. Both scenes are shot in an elegant black-and-white and recall the look of the Golden Age of Hollywood (in "Vogue," many of the scenes are recreations of star portraits taken by famous photographers). In both, Sue is all dolled up in fancy clothes and hair. Nevertheless, those performances are difficult to take seriously. Whereas the young glee club members usually perform 'straight' tribute to the originals they are recreating, Sue's strong persona forces to consider such performance as quintessentially parodic. This tightly links aesthetics and theatricality, the third feature of camp as identified by Babuscio.

This distanced recreation is all the more camp in that those performances have everything to do with gender issues. Indeed, both "Cheek to Cheek" and "Vogue" are answers to Sue's quest for models in femininity. In "Cheek to Cheek," she fantasizes that Will Shuester teaches her to be more feminine as they metamorphose into the iconic Astaire-Rogers couple; in "Vogue," Glee club members Mercedes and Kurt face the challenge of restoring Sue's confidence by putting her in the place of Madonna. Sue is purposely performing femininity and, therefore, highlighting its artificiality. Both performances question their relationship to the originals. In "Cheek to Cheek," Sue subtly queers a number that epitomized the celebration of heterosexual romance. Richard Dyer analysed this Astaire-Rogers' routine as a paroxysm of male domination, where partnering was predominant (Dyer 94). The *Glee* version has much more parallel dancing than the original, and its dancing is much less romantic. For example, *Top Hat*'s final supported backbend was both an occasion to display Roger's back flexibility and to symbolize romantic abandon; in *Glee* the backbend is far less spectacular and a mere wink to the original. Moreover, the partnering moments are less frequent than in the original, and are placed in side-by-side routines where male and female dancers do the same movement, thus tending towards a more "egalitarian" model—for Dyer, a model that Astaire-Rogers sometimes embraces, but in other routines, such as "Isn't it a lovely day to be caught in the rain?," also from *Top Hat* (Dyer 93). This idea of equality is also conveyed through song: in the original version, Astaire was the only one to sing; and singing was separated from dancing: in a common pattern of the Astaire-Rogers films, Astaire is the one who leads into the dance with his singing. In *Glee*, both Sue and Will are singing while dancing; they even harmonize and Sue sings the lower line. All those elements tend to convey an impression of a dance much more egalitarian and without romantic value. Of course, the campiest element is the distance introduced by Sue's visible perplexity at the beginning of the number, and Becky's (Lauren Potter) voice bursting at the end of the sequence and awaking her from her dream.

"Vogue" is perhaps the furthest that Sue has ever been from her usual persona. In this number, she genuinely performs a drag act, as she reproduces some of the most clichéd representations of femininity. Firstly, she wears several blond wigs, of different textures and length. She also wears costumes that are prominent attributes of femininity: lace corsage, satin evening dress with a fur collar, cleavage, corset and Madonna's emblematic pointy black bra. Suggestive shots make this femininity even more glamorous: medium shots show her face and her nude shoulders while she caresses her arm, high-angle shots display her lying on a sofa and touching her breasts, etc. Sue's clip is almost exactly identical to Madonna's; thus, it works on the same myths of femininity, using multiple fragmentations of a stylized feminine body. However, the huge seduction potential of the original clip is completely subverted by Sue's personality, which emerges briefly several times. For example, she changes the content of the lyrics in order to make them fit her identity: "Gene Kelly, Fred Astaire, Sue Sylvester dance on air" expresses her narcissistic megalomania, and "Lauren, Katherine, Lana too, Will Schuester, I hate you!" her pathological resentment of Schuester. She modifies the choreography too: first, by knocking down a young dancer who gets too close to her (it seems she wants to be the only center of attention in the frame), and secondly, by kicking with impatience one of the multiple hands that do her make-up. Like in "Cheek to Cheek," these short moments of discrepancy are pure manifestations of camp theatricality. In addition, this performance also has to be replaced in the story of the original "Vogue" clip. When she released "Vogue" in 1990, Madonna brought the black, queer, underground culture of voguing into the white, straight, mainstream world of pop music. Jane Lynch's rendition in *Glee* can be interpreted as a displacement even further away from those queer roots as Fox's show is targeted at mainstream family television audience. However, it can also be seen as a trickier move: whereas Madonna's performance of femininity can be read as 'straight' (as the pop singer broadly embraced the norms of desirable femininity), Jane Lynch's cannot be seen as anything else than parodic. Thus, *Glee*'s "Vogue" can almost be claimed as giving its queerness back to a number that once lost it.

The last feature of camp as described by Babuscio is humour, which "results from an identification of the strong incongruity between an object, person, or situation and its context" (46). Some of the above examples have already given a taste of Sue's immoderateness, wherein lies much of her comic incongruity. But if one were to locate her camp quality, it would undoubtedly lie in her comic one-liners. Far from being politically correct, they could even be judged offensive by several minorities[18] and are very often graphically disgusting.[19] Such humour can typically be seen as camp by its taste for exaggeration and the hyper-graphic, as well as a tendency to superimpose tragic and comic elements. In "The Power of Madonna," she is offended that Schuester made fun of her hair and reveals she always had to wear it short and that she suffered from it. Her parents being "famous Nazi hunters," thus never at home, she and her sister bleached their hair with "whatever chemicals [they] could find in the house: ammoniac, napalm," in order to pay tribute to Madonna. Her story is over-the top, dramatic and unlikely: Mercedes notes that it would make Sue 30 years old and the coach corrects her: "29" (which is comically absurd because Sue looks at least fifteen years older, actress Jane Lynch herself being 50).

The most overtly humoristic of her performance is "Physical," a re-rendering of Olivia Newton-John's 1981 music video. Sue and Olivia Newton-John are exercising in a gym, surrounded by muscular men in tight briefs. This time, the masculine body is on display with numerous close-ups on strong buttocks, biceps and torsos. The original video had a huge gay and humoristic content: the good-looking men were attracted to each other while Newton-John was stuck with the 'fatties.'

[18] Some examples: "I often yell at homeless people: "Hey, how is that homelessness working out for you? Try not being homeless for once!" (*Showmance* [S1: E2])" or "[Ramps] are what I call lazy-makers. They discourage able-bodied students from getting proper exercise by using the stairs" (*Wheels* [S1: E9]).
[19] Such as: "If I have a pregnant girl doing a handspring into a double layout, the judges aren't going to be admiring her impeccable form, they're going to be wondering if the centrifugal force is going to make the baby's head start crowning" (*Wheels* [S1: E9]); (to Will): "I'm seriously gonna puke in your mouth" (*Journey to Regionals* [S1: E22]).

The new version featuring Sue Sylvester is slightly different: the fat men have disappeared, and a new narrative appears. The discrepancy emerges here in the hiatus between the lyrics of the song and the two female singers' seductive attitude on one hand, and the obvious lack of interest from the men who keep on making mechanical movements on the other hand. This situation is very similar to what Vito Russo pointed out in *The Celluloid Closet* about the musical number "Is There Anyone Here for Love?" which Jane Russell performs in *Gentlemen Prefer Blondes* (1953). Jane Russell walks across a group of semi-nude sportsmen who are "totally oblivious to her charms" and only work on displaying their bodies to one another through the athletic choreography (Russo 78). In "Physical," the only actual physical contact between Sue and the men are a quick spank from Sue to one of them leaving the room, and a curious *porté* featuring Sue sliding on a bumpy line of men rolling on the floor. Once again, the erotic potential theoretically induced by the song is subverted, among other things, by Sue's personality: her vindictive overacting and clumsiness make it impossible to believe in her portrayal of seductive femininity.

These analyses of Sue's performances aim at underlining their constant camp value. This proves that the series knowingly encourages (or, at least, allows) viewers to read Sue as camp. Sue is, with no doubt, the most interesting character in *Glee,* because of her clever use of music and dance to convey gender problematics and her uncanny reconsideration of queer musical culture.

Glee has proven itself to be a prime display window for LGBTQ visibility, by including a record number of LGBTQ characters and by making LGBTQ issues crucial to its storylines. But the most unique accomplishment of the show is to have used its generic specificity to problematize these issues through music and dance. This musicality of *Glee*'s gender problematics is triply valuable. First of all, by transcribing gender issue in musical terms, it unravels how 'masculinity' and 'femininity' are culturally constructed. Secondly, the evolution of power and gender dynamics through musical performance highlights how gender is performative. Thirdly, by openly acknowledging an association between gay/queerness and some musical styles, the series unveils to its young audience the historical roots of gay/queer culture.

Glee has to negotiate constantly between queerness and normativity, more likely because it targets a wide audience. Even if Kurt's performances are meant to discuss existing stereotypes (such as linking male homosexuality and musical theatre), the most gender-troubling are Sue's. As a woman who is neither trans- nor homo-sexual, but can nevertheless be read as camp, she deeply challenges the cultural norms that are acceptable on primetime TV.

The exploration of Kurt and Sue's characters show how heavily *Glee* relies on the existing stereotypes linking sexual identity with musical preferences. It indeed favours show tunes and pop-diva hits every time it tackles gender-trouble issues. However, it does not use these musical styles as mere badges of queerness. Indeed, such associations are discussed at length in the show's narrative, thus acknowledging the gay investments in certain musical styles or stars. Making these associations explicit is typical of *Glee*'s postmodern position: the show introduces a distance with the stereotypes depicted while relying upon them.

Works Cited

Babuscio, Jack. "Camp and the Gay Sensibility." *Gays in Film*. Ed. Richard Dyer. San Francisco: Zoetrope, 1984. 40-57.

Buckley, Katie. "Identity and Solidarity in Online Communities: Queer Identities and Glee." M.A. Thesis, Bowling Green University, 2014.

Butler, Judith. *Gender Trouble* [1990]. New York and London: Routledge, 2011.

Brown Sonya C. "Body Image, Gender, Social Class and Ethnicity on Glee." *Studies in Popular Culture* 36.2 (Spring 2014): 125-147.

Chenn, Stephanie. "The 'Glee' Effect: Singing is Cool Again." *CNN* 15 November 2010. www.cnn.com/2010/LIVING/11/15/glee.effect.show.choir.comeback/index.html.

Clum, John M. *Something for the Boys: Musical Theater and Gay Culture*. New York: St Martin's Press, 2001 [1999].

Dyer, Richard. "'I Seem to Find the Happiness I Seek': Heterosexuality and Dance in the Musical". *In the Space of a Song: The Uses of Song in Film*. New York and London: Routledge, 2012. 89-100.

Fisher, Luchina. "'Glee:' 'Born This Way' Episode Has Sparks Flying." *ABC News* 26 April 2011. abcnews.go.com/Entertainment/glee-lady-gagas-born-episode/story?id=13451313.

Johnson, Brian C. and Faill, Danielle K., Eds. Glee *and New Directions for Social Change*. Rotterdam: Sense Publishers, 2015.

McCracken Allison, "Glee: The Countertenor and The Crooner." *Antenna*. 3 May 2011. blog.commarts.wisc.edu/2011/05/03/glee-the-countertenor-and-the-crooner.

Miller, D.A. *Place for Us: Essay on the Broadway Musical* [1998]. Cambridge, MA: Harvard University Press, 2000.

O'Connell, Michael, "TV Ratings: 'Glee' Exits Stage Left". *Hollywood Reporter* 21 March 2015. www.hollywoodreporter.com/live-feed/tv-ratings-glee-exits-stage-783509.

Parke, Michelle, Ed. *Queer in the Choir Room: Essays on Gender and Sexuality in* Glee. Jefferson, NC: McFarland, 2014.

Rosenberg, Alyssa, "Glee Is an Immoral Television Show and It's Time to Stop Watching It." *ThinkProgress.* 2 May 2012. thinkprogress.org/glee-is-an-immoral-television-show-and-it-s-time-to-stop-watching-it-49f7563ba0ac.

Santori Ann, "Glee's 'Very (Disappointing) Episodes.'" *Half-Way to a Mid-Life Crisis.* 11 May 2012. halfwaytoamidlifecrisis.wordpress.com/2012/05/11/glees-very-disappointing-episodes/.

Wolf, Stacy. "'Defying Gravity': Queer Conventions in the Musical Wicked." *Theatre Journal* 60.1 (March 2008): 1-21.

1980—The Year to Fear the Queer: Violent Responses to Patriarchy and Gender-bending in *Cruising* and *Dressed to Kill*

DAVID KLEIN MARTINS

The year 1980 started with two uprisings of film-historical significance which proved that, after Stonewall, American queer communities had gained a voice to collectively protest the discrimination exerted against them by the media and the government. Unfortunately, this queer momentum was soon to be lost into conservatism's clutch of the unfolding decade.

When filmmaker William Friedkin announced that he was planning to make a cinematic adaptation of the 1970 pulp novel *Cruising* by Gerald Walker, *Village Voice* reporter Arthur Bell, who had years earlier criticized Friedkin for arguably exploiting gay men in *The Boys in the Band* (1970), rose to the occasion to impede yet another homophobic picture in the director's oeuvre (Guthmann 2). Thus, a year prior to the film's release—i.e. even before the first scenes were shot—the movie was "accused of slanderously and dangerously implying a link between the gay lifestyle and violence that would lead to violence against gays" (Davidson 25).

Cruising presents the story of Steve Burns (Al Pacino), a police officer who accepts an undercover assignment to infiltrate New York's gay male sadomasochist and cruising subcultures to solve a number of murders connected to these scenes. Burns hands himself over to this mission, completely immersing into the shadowy world of homosexual kink. Although only suggested but never fully disclosed during the course of action, the viewer gets the feeling that Burns begins to struggle more intensely with his sexual identity and desire the further his mission leads him into the depths of gay nightlife. While he is eventually able to catch a suspect, it is also implied that Burns himself might have turned into a copycat killer. The movie's title is thus a double entendre alluding to both police patrolling and the act of cruising for a sexual partner. Surprisingly, Bell's articles calling for a boycott of the movie mobilized "large segments of the gay male ghetto community in New York City (and, to a lesser extent, in a number of other North American centers)" (Wilson 98). Willing to destroy any possibility of the movie's release, the angry mobs' rage led to a wave of vandalism – "windows were smashed, cars overturned, technical equipment on Friedkin's set damaged" (103). Apart from this urge for destruction, more sophisticated and direct tactics to prevent the crew from filming were developed, such as "shining mirrors onto sets and blowing whistles during sound takes" (Davidson 25). Even though the queer community was able to show that they were indeed a factor to be reckoned with, in regard to their aim to stop the film's production they failed. Despite all interruptions, the film was released on schedule, although approximately sixty percent over budget (Wilson 98; Guthmann 3). The only change achieved was a disclaimer added at the beginning of the movie, explaining "[t]his film is not intended as an indictment of the homosexual world. It is set in one small segment of that world, which is not meant to be representative of the whole" (Davidson 25).

Following the great controversy surrounding *Cruising*, yet another movie that caused a similar, though less radical, scandal was released later that very same year. Although Brian De Palma's *Dressed to Kill* was mainly criticized and protested against by feminists for the film's graphic killing of a woman, it was also condemned by the queer community for resorting to the clichéd idea of a gender-queer killer. *Dressed to Kill* introduces us to Kate Miller (Angie Dickinson), a middle-aged mother and wife, unfulfilled by her marriage, especially in sexual terms. While on a visit to New York's Metropolitan Museum of Art, she encounters a stranger, whom she follows home after a prolonged and sexually charged cat-and-mouse chase, and with whom she spends the day in bed. Unbeknownst to Kate, she has been followed by her gender-confused psychiatrist, Dr. Robert Elliott (Michael Caine). Dressed as his female alter ego 'Bobbi,' Dr. Elliott stabs Kate to death in an elevator right after her sexual encounter.

What infuriated many critics at the time was the fact that Kate's murder seemingly represents a form of punishment for her extramarital sexual activity. The murder is witnessed by the prostitute Liz Blake (Nancy Allen), who now becomes actively involved in the criminal investigation since she, as the sole witness, becomes a murder suspect. However, as sole witness, Liz also becomes the killer's next target. The movie progresses with Liz, and Kate's son Peter Miller (Keith Gordon), trying to solve the mystery of Kate's murder, eventually revealing Dr. Elliot as Kate's assailant. It is then disclosed that Dr. Elliott is indeed a transgender individual with a split personality, too confused to be able to decide whether to go through with sexual reassignment surgery.

Besides the anger stirred by both films, there are a variety of other essential parallels connecting the two. Interestingly, Brian De Palma had written a yet unpublished screenplay for Walker's novel *Cruising* before the directorial rights were granted to William Friedkin. This led De Palma to write another movie instead, namely *Dressed to Kill*. David Greven thus argues that De Palma's film "plays out as a much more heterosexually oriented story, yet it bears some elements of *Cruising*'s plot and is not without a few queer elements of its own" (183). While the films are indeed very different in terms of content and narrative structure, they both play with the sexual act of cruising—be it of heterosexual (*Dressed to Kill*) or homosexual (*Cruising*) nature.

The most important feature connecting *Cruising* and *Dressed to Kill*, however, is the queerness exploited in both films in form of gender- and sexually-confused killers. The question regarding the queer killers' identities and motivations, however, is not as straightforwardly addressed in both movies. In *Dressed to Kill* the killer's identity produces bafflement during the course of the film due to the fact that he is a biological male wearing female attire. However, once Dr. Elliott is revealed to be the criminal behind the mask, the question regarding the killer's identity is immediately settled. When it comes to identifying the killer in *Cruising* the task becomes more ambiguous. As a matter of fact, one might say that it is simply impossible to point out who the one/s responsible for the murders is/are. While the movie provides an answer to an unobservant viewer, namely that the arrested Stuart Richards is guilty of the crimes, this plain and obvious solution seems unsatisfactory since there remain too many unresolved issues.

The movie first establishes the connection between Stuart and the killings in a dream sequence, in which Richards talks to his deceased father. This dialogue is intercut with images of the previous murders, linking Richards directly to these killings. Yet we should not take these connections at face value. One might instead argue that, maybe, the intercut moments in the dream sequence are the concoction of an unreliable narrator aiming at further confusing the viewer. Nonetheless, there is also the hard evidence of his fingerprints on a coin found at the peep show crime scene. It needs to be remembered that nothing in this film can be taken for granted. The fingerprint might thus be a lie made-up by the police. In fact, Edelson (Burns' superior) and Burns are facing great pressure to solve this case. The incarceration of Richards might thus be an act of desperation on the side of the police (Davidson 32; Wood 55-6; Krohn). By solving the murder not only do they both avoid losing their jobs but furthermore it allows "Steve [to gain] his gold badge and clear the books of all murders Edelson has been taxed with solving" (Krohn).

Apart from this, an even weightier discrepancy in the movie needs to be addressed: namely, in each murder scene we see a different actor playing the murderer. The murderer's physical appearance thus varies from murder scene to murder scene, as well as his voice, his clothes, his sunglasses, and even the knives he uses to kill his victims (Snyder 111; Wood 56; Krohn). This leaves us to conclude that "[t]here are, then, probably at least two different killers" (Snyder 111), if not more. Accordingly, this very much reflects the uncertainties of a postmodern world, where "everything becomes a matter of 'if,' 'maybe,' 'let's pretend,' rather than '*this* is what happened'" (Wood 56).

However, the fact that Stuart Richards tries to stab Burns in the scene of their final confrontation cannot be denied, although I would read this as a desperate measure of self-defense, rather than a bloodthirsty attack. It is of importance to remember that Steve Burns has very blatantly stalked and shadowed Richards before this scene, which has naturally come to Stuart Richards' attention. Richards is also shown reading a newspaper that headlines the killings in the gay underground scene while noticing Burns' incessant stare. It is therefore possible that Richards links Steve Burns' stalking to the killings, thus believing Burns to be the serial killer following him. When confronted face to face with Burns, it appears as if Richards feels threatened and only tries to protect himself against his prowler by trying to stab him before his opponent anticipates his killing.

This leads us directly to the assumption expressed earlier that Steve Burns himself might be connected to some of the murders witnessed in the film. Burns was assigned for the investigation because he resembles the killer's victims and thus physically fits the killer's 'type' in men. As will become apparent, by adopting the victims' dress codes and socializing in the same circles as they did, Burns not only becomes a mirror image of the victims, but also of every gay man in the scene, including the killer, since they all look alike. This constant doubling of gay men, as Davidson notes,

> suggests the figure of the gay clone: the same-looking, simulacral gay man, a copy for which there is no original. If the clone was one of the primary modalities through which postliberation gay identity was performed, then this was an identity that pointed up identification's constitutive element of imitation. (47)

In a way, this can be understood as a "seriality and standardization" (47) of the gay 'look' that occurred in the 1970s. In regard to the film this simulacral doubling of gay men symbolizes that anyone can become a victim or a victimizer at any time, leading to total paranoia. The hypermasculine gay clone also presents a conundrum. On the one hand, he oozes masculinity—a desirable characteristic society demands from men. On the other hand, he symbolizes queer desire and, in effect, the inversion of masculinity, as far as the widespread misconception in the public mind goes.

The theory that Burns was possibly involved in a number of murders is moreover based on the fact that, in the course of the film, several parallels between Burns and the supposed killer, Stuart Richards, are created, equating one with the other. Both men are seen "weight lifting to keep in shape, staring at the other through windows, and dressed exactly alike in their highly eroticized, climactic confrontation" (Savran 215), eventually becoming almost physically and behaviourally indistinguishable.

The parallels connecting both men go even deeper into their pasts and psyches: Stuart Richards and, to some extent, Steve Burns, suffer from a trauma connected to unhealthy parental ties. Richards makes believe that his deceased father is still alive, talking to his friends about recent meetings with him. From the letters Richards wrote to his father but failed to mail to him and from their imaginary conversation in the park, one gathers that Stuart yearns for the approval of his father, even exclaiming the wish that "just once you'd say something positive to me."

The same father issues are also reflected by Stuart's doppelganger Steve Burns. Nevertheless, this parallel is only suggested fleetingly, namely, in the scene that first shows him lying in bed with his girlfriend Nancy (Karen Allen). Pleasant violin music plays during a conversation the couple is having about Steve's upcoming mission. However, as soon as Nancy casually mentions that Steve's father called, he appears to get tense, he deeply exhales and, most significantly, the joyous violin music is replaced by threatening, unnerving sounds. Absent-mindedly, Burns tells Nancy: "There's a lot about me that you don't know." When she inquires "Such as?" he simply remains silent. Instead the scene dissolves into the next one, retaining the eerie music. While Steve Burns' relation to his father remains unexplored, these visual and musical cues nevertheless speak of a broken father-son relation.

Ultimately, the father issues that both Richards and Burns experience might represent the struggle of fitting into patriarchal society, as Wood observes:

> Somewhat explicitly but more by implication, the film's real villain is revealed as patriarchal domination, the "Law of the Father" that demands the rigid structuring of the subject and the repression of all conflicting or superfluous realities—the denial of the Other, both internal and external. (60)

The violent killings exerted by these men thus "ha[ve] to be blamed on the culture, not on the individual" (Wood 56), i.e., a culture of homophobia that encourages the fruition of internalized homophobia and self-hatred through its insistence on compulsory heterosexuality. The real disease infiltrating the world of *Cruising* is thus "our refusal to recognize that the human psyche is a blend of masculine and feminine elements, our refusal to accept human sexuality as a continuum, our persistence in assigning to ourselves and others rigid sexual roles" (Hayle 230).

Eventually, the film ends the way it began—with a man walking into a private nightclub in New York's Meatpacking District. Since the scene at the beginning of the film was followed by a murder, one might read this as an indication that the killer has indeed not been captured and that he is on the hunt again. It might also be an assertion that all the signs pointing towards Steve Burns' newfound passion for killing were indeed correct. The circular motion of the movie after all alerts us that evil is unkillable in a society that stirs violence with its rigid gender roles: if one killer has been captured, the next one will continue his game.

Returning to the queerness exploited in both films, it needs to be taken into account that the murderers in *Dressed to Kill* as well as in *Cruising* are all males in gender distress or in a crisis concerning their (hetero-)sexuality. The gender-queer Dr. Elliott is portrayed as a split personality, unable to reconcile his male and female side. While his male identity is the one of a warm and nurturing psychoanalyst, his female side, Bobbi, is an envious, murderous monster. This shows that femininity in a *man* is represented as evil and undesirable. Bobbi is pushing Elliott to accept her sex reassignment surgery, but to no avail. One can presume that Dr. Elliott refuses to go through with the surgery due to the social implications it would bring.

As a psychiatrist Elliott has achieved a certain status in society that he/she would lose after his/her transition due to the raging transphobia of the times. It needs to be remembered that although the gay movement had gained a lot of visibility and tolerance after Stonewall, transgendered individuals were not included into their political agenda, as they supposedly only brought further confusion to the matters for which the groups were fighting (see Skodbo 25). The rising acceptability of the transgender community is in fact a very recent phenomenon, which was unthinkable in the late 1970s or early 1980s.

As a form of revenge, whenever Dr. Elliott becomes sexually aroused, Bobbi sees it as her mission to eliminate the cause of Elliott's erecting penis. The awakening of Bobbi happens the instant he becomes sexually stimulated and this shift is visualized each time. We can first witness this transformation when Kate offers to sleep with Dr. Elliott. He then pauses and looks into a mirror with an ominous expression on his face, the gesture that signifies his identity switch. This happens again when Liz pretends to want to have sex with him. It hence appears as if it is in a mirror that Dr. Elliott reaches out to his female shadow-self Bobbi, the flip-side to his gentle male self. Mirrors can serve to create the doubling of the person regarding his reflection. In the present case, the mirror not only puts the spectator (Dr. Elliott) in face of himself to reveal a side of him that he cannot recognize, but it also speaks of inverted narcissism—a form of self-identification closely linked to self-hatred, or rather, internalized transphobia.

In fact, Bobbi is constantly associated with mirrors during the film. In the elevator scene, for instance, the camera focuses on a small circular mirror to show the reflection of the murder taking place. During Liz's final nightmare, Bobbi again first appears in a mirror before we see her slit Liz's throat. Interestingly, this evokes scenes from *Cruising*, in which we can observe Steve Burns working out in front of a mirror or applying makeup before going out to gay clubs. Here as well, the mirror is used as a tool for transforming oneself. Burns namely uses the mirror to become the stereotypical gay clone. This leads to the conclusion that mirrors can bear the connotation of a closeted double life led by a double-faced person.

Not only is Bobbi vengeful but she is also deeply envious of hyperfeminine women and the opportunities they have to express their gendered desires and charms. Above all, "[t]hese fantasies of women's luxuriant power within and over social and sexual realms only fuel the killer's misogynistic and self-hating rage" (Greven 233). Kate, who arouses Dr. Elliott and immediately afterwards is able to cruise a man and live out a pleasurable sexual fantasy, thus perfectly falls into the pattern of Bobbi's wrath. Since Bobbi is unable to express her sexuality and gender freely, sexuality of any kind infuriates her.

Nonetheless, Bobbi utilizes her gender-nonconforming body to wreak havoc in *heterolandia*. Being a woman in a biological male body, Bobbi takes advantage of her "phallic power that the hyperfeminine Kate does not possess" (Greven 240) by symbolically killing her with a blade, an obvious phallic symbol. This underlines the fear of a queer individual living in the liminal space between genders, or more specifically, the misogynistic anxiety of a woman enjoying the prestige of the phallus.

The same equation of sexuality and violence/murder is presented in *Cruising*. However, since there are, as determined, several killers in the film, it is of importance to approach this discussion in two steps. First, I will consider the sexualized murder scenes. Following this, I will take a closer look at Steve Burns' sexuality since he has possibly adapted the killer's identity.

Cruising takes place in the promiscuous S&M and cruising scenes of late 1970s New York City and thus presents a world tinged with sexual desire. Front and center to this world stand "the possibilities of the male body as a site of worship and a geography of distinct pleasures" (Greven 188). The male body is presented as appealing and always ready to be consumed by other men. The gay male body moreover becomes attached with a plethora of signifiers deconstructing the idea of the 'homosexual physique.' As Greven argues, "[t]he film refuses conventional notions of gay masculinity by making the actor[s] strong and buff rather than pitiably weak-looking, as so many gay males in film have been depicted, particularly in this period" (197). There is also an element of parody present, because the actors epitomize masculinity through their performance of gender, while engaging in a variety of homoerotic acts (200).

This overturns the dominant understanding that masculinity and male homosexuality are incompatible, as homosexuality is widely perceived as the ultimate failure in terms of masculinity. Yet the sadomasochistic urges ever-present in the film also speak of the destructive tendencies directed towards a sexual partner. In a sense it is possible to wonder, with some plausibility, if this proclivity for destructiveness in the film stems from the misconception that S&M practices are closely related to the internalized homophobia felt within the gay community. In this respect, sadomasochism is often criticized as "*the* privileged instrument for the stabilization of heterosexual patriarchy, the false consciousness that eroticizes power and powerlessness" (Savran 217). According to this, S&M perpetuates the submission of the feminine through the masculine. In a gay relationship this would mean that the sadistic part of a couple can only upkeep his masculinity if his masochistic counterpart is humiliated and therefore feminized. This, however, appears to be an utmost reductive form of sexual shaming, ignoring realities such as lesbian S&M practices as well as female domination as epitomized by the figure of the dominatrix. Besides, equating femininity with humiliation is regressive misogynistic thinking. It needs to be highlighted at this point that although sexual S&M plays nowadays find more acceptance, in the early 1980s the equation of S&M and LGBT people was highly damaging for the community's reputation.

Building upon these negative connotations associated with sadomasochism, in the movie the connection between S&M and violence goes as far as to suggest that "sexual violence and S/M are finally indistinguishable, that homicide is simply an extension of rough sex" (Savran 217). The queer underground scene is hence not only extremely sexualized but also highly violent to the extent of murder. Most conspicuously, every murder is committed during a sexual act of homoerotic nature. In all three murders depicted in the movie, the killer stands behind his victim and stabs him in the back—a gesture clearly alluding to anal sex.

In order to further highlight this, Friedkin intercuts these stabbings with subliminal pornographic images of actual anal penetration, which cement the aforementioned connection between stabbing and sexually penetrating a male body. In turn, the subject of pornography is also repeatedly associated to the murders. In the St. James Hotel murder scene a series of pornographic magazines titled *Wrestling* are scattered all around the floor. The image of wrestling again evokes the conflation of glorifying violence and the objectified male body. Next, in the peep show scene a pornographic film is projected onto the wall. Porn in this context becomes a metacommentary on how a certain sense of pleasure is literally derived from the act of looking.

During the stabbing, blood splashes directly onto the projection, again creating an obvious association between sexuality and murder.

Above all, this brutalized display of pornography can be read as a self-reflexive critique regarding our sexualized and violent cinematic viewing habits. After all, it is the sex and the violence that make movies such as *Cruising* appeal to large audiences, regardless of their sexual orientation or identity. It is therefore safe to assume that a movie with queer content would not attract large segments of moviegoers if it were not for its graphic depiction of violence and sex.

Similarly, Steve Burns also falls victim to the understanding of sexuality as a violent practice. Burns starts out as a seemingly heterosexual man enjoying an amorous relationship with his girlfriend Nancy. When his boss, Captain Edelson, inquires if he has ever engaged in sexual relations with other men, Burns decisively denies the implication. Soon, this self-assured heterosexuality starts to dwindle. The further he gets drawn into his mission and into the queer underground world, the more the defining categories between heterosexuality and homosexuality get blurred. Although Burns' arising homoerotic feelings are never explicitly expressed at any point in the movie, they are, however, suggested on various occasions. Midway through the narrative, Burns goes beyond his mission to solely observe the men surrounding him and begins to actively partake in the queer conglomeration of men by accepting an invitation to dance. This dance then turns into an energetic 'initiation ritual': "His movements are uninhibited, forceful, and sexual. Now he meets directly and unabashedly the eyes of those who observe him. Ostensibly the immersion is necessary so that he can do his job; but its [sic] totality goes beyond duty" (Hayle 229).

It is also suggested that Burns accepts sexual invitations by other men. More precisely, "one scene, set in a bar, ends with him allowing a man to fondle his chest; another ends with him walking off with a man he meets in the Rambles in Central Park" (Davidson 31). These sexual encounters, however, are never explicitly shown and only remain on a suggestive level. Burns' identity crisis becomes most apparent when considering his symbolic cries for help that reveal his uncertainty regarding his sexual orientation. To prove his heterosexuality (and the implicit sense of masculinity he receives from it) to himself, Burns returns to his apartment to have "rough sex with Nancy, the camera lingering on the leather wristband that is part of his cover" (Davidson 31).

The camera's lingering thus visualizes Burns' true sexual desires that are now connected to the violence he experienced in the sex clubs and which he wishes to transfer to his own sexual relation with his girlfriend. In another scene, Nancy performs fellatio on him. We first hear the harmonious violin music, a sort of leitmotif that represents their heterosexual relationship. Soon, however, the music is drowned out by sounds of the nightclub scenes. Burns then closes his eyes, as if to fully submerse into the homoerotic fantasy without having to be confronted with the actual heterosexual sex he is having.

Eventually Burns reaches a state of despair, a point at which he needs to express and voice his confusion about these new feelings he is facing, declaring "What I'm doing is affecting me," as well as, "Something's happening to me—stuff going down, I don't think I can deal with it." It appears as if the gay ghetto is rubbing off on Burns, as if queerness was contagious—a fear evocative of that of the 'gay agenda,' which claims that there is a queer conspiracy to overthrow heterosexuality.

Burns' sexual uncertainty coupled with his internalized homophobia eventually lead to his growing destructive tendencies. The killing of Burns' neighbour Ted Bailey gives more insight into this matter. After Ted's mutilated body is found, Captain Edelson finds out that Steve Burns was the victim's neighbor. As a reaction to this, Edelson utters a shocked "Jesus Christ!"—a clear indication that he connects Ted's death to the fact that he knew Burns, who in turn seemed increasingly confused and anxious (see Wood 55).

Burns' involvement in the killing of Ted might be linked to Burns' homosexual desires he felt towards Ted. This becomes evident in an earlier scene, in which Burns "has broken down the door of Ted's apartment to fight Ted's jealous boyfriend, who has goaded him with the accusation that Burns and Ted are involved" (Davidson 31). Does Burns' repressed anger allude to the fact that Ted's boyfriend indeed touched a raw nerve by exposing his queer desires? Is Burns unable to cope with his homoerotic feelings for Ted and as a compensatory act needs to resort to violence? It is also possible that, to some extent, Ted's murder might have been an act of jealousy committed by Burns, who is unable to openly express his sexuality. After all, if we look at it from our present standpoint without any prejudice, Ted is constructed as a positive gay character that is allowed to embrace his homosexuality and live it out openly, as opposed to the repressed Steve Burns.

Ted's death thus builds a bridge to the killing of Kate Miller in *Dressed to Kill* in so far as ultimately the feminizing attributes of his gayness are punished, i.e., "vulnerability, gentleness, 'femininity' (all intolerable within the world of the film)" (Snyder 112). This above all represents the fear of failing masculinity. Burns' sense of belonging to the hypermasculine primarily clashes with his fear of being feminized due to his queer desires. Again, this reveals Burns' difficulty to reconcile his apparent bisexual desires, just as Dr. Elliott struggles to accept his feminine side. Instead, both characters perceive homosexuality and heterosexuality (as well as masculinity and femininity) to be two isolated categories unable to be merged into a single sexual- and gender-fluid unity. The two characters are thus put into a figurative closet, their jealousy not only preventing any type of freedom of gender expression but also turning into (self-)hatred stirred by a deep frustration.

What is remarkable when looking at both films is the sexualized voyeurism attached to the violence at hand. In fact, the idea of scopophilia addressed in *Cruising* functions as an allegory of spectatorship: the entire cruising scene as well as the sex clubs with their diverse public sex acts, all serve the purpose of pleasing the gay male gaze.

During the movie the viewer is not only put into the position of detective Burns observing the queer goings-on but constant subjective shots of the men checking Burns out also place us in the position of the ones cruising. This even leads to moments of queering of the heterosexual male viewer.

In other words, together with Steve Burns the viewer also goes through a transformation of queer nature throughout the course of the film, since, through the camera work, he actively cruises and is cruised by many men. By breaking the boundaries of the diegetic world, in the final scene Burns makes us aware of our shared transformation through his gaze: "Burns's stare into the mirror and into the camera means that this sense of possible transformation potentially applies not only to the subject in the film (Burns) but also to the subject watching the film" (Davidson 45). Taking into consideration that Burns is a potential killer, Burns' point-of-view also aligns the viewer with the killer.

In *Dressed to Kill* the voyeuristic gaze is very openly scrutinized and criticized. By emphasizing the gaze, Brian De Palma "underlines the fact that voyeurism is integral to the nature of movies" (Kael 37). This is highlighted through the plethora of close ups and extreme close ups of eyes we find in the film. Furthermore, the plot is greatly based on spying, another form of employing the gaze. Amongst others, these spying scenes include the one in which a cab driver gazes at the sexually engaged Kate Miller and her lover on the back seat of his taxi, the scene in which Peter secretly takes pictures of Dr. Elliott's patients through his timed camera, or the scene in which Bobbi spies through Liz's window—a scene which mirrors the one in which Burns spies on Stuart Richards through his window in *Cruising*.

Simultaneously, all the characters' gazes are doubled by the viewer's gaze. Yet, the gaze of the audience goes beyond merely reflecting that of the characters, since audience members are able to witness every intimate moment in the film. Brian De Palma cleverly uses this insight to create a complex intersection of all these gazes. The movie begins with an erotic dream sequence, in which Kate's body is objectified for the viewer to indulge in her beauty. Kate in turn gazes at her husband in the hope of sexually stimulating him; too self-absorbed to even notice the desires of his wife, he only looks into a mirror to see his own reflection. The motif of the invisible desires of a woman is then repeated when Kate enters her son's room to remind him of their plan to visit the museum that same day. He, however, is too captivated by the world of his computers to even look at her. Kate needs to ask him to "put that down and look at [her]" (De Palma 1980). Both scenes go hand in hand with Laura Mulvey's notion of the "active/male and passive/female" in film—or rather the idea that a woman in film serves only as an object, a so-called "to-be-looked-at-ness" (19), to male characters and viewers.

While Kate's beauty can be admired, her own desires remain unfulfilled. Just like a passive doll, she is thus used by her husband to reach orgasm in bed while she has to remain sexually unsatisfied. Her son's promise to spend the day with her at the Metropolitan Museum is not met. Moving on, when at the museum all by herself, De Palma focuses on Kate's wishful gaze while observing all the different couples and families around her, representing the happiness her life is lacking. The subsequent chase between her and her suitor is again based on the opposition between a man that actively sees and a woman unable to see.

Linda Williams explains that in this scene Kate's point-of-view shots allow the viewers to adopt Kate's field of vision "only to demonstrate her failure to see" (574). Once Kate breaks out of the passivity her life has so far entailed and finally pleases herself by following the stranger's sexual invitation, tragedy strikes. Right after her sexual encounter, Kate meets a little girl in the elevator who refuses to stop staring at her. The stare of an innocent girl personifies the guilt, humiliation, and shaming that Kate feels after having had sex with a stranger and finding out that he has possibly infected her with a venereal disease.

Next, Bobbi appears onto the scene to bring Kate's final demise. During the slashing of Kate in the elevator, De Palma chooses an extreme close up of Kate's eye gazing directly into the camera while the killer slits her face. One might wonder if her confrontational stare breaking the fourth wall is an accusatory commentary on the thirst for blood of an audience that has grown callous to such high levels of violence as shown in this scene. When Liz enters the narrative a transference from one character to the next occurs through visual cues. It needs to be stressed at this point that the transference is only possible due to the fact that the main protagonist is killed off and disappears midway through the plot (the same way as in *Psycho,* the text *Dressed to Kill* repurposes).

Kate namely reaches out her hand to Liz, a clear cry for help. Next we see an extreme close up of Kate's eyes. In a reverse shot, Kate's look is met by Liz's stare in a similar extreme close up. In this way, De Palma creates a moment of female bonding (see Greven 238). It is now Liz's task to avenge Kate's murder and to solve the mystery surrounding her death. On a symbolic level Kate has granted Liz entrance into her life and family. Liz will not only avenge Kate's death but also, more importantly, bring redemption to the regressive way Kate as a woman has been portrayed in the first half of the movie. Although Liz is a professional prostitute, she is not as easily labeled as an object: this is related to the controlled manner in which she handles her sexuality.

Liz understands her sexual power and erotic potential as well as male desire, all of which she uses for her own benefit. Instead of a passive character, the viewer is now confronted with an active woman who helps to advance the investigation of Kate's murder and, with it, the entire plot development. In this way, Liz inverts Mulvey's concept of the inactive woman in film.

Although Peter accompanies Liz's quest during the course of the movie, it is Liz that stands out as the true hero of the story. After all, it is she who meets Dr. Elliott in his counseling office. She goes even further and rummages through Dr. Elliott's documents to find out more about Bobbi's identity. It is here that she adopts the investigating gaze that is traditionally withheld from women in film. By becoming the investigating woman, Liz is able to uncover the mystery behind the murderous Bobbi. It is namely through Liz's eyes that we witness the unmasking of Bobbi/Dr. Elliott in the final confrontation.

Liz's gaze thus deconstructs the killer's invisibility obtained through the costume he/she wears. Interestingly, when Bobbi attempts to attack her she is saved by another female character. Although Peter screams and taps on the window in order to warn Liz from the impending danger, Liz fails to understand what he is trying to communicate. Instead, a policewoman shoots the assailant in a last-minute rescue, preventing him/her from stabbing Liz. Here again, the movie speaks of sisterhood:

once more it is a woman that helps out another woman in distress. This is to say that this scene might be perceived as an equivalent to the scene in which Kate transfers her role to Liz, so that Liz can avenge her. In the world presented, men, on the other hand, are unable to do so since they are blind to women's fears and desires and use them for pleasure only.

Liz's job further enhances her qualities of a gender-bending heroine. Liz is a prostitute earning her living by providing sexual services. More than only making ends meet, Liz sees her job as a vehicle to aim for higher financial goals, which links her significantly to the male sphere. She invests much of her earned money into stocks and into her private art collection, a fact that she mentions on various occasions during the course of action. Indeed, in the scene in which she is first introduced to us, we see her talking to a client of hers about recommendations regarding the stock market while she is waiting for the elevator in which Kate Miller is being stabbed. This reveals that Liz not only uses men for financial profit but also to extract valuable information. Liz is thus first presented as a business-oriented, cunning woman. Next, this dialogue is interrupted by the discovery of the mutilated Kate. As already expected from men in this film, Liz's client immediately runs, leaving Liz to manage the situation alone. With the help of cross-cutting—a succession of shots jumping between Liz waiting for the elevator and Kate's death inside the elevator—De Palma further highlights Liz's masculine traits by comparing and contrasting the two women.

In other words, in this montage sequence the dependent, silenced, and sexually unfulfilled Kate is counterposed to the independent, confident, and sexually empowered Liz. The elevator, with its confining framing power, symbolically represents Kate's restricted life and her constant feeling of entrapment. Thus, the montage sequence ends in a convergence of both paralleled actions, alerting the viewer that the repressed life Kate leads will end in her destruction, while the emancipated Liz survives by not entering the elevator—or, symbolically, the restricted life society demands from a woman. Instead, Liz has become an expert when it comes to adapting her gendered performance to different situations in which she finds herself. When interrogated by Detective Marino, for instance, she starts off playing an innocent girl.

However, as soon as Marino reveals that he knows about her profession, she instantly grabs a cigarette—a phallic symbol representing her gender-bending potential—lights it up and switches into the role of the self-confident, empowered businesswoman. This gender shifting is later epitomized in a scene in which Liz handles two telephone calls simultaneously, each representing a different social interaction. On one phone Liz is speaking to her employer, Norma, sweet-talking her into making an arrangement with a client for her. On the second phone Liz discusses business with her broker, adopting a cold voice, and handling the call in a very straightforward manner. It is indeed quite significant that she can switch from one gendered behaviour to the next within seconds.

Liz has mastered the artistry of gender performance and uses it to make it in a world ruled by patriarchy. In this scene Liz's potential regarding her switching between genders is furthermore highlighted through the use of the split screen. While Liz's telephone call takes place in the right hand side of the split screen, on the left we see Dr. Elliott listening to a hateful message Bobbi left on his answering machine. He then turns on his television to watch *The Phil Donahue Show*, which Liz is also watching.

Most importantly, on the show a transgendered woman, Nancy Hart, is interviewed, explaining that she used to be a "macho man," which again stresses the ways in which gender can be performed and moulded. It is also a comment on societal expectations regarding the hypermasculine behaviour a biologically born male is demanded to perform, leaving no space for the flourishing of the gender form with which he/she truly identifies. Through the split screen Liz is consequently equated with two other genderqueer characters—Dr. Elliott/Bobbi and Nancy Hart.

Yet, as opposed to Liz and Nancy, Dr. Elliott/Bobbi is unable to combine the masculine and the feminine aspects within himself/herself; a fate speaking of great frustration reminiscent of the one felt by Kate Miller, who also felt trapped by the confinements of gender expectations. During the split screen sequence, Liz also places herself in front of a three-piece mirror. By tripling her image, the mirror reflects on the idea of the fragmentation of her identity by showing that neither identity nor gender are stable or can be pinned down in any way, making her the queer hero of the movie. Nevertheless, unlike Dr. Elliott, she has the potential to choose which gender to inhabit. It is namely in front of the mirror that Liz applies her makeup, an act symbolizing her self-chosen transformation into a feminized self. This way the mirror is again linked to queerness.

Inherent in the murders there also exists a strong critique of patriarchal authority. In *Dressed to Kill* it is Kate in particular that falls victim to patriarchy. The first father figure that appears in the movie is

Kate's husband Mike. As has been previously mentioned, during Kate's sexual fantasy, he completely disregards Kate's obvious yearning for affection and sexual release. The dream sequence ends with a stranger appearing in the shower behind Kate, covering her mouth, raping her.

This gesture establishes the subject of the silencing and the careless abuse of women that will be repeatedly addressed throughout the film. Instead of playing the role of the protector, Mike merely continues shaving. In the very next scene, the warnings of the dream sequence turn into reality when Mike has actual, unsatisfactory intercourse with Kate to the background noise of a radio weather forecast ironically speaking about fireworks that Kate is not feeling. Moving forward, Kate is once more betrayed by a man when she finds out that she has contracted a venereal disease from her one-night stand.

The letter she finds in his desk proves that he knows about his health issues. Nevertheless, he fails to warn his sexual partner (Kate) about the risk she is about to take when sleeping with him. His indifference towards her "shows that she continues to be victimized by the varieties of male arrogance and indifference to women's well-being" (Greven 215). This scene, however, takes on even more symbolic importance when taking into consideration that the medical results Kate finds in her lover's drawer lie right next to a magazine headlining "Ted Kennedy's challenge to Jimmy Carter for the Democratic presidential nomination." To this end, Greven further reasons that "[w]hatever the specific import of this cover, in political terms, it alerts us to impending waves of change that affect even this post-coital scene presumably distant from changes in the national and political life" (215-216). What he means by this has to do with the changes from 1970s liberalism to a rising conservatism already felt at the time of the movie's production. More precisely, "[w]ith uncanny precision, *Dressed to Kill* anticipates the sexual panic and moral condemnations—largely directed towards gays—of the imminent AIDS era" (Greven 216). The coupling of the news report with the venereal disease then further underlines this message since it "anticipates a new culture of morality and condemnation about matters of sex. . . . The possibility that Kate has contracted it suggests her fall into a culture of repressiveness and judgment about sexuality" (216).

Kate's ultimate betrayal by a man she trusted and confided in—i.e. her psychiatrist who is supposed to help her to mental stability—is then epitomized by her murder. Even the well-adapted, gender-fluid Liz is not fully immune to the trap of patriarchal dominance and betrayal. In her case, she is used by the police force, represented by Detective

Marino, who irresponsibly sends Liz into dangerous situations to help him solve the murder case while knowing that she is not involved in the murder in any way (see Greven 227). Another police officer appears in the subway chase scene. Here Liz calls out the inefficiency of the police by stating, "Where the fuck are you guys when somebody needs you?" Indeed, the officer then disappears right at the moment that Liz's tormentors reappear and she finds herself on her own again.

In *Cruising* authoritarian figures are ridiculed and portrayed as corrupt and evil. Although the film is often derided for depicting the queer community as violent, we need to bear in mind that before any violence in the queer community is shown it introduces male heterosexual violence employed by the police force. Stephen Snyder connects this omnipresent violence that transgresses sexual orientation to the compulsory hypermasculinity in American society:

> [T]he heavy-leather gay community depicted in the film can be seen as an extension of the aggressive macho-oriented society of the heterosexual world, typified by the police, which tends to suppress femininity in favour of masculine aggressiveness. The result in either world is a displacement of affection by aggression. (103)

Hence violence is omnipresent in the movie, transcending sexual orientation. The movie opens with the finding of a severed arm in a river, which is then brought to a forensic doctor for analysis. The doctor explains that the arm clearly points to a homicide, yet the police refuse to open up a murder investigation. Instead the arm is stored in the forensic facilities. This scene thus introduces the topic of authoritarian corruption that is then further explored in the next scene, in which we see two police officers driving in a patrol car. One policeman, DiSimone (Joe Spinell), rambles on about his wife leaving him and how he is going to "get that bitch." He then goes on to explain how the city has changed and degradingly comments on the gay men he sees roaming the streets. When two transvestite prostitutes cross his way, he stops and, after a short dialogue, forces one of them to perform oral sex on him.

In the same manner as women are abused in *Dressed to Kill*, authority figures discriminate against and harass homosexual men in *Cruising*, thus failing in their task to protect civilians. In the further course of the movie the same police officer "turns up twice in the context of the gay subculture, cruising Burns once in a bar (where he is closely juxtaposed with Stuart Richards) and once in Central Park" (Wood 27). This further establishes the bridge between gay underground life and the police force. The ultimate clash between both worlds happens during so-called "Precinct Night," a themed party in a gay club where guests dress up as policemen.

This scene "so flagrantly reveals (long before *Gender Trouble*) not only the necessarily performative nature of identities (sexual, gendered, and otherwise) but also the intense homoeroticism that is sublimated in what passes for normative male homosociality" (Savran 216). In other words, although greatly denied and fended off in heterosexual culture, homoeroticism is omnipresent. Furthermore, the idea of 'precinct night' exposes S&M to be a possible inherent constituent of cultural hierarchies in the US. The same idea is again returned to in another scene in which an innocent suspect, Skip, is brutally abused by policemen during his interrogation, as Wood comments:

> Finally, the grotesque scene in which both Burns and the innocent suspect are beaten up at police headquarters by an immense black policeman dressed only in a cow-boy hat and jockstrap has only the vaguest narrative plausibility, and seems to be there primarily to underline the connection between the two worlds. (57)

In this manner, police forces are thus just an extension of the sadomasochistic power rituals going on in everyday life. Besides, the police brutality witnessed throughout the film underlines the idea explored earlier that violence is omnipresent in the American framework. Not only is it found in every stratum of society, it is even institutionalized, thus permeating and corrupting American law enforcement.

In conclusion, although *Cruising* and *Dressed to Kill* have, to some extent, rightly been criticized for being misogynistic, homo-, and transphobic, one needs to look beyond the superficial events in both films and detect the feminist nuances and the subtle critique of a patriarchal system suffocating women and queers in the films. The films explicitly use queer killers to show how compulsory heterosexuality and patriarchal authority employ restrictions on those perceived as 'Others,' which eventually leads to self-hatred and violence against fellow human beings.

N.B. Parts of this essay were used in different chapters of "From Monsters to *Monsters*: Perverted Predators and Diseased Deviants—Queer Representations in American Slasher Films of the 1980s" (MA thesis, Universidade de Lisboa, Faculdade de Letras, 2016).

Works Cited

Davidson, Guy. "'Contagious Relations': Simulation, Paranoia, and the Postmodern Condition in William Friedkin's *Cruising* and Felice Picano's *The Lure*." *GLQ: A Journal of Lesbian and Gay Studies* 11.1 (2005): 23–64.

Greven, David. *Psycho-Sexual: Male Desire in Hitchcock, De Palma, Scorsese, and Friedkin*. Austin: University of Texas Press, 2013.

Guthmann, Edward. "The *Cruising* Controversy: William Friedkin vs. the Gay Community." *Cinéaste* 10.3 (1980): 2-8.

Hayle, Nancy K., & Katherine D. Rindskopf. "Movies: Cruising the Shadows." *Psychological Perspectives: A Quarterly Journal of Jungian Thought* 11.2 (1980): 227-31.

Kael, Pauline. *Taking It All in*. New York: Holt, Rinehart, and Winston, 1984.

Krohn, Bill. "Friedkin Out." *Rouge* 3 (2004). http://www.rouge.com.au/3/friedkin.html

Mulvey, Laura. *Visual and Other Pleasures*. Bloomington: Indiana University Press, 1989.

Savran, David. *Taking It like a Man: White Masculinity, Masochism, and Contemporary American Culture*. Princeton, NJ: Princeton University Press, 1998.

Skodbo, Thomas. "Nan Goldin: The Other Side: Photography and Gender Identity." MA thesis, University of Oslo, 2007. http://urn.nb.no/URN:NBN:no-16747

Snyder, Stephen. "Cruising: The Semiotics of S & M." *Canadian Journal of Political and Social Theory* 8.1-2 (1989): 102-114.

Walker, Gerald. *Cruising*. New York: Stein and Day, 1970.

Williams, Linda. "When the Woman Looks." *Film Theory and Criticism: Introductory Readings*. Eds. Gerald Mast, Marshall Cohen, and Leo Braudy. New York: Oxford University Press, 1992. 561-77.

Wilson, Alexander. "Friedkin's *Cruising*, Ghetto Politics, and Gay Sexuality." *Social Text* 4 (Autumn 1981): 98-109.

Wood, Robin. *Hollywood from Vietnam to Reagan*. New York: Columbia University Press, 2003.

Filmography

The Boys in the Band. Dir. William Friedkin. Perf. Kenneth Nelson, Frederick Combs, and Cliff Gorman. Cinema Center Films, 1970. DVD.

Cruising. Dir. William Friedkin. Perf. Al Pacino, Paul Sorvino, and Karen Allen. United Artists, 1980. DVD.

Dressed to Kill. Dir. Brian De Palma. Perf. Michael Caine, Angie Dickinson, Nancy Allen. Filmways Pictures, 1980. DVD.

Psycho. Dir. Alfred Hitchcock. Perf. Anthony Perkins, Janet Leigh, and Vera Miles. Shamley Productions, 1960. DVD.

"So You Thought We Would Go Away?" Confronting Shaming in Lillian Helman's *The Children's Hour*[1]

Anna Fahraeus

MARTHA (slowly): So you thought we would go away?
MRS. TILFORD: I think that would be best.
MARTHA: There must be something that we can do to you, and, whatever it is, we'll find it.
MRS. TILFORD: That will be very unwise.
KAREN: You are right to be afraid.
MRS. TILFORD: I am not afraid, Karen.
(Act 2, *The Children's Hour*)[2]

Introduction

In 2014, the Rideau Vert's theatre director René Richard Cyr was asked if it wasn't a poor idea to stage a play about the culpability of a woman who is ashamed of being lesbian at a time when we have just started to see positive images of lesbians (Boulanger).[3] He responded that that was not how he looked at it. Instead, he sees Lillian Hellman's *The Children's Hour* as being about a woman who comes to realize something about herself because of a lie,[4] and that the experience is still applicable today: *"Il y a encore des gais aujourd'hui qui, du jour au lendemain – à 35, 40 ans –, se déclarent homosexuels. Même dans le milieu du théâtre!"* The addition of "Even in the theatre!" can be seen as an

[1] I want to thank Bruce Drushel for the opportunity to present some of the ideas in this article at a Gay, Lesbian & Queer Studies Area panel at the Popular Culture Conference in Seattle in March of 2016. The encouragement and support that I received there, in particular from Bruce and Thomas Piontek, was invaluable. Danielle Cudmore was also kind enough to read this chapter in draft form and to make valuable comments. Any remaining errors or imperfections are mine.

[2] The edition used in this chapter was first published in 1934.

[3] The Théâtre du Rideau Vert is located in Montreal. The French phrase is hauntingly evocative in a disturbing way: "la culpabilité d'une lesbienne honteuse."

[4] The original text reads: "Je ne le vois pas sous cet angle, répond Cyr. Pour moi, c'est un aveu que Marthe se fait à elle-même. Une vérité qu'elle apprend sur elle-même à cause d'un mensonge."

afterthought but there is a sad wealth of studies that document the frequency with which coming out to the self and to others is a struggle in a heteronormative culture that is still clingingly oppressive despite all the strides made for greater visibility and equality for queer minorities.[5] No matter how much we might wish it wasn't, shame is still a part of many people's experience in first realizing they are lesbian, gay, gender queer, trans—different from what society insists is the norm. What caught my attention in Hellman's play was the ways in which the shaming fails. Martha and Karen do not cower or hide. They lose the court case, but that loss in 1934 makes the play historically realistic, which is sad but not necessarily a bad thing in terms of representation.

Janet Chusmir calls the opening night of *The Children's Hour* at Maxine Elliott's Theatre in New York City on November 20, 1934, the birth of Lillian Hellman as a playwright. Described as a "smash" hit in a brief retrospective on Hellman in the *New York Times* in 1941 (Bryer 12), the play was a critical as well as popular success and rumoured to be a possibility for the Pulitzer (24). Maxine Elliott's Theatre had a seating capacity of 935 and the play had a documented run of 691 performances.[6] Even at two-thirds capacity over 400,000 people would have seen the play, talked about the play, and had opinions about it. The play would be banned in Boston and Chicago but the drama of two teachers accused of being lesbian would pop up again and again in Paris for forty years.

[5] See e.g. Mallon 2001, Crisp and McCave 2007. Mallon provides a five stage model for the coming out process when it is accompanied by ambivalence. Crisp and McCave belong to the numerous studies that document depression and suicidal ideation among LGBT youth. See also the 2008 Stonewall report, which sadly reiterates that lesbians and bisexuals are more likely than straight women to develop problems with depression, anxiety and thoughts of suicide (Hunt and Fish). For an insightful, provocative discussion of shame, see Moon (2009). She looks at Jonathan Tolin's play *The Last Sunday in June*, which dramatizes shame as an alienating force for gay men both within the gay community and in society. Moon's point is that the experience of shame in a heteronormative society has the potential to create alliances within the community and that that should be our focus rather than using shame against each other within the LGBTQIA community. Moon talks about a "policing of boundaries" (360), but I think that it is more accurate to say that intragroup shaming exacerbates alienation between the subgroups in undesirable ways. Boundaries, in themselves, are not a bad thing.

[6] Gilroy reports this number in his article "The Bigger the Lie," first published in *The New York Times* 14 December 1952 (Bryer 24). Hellman herself stated that "it did very large business for six to eight months, then fell off" but that it made a profit for over two years (76).

Harry Gilroy reports that it was "impossible to get any of Broadway's leading ladies to take roles in the original production" of *The Children's Hour* because they feared police would shut the play down (Bryer 24). Two earlier tragedies had had significant gender queer roles and themes related to same-sex desire in New York. Sholem Asch's *God of Vengeance*,[7] a play about the downfall of a man who wants to be respectable but owns a brothel. Depending on your perspective, his daughter is seduced by the immoral lesbian prostitute or falls in love with a glamorous older woman.[8] Asch's play ran successfully from December 1922 for eleven weeks at the Provincetown Playhouse in Greenwich Village but when it was moved to the Apollo on Broadway, the NYPD sent officers to arrest the theatre owner and the cast. They were judged guilty of obscenity (Sova 102). Édouard Bourdet's *The Captive*, in which a young woman falls in love with the wife of a friend of the family (or is seduced by the immoral older sophisticated lesbian, again depending on your perspective) drew huge crowds in the 1926-27 season (Sova 38).[9] Basil Rathbone comments that it was "standing room only" for seventeen weeks but that the play was shut down for immorality after 160 performances and everyone in the cast was arrested (101). Clearly, popular appeal and the guardians of heteronormative morality were at odds with regard to the suitability of representing lesbians on stage.

Hellman's script shows the influence of both the Asch and Bourdet productions and their legal repercussions. The Shubert Organization, half-owners of the Maxine Elliott Theatre, had already been involved in at least one obscenity case and had a theatre shut down in 1928.[10]

[7] Originally written in Yiddish but translated by Isaac Goldberg and published in English by Stratford Co. in Boston in 1918. First performed at the Kammerspiele Theater in Berlin in 1907.

[8] Several studies have been written that document the negative representation of lesbians. For a very solid discussion of fictional images (positive as well as negative) in the 1930s see chapter 4 in Faderman (1992). Inness (1997) gives a good introduction to the negative image of the lesbian as a teacher in the early 20th-century American imagination (see ch. 2). Donoghue (2010) puts the image of the lesbian as a social monster in a broader literary historical context (see ch. 2).

[9] *The Captive* was first performed at the Librairie théâtrale in Paris in 1926. Translated into English by Arthur Hornblow, Jr. and published by Brentano's in New York also in 1926. For a discussion of reviews of the plays, see Sova (38-39).

[10] The play was *Maya* by Simon Gantillon. See: Censorship Files on the play, *Maya*, Billy Rose Theatre Division (The New York Public Library. T-Mss 2001-022).

Against the backdrop of repeated censorship, and the threat of the padlock law, which meant that a theatre could be shut down and its cast arrested for indecency, it is not surprising that Hellman's playscript is cautious and does not use overt references to same sex desire such as the word 'lesbian' or any other references common at the time such as 'sapphist' or 'invert' but nor does it use the word 'degenerate,' the term used in Bourdet's play, or 'pervert.' There is also no passionate kissing on stage or discussion of lovely breasts woman to woman as directed in Asch's play.[11] Almost everything related to lesbian desire is said indirectly and by insinuation. The extent of the circumspect language is common for stories about two women who desired each other at the time but should be seen as a product of the resurgence in institutional censorship of public performance rather than as a sign of a general historical reticence.

Hellman's play was topical for its focus on society's reaction to an accusation of lesbian desire and its interest in the expectation of shame. Robert Garland, reviewer for the *New York World Herald-Telegram*, is explicit in referring to lesbian desire as "the affection that passes normal understanding" (Hodges 15). Another contemporary reviewer for the *New York Herald Tribune*, Percy Hammond, describes *The Children's Hour* as an "agitating tale" stating that Hellman shows "a gallant indifference to what has been termed the proprieties" (Hodges 16). In other words, its characters talk about and the play deals with that which is considered outside acceptable social and moral behaviour. Cultural proprieties are socially constructed and temporally contingent. Jennifer Jacquet defines them with stark simplicity as "majority behaviour" (82). Despite being an informal collective understanding, the proprieties are a powerful social force and the general goal of shaming is to coerce conformity to these social norms. To effectively shame another is to achieve power in the localized relationship and to confirm one's belonging to the larger group. To be effectively shamed is to lose power. It is, however, also possible to refuse to be shamed. Like George Chauncey I am interested in shaming as a social practice where it is possible to refuse the role one is assigned. In this chapter, I look at shame not as a psychological phenomenon but as a social one and at Hellman's play as a series of linked social situations where social shaming comes into play in different

[11] The stage direction "Manke kisses her passionately" can be found at the end of Act I (35) and the discussion of breasts occurs in a rather long love scene between Manke and Rifkele in Act II (60-64).

ways but also does not operate as expected from a heteronormative point of view. What can thinking through these imagined scenarios teach us about the role of shaming in anti-gay practices in the past and in the present?

Defining Social Shame

There are a number of theoretical approaches to shame, but social shame is most frequently studied in sociology, social psychology and anthropology.[12] The 2009 collection, *Gay Shame*, encompasses a wide range of studies and perspectives on shame in the LGBTQIA community. Most of the contributions are focused on sources of self-hate between subgroups and intergroup shaming as legitimate sources of shame that need to be addressed. The result of a landmark conference, this organized and public self-critique is welcome and necessary. It reflects the growing concerns about negative discursive practices, prejudices and even (ironically) norms *within* the community. However, Jennifer Moon raises two equally legitimate concerns that shaming each other for shaming is still shaming and thus alienating, and that we are still facing intolerance and oppression from living in a heteronormative society, and that turning on each other is non-productive. She suggests that the shared experience of being shamed for non-normative gender identities, gender expression or sexual practices has the potential to be unifying if we let it, and that there are many sub-groups nationally in the US and LGBT communities globally that need our support.

Shaming is meant to lead to social shame, which is not the same as to experience the affect shame. Silvan Tomkins defines shame as "the affect of indignity, of defeat , of transgression, and of alienation" (134). Social shame is about perceived transgressions and the unequal relationship produced by what is socially considered shameful. It is the product of interaction. As an instrument of control based on social norms, it is a relational state over which the target has limited control. The repercussions of social shame are that one's transgression of a norm is given focus, that one is viewed as abject and that a distance is imposed between the self and society. In a state of social shame, the negative emotional component of shame is not necessarily felt or even necessary

[12] For a good overview of studies on shame see Gilbert (1998) and for a cultural study of sexual dissent in relation to shamelessness, see Stein (2006).

from a social point of view. It is enough that the target of shame accepts either the norm or the undesirability of being marginalized by the social shame that adheres to transgressing the norm. Or the undesirability of being punished, which is why a case like Gloria Morgan Vanderbilt's would have been so devastating to lesbians in the 1930s.

The justification for social shame is that social norms are necessary to maintain order. Jacquet's work on shame supports its usefulness in society. She presupposes that there are "bad apples" and suggests that, "Exposure is the essence of shaming" (9), but while exposure or the threat of exposure can be a means to arouse actual shame, the threat of exposure is not what makes social shaming possible. Exposure in the context of social shame is about revealing *perceived* bad behaviour and presupposes that there is a social transgression involved, i.e., that the behaviour is considered shameful. This means that the power to define what is and is not a transgression is at the core of shaming rather than exposure, because exposure does not matter if there is no social agreement regarding what is shameful. As a field of potential social struggle, what is shameful has to be produced and reproduced through social interaction. Jacquet recognizes that "shame is inextricably linked to norms" (9), but fails to acknowledge that norms can privilege certain social groups and disadvantage others.

In *Straight Expectations*, Julie Bindel asserts that the fuel behind the anti-gay agenda in relation to lesbians and bisexual women appears to be "the need to keep women in their place—in other words within heterosexual relationships—to ensure that patriarchy survives and is effective" (34). This includes a vision of male dominance and female dependence on traditional heterosexual structures. Historically social shame in relation to sexuality in the West is based on the Judaeo-Christian system of values that presumes heterosexuality and places a premium on heterosexual marriage, particularly for women. Female identity is meant to find its closure in wifehood and female sexuality to find its purpose and fulfilment in motherhood. This narrow male-centred but also opposing sex-dependent system of values has been and is determinative in what constitutes shameful in relation to both men and women but for women it has far-reaching consequences for identity. For women, what is shameful is defined in relation to men and their presumed desires and needs: being deemed unattractive by the opposite sex, being single for too long, and being barren. Independent female sexuality is itself suspect. Adrienne Rich wanted to draw attention to the bias in heterosexuality against same-sex desire but also against women as independent subjects. She called this pervasive but normalized and therefore invisible system, "the institution of heterosexuality" and emphasized how its norms rise above the level of expectation to the level of being "compulsory." Rich argued that the norms are by turns "imposed, managed, organized, propagandized, and maintained by force" (135).

Scheff's sociological work on shame shows how conformity is compelled through a deference-emotion system leveraged by the norms themselves. He presents social norms as operating on two levels, in one-to-one encounters but also in self-monitoring (395). Implicit in his work is Michel Foucault's elaboration of the "panoptic schema" with its purpose to "raise the level of public morality" (Foucault 208). This model emphasizes that the social arrangement of a community and the physical proximity of others, regardless of who they are, make us vulnerable to surveillance and thus more likely to monitor ourselves. Disconcertingly, as Foucault observed, "Any individual, taken almost at random, can operate the machine: in the absence of the director, his family, his friends, his visitors, even his servants" (202). The social panopticon has no single director. Power is instead disbursed throughout the community but individual motivation is also irrelevant to the ability to work the apparatus once it has a protocol. A person can, as Foucault observed, be motivated by "the curiosity of the indiscreet, the malice of the child, the thirst for knowledge of a philosopher [or medical professional] who wishes to visit this museum of human nature, or the perversity of those who take pleasure in spying and punishing" (202). Social judgement can lead to socially overt or covert shaming.

The title for this article "So you thought we would go away?" implicitly refers to heteronormative expectations and is taken from the confrontation between Martha, Karen and Mrs. Tilford (Hellman 69). She hopes they will respect the rules of social politeness and not make her talk about what is socially taboo despite her willingness to talk to third parties about her suspicions about their sex life. They are angry that she has spread the rumour that they are having a lesbian affair and have confronted her in her home. She wants them to leave. She does not want to see them or talk about the accusation she has made. To her mind, they are lacking in shame: "it was wrong of you to brazen it out here tonight; it would be criminally foolish of you to brazen it out in public" (214). To brazen is to act shamelessly. It is to be impudent or to defy boldly. Shamelessness is a key motif in fiction about being lesbian and in lesbian fiction. In 1930s fiction, it can be as simple as wearing pants, drinking in the daytime and smoking cigarettes like Lily in Dorothy Parker's "Glory in the Daytime" or leaving a marriage to pursue a relationship with a woman like Robin in Djuna Barnes' queer novel *Nightwood.*

Part of the definition of 'shameless' includes the tension between 'impudent' and 'bold.' The word 'impudent' is more negatively loaded than 'bold' and is an important characteristic in the narratives about lesbians. Lesbian subjects and lesbian desire are represented as impudent in the sense of intruding into spaces where normative heterosexuality is expected, desired, sought after, in story after story.[13] To voice resistance to heteronormativity and claim a space for different choices is to be presumptuous, rude, uncivil and inappropriate from a hetero-normative perspective. In the 1930s, this produced stories like Idabel Williams' *Hell Cat.*[14] From a heterosexual point of view, the main character Scoot embodies the bisexual threat and lesbian desire as socially destructive. She is portrayed as sociopathic and mentally unstable. She is the woman who preys on innocent heterosexuals to engage them in illicit sexual acts. She is punished by incarceration. She is also strong, independent and her core is indomitable. Even at the end, she would "claw you to pieces if she could get at you" (160), but from a 1930s perspective, the representation is very negative and heteronormative. Hellman defamiliarizes this impudence motif—lesbianism as socially bold and transgressive—by making Karen and Martha two hardworking, respectable women who are accused of being lesbians and refuse to take it silently. They are bold enough to object to being shamed.

Refusing to Agree to Shame

In Hellman's play, it begins with the malice of an eavesdropping child but moves to the perversity of a woman who sees herself as a moral guardian for society. With the First Amendment Defense Act making

[13] See note 8.
[14] From a counter-discourse perspective on shamelessness and impudence, Williams' work bears a marked resemblance to the lesbian pulp fiction of the 1950s and 1960s.

its way through Congress as this article is being written, Hellman's portrait of a moral guardian against same-sex desire seems sadly topical even eighty-two years after the play's première. It is disturbing how applicable the approach Hellman has still is. In Act 2, Karen and Martha arrive at Mrs. Tilford's home (Mary's grandmother) in order to confront her about spreading the rumour that they are involved in a sexual affair. Mrs. Tilford tries to prevent them from coming into her home, stating, "I won't have her here" to her nephew Joe Cardin, the doctor that is engaged to Karen. She ignores the presence of Martha focusing solely on Karen. Cardin states that if she cannot come in, then he is not welcome either. Because she refuses to see them, the teachers are left with two choices: either break the rules of social decorum and barge in, or allow her accusation to stand uncontested. They choose to defend themselves and make her talk about it with them. She confirms that she made the accusation and believes it, and then states, "And that's why I don't think you should have come here." The logic behind her reasoning appears to be that they should feel too ashamed to confront her: committing homosexual acts is wrong; she believes they have committed them; and they should be ashamed. Additionally, she seems to feel that her belief gives her the right to publicly accuse them but it does not give them the right to talk to her about it. Her reasoning is based in a sense of moral rectitude that perverts fairness and ultimately justice.

There are four additional statements made by the actress playing Mrs. Tilford in this confrontation that echo sentiments and discursive practices that are based in this sense of a moral rectitude that finds within itself its own justification:

1. "What they are may possibly be their own business. It becomes a great deal more than that when children are involved."
2. "There won't be any punishment for either of you. But there mustn't be any punishment for me, either—and that's what this meeting is."
3. "This—this thing is your own. Go away with it. I don't understand it and I don't want any part of it."
4. "I shall not call you names, and I will not allow you to call me names. It comes to this: I can't trust myself to talk about it with you now or ever." (Hellman 68-69)

Mrs. Tilford expresses the position that homosexuality is socially irresponsible and that it is dangerous to expose children to it, but the statement that it "may possibly be their own business" suggests the opposing position that sexuality is a private matter rather than an issue that should be of public concern. The conflict between these two positions is still ongoing. Mrs. Tilford assumes that her belief gives her the right, even the obligation, to intercede on behalf of what she believes is best for the children. The underlying conservative assumption is that a person's sexuality is relevant to legal discourse. Anti-gay positions are now coached within an explicit religious liberty framework where the right to instituting sanctions privileging heterosexuality based on belief is leveraged in public discourse on civil rights. States like Utah, for instance, continue to allow discrimination against gays and lesbians in certain types of employment, including education.[15] In Hellman's play, the preoccupation with gay and lesbian sexual activity is shown to be an exaggerated concern, a form of public hysteria. Hellman communicates this through Martha and Karen's incomprehension when they recount how the parents pulled their daughters out of the school after Mrs. Tilford's spreading her belief about their sexual activities. The descriptors used are e.g. "crazy," "insane asylum" and "madhouse" which all suggest a wild panic (Hellman 66-67). Mental instability is a traditional anti-gay motif but in this 1930s play, it is mobilized to ridicule anti-gay action. The heterosexual parents are the mad ones. The title of the play, *The Children's Hour*, suggests the same idea, that the world has gone topsy-turvy in terms of maturity and judgement.

The second statement brings out a debate that is very relevant today and where sadly gays and lesbians can be found on both sides of the divide. The core issue is whether different opinions about the nature of homosexuality should be allowed to openly exist. Mrs. Tilford will not seek punishment for the two women for being lesbians (by incarcerating them in prison or an insane asylum) but they should not in turn impose their presence on her. Today the concession seems to be that while gays and lesbians have been granted legal rights and cannot be made invisible in society, they should not be allowed to encroach on the lives of conservative straight people. Mrs. Tilford states baldly that by coming to her house Martha and Karen are forcing her to spend

[15] The Anti-Discrimination and Religious Freedom Act that was passed in 2015 in Utah provides some measure of protection for LGBTs but there are exemptions for religious institutions, societies and "any corporation or association constituting an affiliate, a wholly owned subsidiary, or an agency of any religious organization." For a state like Utah, that includes among others a number of housing owners, educational institutions and even stores.

time with them, to talk to them and that this is a form of punishment for her. The third statement rephrases the same idea: that they should go away and not impose their presence on her or force her to deal with the idea that people with alternate sexualities exist in her own social sphere. What this play highlights, however, is that personal is political. Mrs. Tilford not only wants to control her own space, her home, but also what she hears, and to retain the right to refuse to inhabit the same public space as lesbians, i.e., the school. Not wanting to be exposed to actual lesbians or the idea that same-sex desire exists and is not wrong is a belief that has practical consequences. If these belief-based practices are granted public legitimacy, they undermine anti-discrimination legislation.[16]

The fourth statement is along the same vein. It is another apparent concession to social decorum or political correctness. Mrs. Tilford will agree to not call them names, but she will also not allow them to call her names. This is also reminiscent of the public debate today where the religious right and conservative bigots pay lip service to the idea that LGBT citizens do have rights but where they simultaneously feel that those rights should not mean that religious citizens should have to accept that homosexuality is okay. Anti-gay attitudes should be allowed to exist without the adherents being called homophobes. It is oxymoronic but nevertheless it is being encoded and proposed for US legislation in 2016. In Hellman's play from 1934, Mrs. Tilford wants to be able to act on her anti-gay beliefs by shutting lesbians out, but not be punished for it. Drawing this physical and verbal boundary around herself and heteronormativity expresses a desire for social segregation.

Cardin, Karen and Martha reject the abjection that Mrs. Tilford intends for the women to feel and for Cardin to feel as justified. Despite the fact that her position is supported by the major social institutions (which ironically includes even the theatre milieu in which the play was first performed) and the panoptic schema that is meant to support the

[16] See Bindel for an insightful discussion of the pitfalls of supporting the right to espouse anti-gay belief systems. She uses the term "Christian bigots" deliberately, and provocatively in today's climate when religious freedom advocates and institutions are claiming their right to not be defamed (or called out depending on your perspective) on their anti-gay beliefs. Implied in Bindel's discussion is the strong disavowal of the right of religious institutions to create 'safe' spaces for discrimination and gay bashing. One example is the assertion by the Church of Jesus Christ of Latter-Day Saints to retain the right to urge its members to fight same-sex marriage legislation in Mexico now that the fight is lost in the US (Stack 2016).

state apparatus against same-sex desire, Hellman creates a scene that illustrates a social environment where a rebuttal of the expectation of social shame is possible. The discursive motifs that are levied against Mrs. Tilford are worth looking at:

a. CARDIN: "Are you sick?"

b. CARDIN: "… you are irresponsible."

c. KAREN: "… I don't want to have anything to do with your mess, do you hear me?…"

d. CARDIN: "… they've worked eight long years to save enough money to buy that farm, to start that school. They did without everything that young people ought to have. You wouldn't know about that. That school meant things to them: self-respect, and bread and butter, and honest work. Do you know what it is to try so hard for anything? Well, now it's gone. [*Suddenly hits the side of the table with his hand.*] What the hell did you do it for?"

e. CARDIN: "Righteousness is a great thing."

f. MARTHA: "Tomorrow, Mrs. Tilford, you will have a libel suit on your hands."

Both the first and second rebuttal of social shame turns two of the common ideas about gay people against Mrs. Tilford. Her sanity is questioned and she is accused of being irresponsible in her treatment of Martha and Karen. Similarly in (c), it is Mrs. Tilford as the conservative straight person that is made responsible for the social havoc created by her attempts to leverage norms about sexuality against the teachers. In (d), Cardin makes the argument that is still a standing discursive practice in the fight for equal rights for diverse sexualities: the alternate sexual identities are not incompatible with being socially responsible and with the traditional values of self-respect, ambition, and honest work. In (e), he makes the observation that Mrs. Tilford is being self-righteous, which will become and continues to be a common failing and thus narrative motif in the characterization of anti-gay stereotypes and broader social types in fiction and non-fiction. In (f), Martha threatens legal action. She will follow through and fail in the play, but the idea of lesbians filing suits against heterosexuals is prescient of future legal cases where lesbians will be on the offense side of the legal bench.

A point that can be made about the resistance towards accepting the social shame that Mrs. Tilford deems appropriate for Martha and Karen to feel is that several of the points are made by the doctor, Joe

Cardin. From a narrative point of view this is significant because as a man and a doctor, he represents a voice of traditional authority so to have him speak in defence of the women and against the idea that they should feel shame is to give weight to the ideas. The method of doing this is not radical and it is not in keeping with a feminist politics. The two women who are independent teachers should speak for themselves. This may be, but from the perspective of wanting the arguments to appear significant and noteworthy, it could also be that Hellman is simply following the gender-normative rules of storytelling and avoiding the association of overly opinionated independent women with the negative understanding of lesbianism. In choosing a man to attack homophobia, she creates the mirror image of giving the mendacious child, Mary, and her gullible grandmother the roles that represent society's normative view. Neither choice is flattering to women but from a gender-normative perspective the choice of which character plays each role is a clear sign for what evaluations the author expects the reader/audience to reach about who is on the side of justice.

The Triangle of Shaming

Shaming is usually discussed in terms of the interactional dynamics between the shamer and the shamed (e.g., Fossum and Mason 1986). However, a third party is always involved—the community which is leveraged against the target of shaming. I want to propose a triangle model with three axes, representing the relationship between the three parties: the shamer and the target (A-B), the target and the social community with which the target is threatened (B-C), and the shamer and the community (A-C). Because the intent of the protocols that make shaming possible is to uphold the status quo, all that is required for social shaming to be effective is that one of the axes of shame is satisfied. This complicates things because while the agreement on what is shameful is needed for social shaming to be successful, it is only needed between two parties and it does not matter which two. This means, for example, that it is possible to be socially shamed effectively without agreeing that what one has done is shameful, if the social community agrees with the shamer.

The existence of the three axes means that there is always room for a negotiation of whether shame is warranted. The negotiation is a complex activity with a number of variables but for now I want to focus on the four possibilities for social shame that exist in the triangle:

1. B and C agree on what is considered shameful, A dissents
2. A and B agree on what is considered shameful, C dissents
3. A and C agree on what is considered shameful, B dissents
4. A, B and C agree on what is considered shameful

The first possibility highlights that social shame does not actually require that the target feel any actual shame or agree with the definition of what is shameful. This is what Chauncey sets out to show in the study, "The Trouble with Shame." Writing about the 1950s, he challenges the assumption that gay men were ashamed of being gay. He works from the premise that while "self-righteous heterosexuals wanted to believe that the homosexuals they loathed suffered from self-loathing and shame," this was not necessarily true (277). This is the core struggle and failure of social shame if it is defined by affect in *The Children's Hour*. Karen and Martha refuse to agree that they have done anything shameful. This is the basis for their confrontation of Mrs. Tilford and the basis for their shared confusion in the opening of Act 3. If the person(s) doing the shaming and the community to whom the secret is exposed agree that what has been done qualifies as a transgression and deserves shame, the shaming can still be effective. It can still result in social disgrace and alienation. This is the outcome in *The Children's Hour*. Social shame is enforced from the outside without the assent of the targets.

Though Jacquet suggests that deploying shaming rituals in a social context is not effective when institutional punishment is not anticipated (Jacquet 100), the two are linked in *The Children's Hour*. Martha and Karen bring a libel suit against Mrs. Tilford to punish her for defaming them. The trial is not staged. In the play, the function of the trial is to confirm the verdict of the social judgement passed by Mrs. Tilford. This is underscored by the lack of roles provided for official representatives of the legal system. Shaming in relation to same-sex desire in the 1930s was supported by religion, law and medicine. Interestingly, Hellman eschews all of these in her play. The focus is on social judgement and the effects of that judgement.

The second possibility suggests that the person doing the shaming does not actually have to believe that what A has done is shameful. If the target (A) believes it and the audience to whom the secret is exposed (C) believes it, shaming can still be effectively deployed. This is the main plot of the play in relation to social shaming. When Mary tells her grandmother, Mrs. Tilford, that Martha and Karen have had late-night amorous trysts, she knows that what she is saying is not true, but it does not matter because she knows that if it were true it would be considered shameful—in other words, society or, in this case, the broader community of the fictional town of Lancet, would condemn them for it. Mary simply wants to gain an advantage over her teachers and not have to go back to school. The scenario shows one of the peculiarities of social shame; the instigator does not have to believe or care about the effects of the shaming on the target: shaming can be an indirect tool to gain some social advantage. In Mary's case, she simply does not want to have to go to school.

The third possibility suggests that it does not actually matter if the community (C) thinks that what (A) has done is shameful; it only matters that (A) accepts the proposition given by (B) that it is shameful, i.e., that the imagined community in front of whom the target is exposed will find it shameful. This can apply to Hellman's play if the community function is shifted to Dr. Joe Cardin as either a private individual who does not believe that they have been lovers or as representative for a cohort of his profession which recognized that homosexuality was not morally reprehensible. In the final act, Karen treats Joe as if she is convinced that Joe either believes that she and Martha have been lovers or is ashamed of them because they have been publicly shamed. In this case, the accuser is the court system and Joe is the social group in front of whom Karen and Martha have been shamed. Karen expresses this outright, "I was watching your face in court. It was ashamed—and sad at being ashamed" (97-98). She recognizes his ambivalence and believes that he is just trying to "spare" her feelings (99). The dialogue is such that the reader cannot be sure and an actor would have to interpret how to play Joe. Is he actually reluctant to leave or is he relieved? For the social shaming of Karen to be effectual, it does not matter. Her belief in her irredeemable status as abject and their relationship as unworkable as a result is the one thing that does not change: "we won't be all right. Not ever, ever, ever."

The fourth possibility is the easiest to understand why it would be effective. If the target of shaming believes what they have done is shameful, and the person(s) doing the shaming believe it, and they know that the audience believes it, there is a *de facto* agreement that the behaviour is shameful and shame will be the result if/when it is exposed. By Act 3 of *The Children's Hour*, after the trial that the audience does not get to see, Martha seems to have internalized the negative evaluation of her community, that is the shame she is expected to feel, and refers to herself and Karen as "bad people" (103), and they both show signs of abjection; apathy, depression and a reluctance to socialize. Martha's sense of shame seems to be confirmed later when she confesses that she is "guilty" because she has always loved Karen and that she feels "sad and dirty" while in her mind Karen feels "sad and clean" (105).

However, context is vital to understanding how shame is operating in this scene. Martha has not completely internalized the shame despite these seemingly apologetic words. Paul Gilbert suggests that in relation to shame, there exists a self-other evaluative domain with three cognitive aspects: how we think we appear to others, how we think they see us, and how we think about what (we think) they think (17). He suggests the term "external shame" for when we perceive we have been judged and found wanting (17). In Hellman's play, the negative judgement of lesbian behaviour has been explicitly expressed not imagined. It is possible to think of the knowledge of this judgement by the other as resulting in an imposed sense of shame or external shame to use Gilbert's term. I would suggest calling it a taint of shame to further emphasize that while external it does enter the self, but it is not self-generated. It has been transmitted from the outside. While internalized implies that something has become part of the self, to be the object of a transmitted substance is to recognize that substance as foreign to the self. If we look at Martha's phrases one at a time, this is how they appear:

> There'll never be any place for us to go. We're bad people. We'll sit. We'll be sitting the rest of our lives wondering what's happened to us. (103)

This is not the full speech at the opening of the scene when Karen has asked if there isn't somewhere they can go, but it is sufficient. The statement "We're bad people" is framed, on the one hand, by the recognition that socially their names have become too publicly associated with the scandal of the trial and there is nowhere they can go where what has happened will not follow them. They have lost the court case for libel and the charge of indecent and immoral behaviour has been made to stick. They have become known as two lesbian women in a society that does not accept lesbian women; in a society that jails them or puts them in mental institutions. The evaluation that Martha is given in the dialogue seems fairly on point and probable as an immediate reaction under the circumstances. There initially does not appear to be anywhere for two teachers to go where the trial will not follow them, and it is definitely unlikely that there is anywhere for them to find work teaching again. In their middle-class world where work is necessary and there is no family money to fall back on, they have a choice between living apart in isolation in poverty or living daily among people who openly reject them. With this frame, it seems possible that the statement "We're bad people" is shorthand for, "We're marked as bad people," which is not the same thing. To be marked is to be socially identified in a specific way and expected to feel shame but it does not necessarily mean an acceptance of the designation. Her use of the pronoun "We" can be read as a recognition that the designation has been made and is unavoidable. However, it does not seem to indicate self-identification as "bad" since Martha says that she and Karen will wonder what happened to them, indicating an event from the outside.

A legitimate question is why would Hellman represent them as avoiding going out if they are not to be read as ashamed of accusations of lesbianism? There are two possible perspectives on that. One is that they are ashamed only of having lost the trial, not because they know they are lesbians. Mrs Tilford's unsubstantiated point of view has been upheld in court. They have lost to a system where they expected to be justified because the accusations were based on a lie. They will no longer be allowed to teach. That is humiliating. Tomkins remarks that it matters how we are evaluated in our work. He has astutely observed, "If I wish the initiation or continuation of my work to be demanded by others, their indifference can evoke shame" (Sedgwick and Frank 150). The outcome of the trial is more than indifference, it is rejection. I would add that it matters by whom and how competent we judge the accusers to be. Being condemned by an incompetent and then having their critique publicly upheld is humiliating. Hellman has created a scenario where two resourceful and successful professional women lose a case to an older gossipy woman and a lying child. They have failed to rescue their reputations and lost their school and their financial security irrevocably to a case that they should have won on professional merit. That this is a source of shame to the point where going out and holding your head up high would be difficult seems plausible. The nature and outcome of the event is a source of shame as a sense of social isolation and vulnerability, but this outcome is not necessarily a sign of an actual sense of guilt.

A second perspective on why Martha and Karen would avoid

going out is thus that Hellman is writing a scenario that shows the toxic cycle produced by living in a society with institutionalized shaming apparatus for same-sex desire. The symptoms of abjection can also be signs of social disgrace, e.g., to be stripped of material goods and social support. There is a deliberate focus on the force of social shaming rather than shame as having the potential to humiliate the individual into compliance, denial, silence and self-erasure. After the trial, Martha suggests with biting self-mockery: "Let's pinch each other sometimes. We can tell whether we're still living." Karen is described as acting "listlessly" and "vaguely" (103). Both women are in a state of abjection. They show the signs: apathy, desolation, lifelessness, insufficiency, lethargy, sadness. By a dictionary definition, it is a state produced through the act of humiliating or being humiliated. Humiliation is the same as shame except for one important component: the feeling that it is undeserved. That what they are feeling is humiliation rather than shame is evident in Karen's attempt to resist the toxic cycle that she has been made a part of and the intensity of the shame imposed by the trial they have just lost: "But this isn't a new sin they tell us we've done" (103). This suggests that, despite the knowledge that same-sex desire is illegal and is considered immoral, Karen had some reason to anticipate a different outcome because the views on homosexuality had evolved somewhat. This is supported by her recognition that there are lesbians in society and that "Other people aren't destroyed by it."

Conclusion

Conformity and the right of stewardship of the norms governing conformity, i.e., what is considered shameful, were a middle-class expectation and an invisible heterosexual one in the 1930s. In this chapter I have argued that Martha and Karen reject the accusation of lesbian behaviour but also the shame associated with same-sex desire. In France, this will lead to the title of the play being changed to *Les Innocentes*, which has a pleasing ambiguity making it able to appeal to contemporary and modern audiences who choose to interpret it in favour of lesbian behaviour itself as innocent and unworthy of the shaming in the play. Of course, heterosexuals are free to interpret it as meaning that Karen and Martha are not lesbians and ignore the confession of same-sex desire and self-reflection behind it in the final act.

When I first started to think about shame in relation to *The Children's Hour*, I focused on Martha's confession in Act 3 and the dialogue where she expresses her sense that she feels "dirty." It bothered me because it saddened me and made me vicariously angry and a little exhausted. I would ensure that my students understood that the seemingly obvious idea that Martha commits suicide because she is ashamed of finding out that her feelings for Karen transgress the boundaries of the heterosexual must be interrogated over and over again. We would look at and talk about the culpability of the community in which the teachers lived, of Mary, Mrs. Tilford and the anonymous Lancet court system in Martha's suicide. Gradually, because Mary's motivation is not really to cause her teachers to be ashamed but to make her grandmother allow her not to have to go to school, I started to think about the relationship between shame and what happens in the play. By distinguishing social shame from the affect of shame, it became possible to see the different operations of a triangle of interacting parties involved.

One of the most valuable insights that Hellman's play offers is a way to think about the discourse about lesbian desire in the 1930s as encompassing visions of the failure of social shame, and social shame as an arena where norms about sexuality could be wielded to achieve social ends that are unrelated to sexuality. In looking at the different scenarios in this play to see where the women are expected to feel shame and do not, and where shame is expected to affect certain ends but does not, the resistance motifs that Hellman has put in the dialogue became more apparent. Each discursive practice outside the court room that seeks to leverage shame against same-sex desire in Hellman's play is countered in one or more ways:

1. the shame motif <> the indignation motif because shame is not warranted
2. the failure of civilized behaviour <> the right to defend oneself against attack
3. the social irresponsibility motif <> the social irresponsibility motif as counter-argument
4. the social disorder motif <> the social disorder counter-argument motif, that is social disorder as caused by anti-gay panic

This short list of competing motifs related to shaming in the representations of lesbians in the 1930s can be augmented but each of these also needs to be further explored. One that is not listed is the failure as woman motif, which is central to shaming in many of the stories in the time period and thus should be investigated and interrogated. For this chapter, I have wanted to begin this process of relating the negative motifs explicitly to shaming and the rejection of shaming. The re-evaluation of the reasons for Martha's abjection and Karen's apathy in the final act, for example, shows that shame can exist in a story about lesbian desire but not be about lesbian desire. There can be shame about being socially alienated without someone being ashamed of what they feel. There can be shame about who you are and what you feel in a personal relationship but it is caused by the other person's reactions, not because it fundamentally feels wrong. Shame can be present for the community that treats you unfairly. Shame is complicated and social shame makes it more complicated.

Works Cited

"Antidiscrimination and Religious Freedom: Amendments." S. B. 296. 2015 General session. State of Utah. Chief sponsors: Stephen H. Urquhart and J. Stuart Adams. House sponsor: Brad L. Dee. http://le.utah.gov/~2015/bills/sbillenr/SB0296.htm.

Bindel, Julie. *Straight Expectations: What Does It Mean to Be Gay Today?* London: Guardian Books, 2014.

Boulanger, Luc. "Les innocentes: sentiments inavouables." *La Presse* 12 May 2014. http://www.lapresse.ca/arts/spectacles-et-theatre/theatre/201405/12/01-4765943-les-innocentes-sentiments-inavouables.php.

Bryer, Jackson, R., Ed. *Conversations with Lillian Hellman.* Jackson, MI: University Press of Mississippi, 1986.

"Censorship Files on the Play, Maya, 1927-1928." Billy Rose Theatre Division, The New York Public Library Archives and Manuscripts. Archives.nypl.org/the/21536.

Chauncey, George. "The Trouble with Shame." *Gay Shame.* Eds. David M. Halperin and Valerie Traub. Chicago: Chicago University Press, 2010. 277-82.

Crisp, Catherine and Emily L. McCave. "Gay Affirmative Practice: A Model for Social Work Practice with Gay, Lesbian and Bisexual Youth." *Child and Adolescent Social Work Journal* 24.4 (2007): 403-321.

Donoghue, Emma. *Inseparable: Desire between Women in Literature.* Jersey City, NJ: Cleis Press, 2010.

Faderman, Lillian. *Odd Girls and Twilight Lovers: A History of Lesbian Life in Twentieth-Century America.* New York: Penguin, 1992.

Fossum, Merle A. and Marilyn J. Mason. *Facing Shame: Families in Recovery.* London: W.W. Norton & Co, 1986.

Foucault, Michel. *Discipline and Punish: The Birth of the Prison.* London and New York: Penguin Books, 1977.

Gilbert, Paul. "What is Shame? Some Core Issues and Controversies." *Shame, Interpersonal Behavior, Psychopathology, and Culture.* Eds. Paul Gilbert and Bernice Andrews. Oxford: Oxford University Press, 1998. 3-38.

Hellman, Lillian. *The Children's Hour* [1934]. New York: Alfred A. Knopf, 1936.

Hodges, Ben, Ed. *Forbidden Acts: Pioneering Gay & Lesbian Plays of the Twentieth Century.* Milwaukee: Applause, 2003.

Hunt, Ruth and Julie Fish. *Prescription for Change: Lesbian and Bisexual Women's Health Check 2008.* London: Stonewall, 2008.

Inness, Sherrie, A. *The Lesbian Menace: Ideology, Identity and Representation of Lesbian Life.* Amherst, MA: University of Massachusetts Press, 1997.

Jacquet, Jennifer. *Is Shame Necessary? New Uses for an Old Tool.* London: Allen Lane, 2015.

Mallon, Gerald, P. *Lesbian and Gay Youth Issues: A Practical Guide for Youth Workers.* Washington, D.C.: Child Welfare League of America Press, 2001.

Parker, Dorothy. "Glory in the Daytime." *The Portable Dorothy Parker.* New York: The Viking Press, 1973. 276-90.

Rathbone, Basil. *In and Out of Character* [1956]. Milwaukee: Limelight Editions, 2007.

Rich, Adrienne. "Compulsory Heterosexuality and Lesbian Existence." *Feminism and Sexuality.* Eds. Stevi Jackson and Sue Scott. New York: Columbia University Press, 1996. 130-42.

Scheff, Thomas, J. "Shame and Conformity: The Deference Emotion System." *American Sociological Review* 53.3 (1988): 395-406.

Sova, Dawn B. *Banned Plays: Censorship Histories of 125 Stage Dramas.* New York: Checkmark Books, 2004.

Stack, Peggy Fletcher. "Leaders Urge Mexico's Mormons to Fight against Push for Same-Sex Marriage." *Salt Lake Tribune.* 2 June 2016. archive.sltrib.com/article.php?id=3957702&itype=CMSID

Stein, Arlene. *Shameless: Sexual Dissidence in American Culture.* New York: New York University Press, 2006.

Tomkins, Silvan. "Shame—Humiliation and Contempt—Disgust." *Shame and its Sisters: A Silvan Tomkins Reader.* Eds. Eve Kosofsky Sedgwick and Adam Frank. Durham, NC: Duke UP, 1995. 133-78.

Williams, Idabel. *Hell Cat.* New York: Dell, 1934.

Coming Together: *Pride* and Queer Social Realism

FLORIAN ZITZELSBERGER

In the introduction to *British Queer Cinema* (2006), Robin Griffiths bemoans the fact that, although Great Britain has seen considerable advancement in terms of both cinematic production and cinema studies, deviations from heteronormativity are still relegated to niches and are either covered peripherally or, more alarmingly, omitted entirely (1). This is not surprising, however, if we assume that mainstream cinema follows what Judith Roof calls an "ideological version of (re)production produced by the figurative cooperation of a naturalized capitalism and heterosexuality" (xvii). In other words, mainstream cinema produces films conforming to a heteronormative ideal, simply because those films are more likely to gross more money. Queer cinema subverts this doctrine by "deconstruct[ing] notions of narrative teleology as both masculinist and heterosexist" (Warhol and Lanser 8), focusing on a part of society rarely represented on the silver screen. This article looks at the 2014 film *Pride*, directed by Matthew Warchus, as an example of queer social realism and examines the intersections of queer cinema and the genre of social realism. I will argue that *Pride* uses its hybrid generic status to juxtapose the experiences of the working-class miners and the LGBTQ community, represented in the film by the group Lesbians and Gays Support the Miners (LGSM), in order to highlight the solidarity that emerges between these groups and thus to pass criticism on (contemporary) society.

Realism's "very premise is contradictory" (Lee 5) because feature films can only strive to depict reality, i.e., autopoietically recreate a world that resembles the extratextual. Realism in film can only be achieved through textual markers or generic conventions that create a sense of authenticity, truthfulness or, above all, reality. Films undergo the filters of mediatization and to some extent manipulation, so that realism is, especially in period films such as *Pride*, about "the representation of history and our thought about it in visual images and filmic discourse"

(White 1193). That is to say, filmic realism has the potential of reflecting upon reality. Focusing on British social realism, Paul Dave hints at the historical dimension of this reflection when he states that "the tragic inflections of the representation of the working class in these films . . . are helping to stimulate a sense of the historic centrality of the working class experience of the contemporary crisis of the social" (52-3). Social realist films not only tend to look back at, for example, the conditions of the working class in a certain era but also at the society within which they are created. Moreover—and this link is important for a queer social realist film like *Pride*—"[a]ttention to temporality also raises questions about queer histories and the ways that gay, lesbian, bisexual, and transgendered experience have been effaced by mainstream accounts of the past" (Warhol and Lanser 8). Realism as a generic or representational category may, especially when it is directed against mainstream cinema, integrate (sexual) minorities in order to paint a heterogeneous and therefore implicitly life-like image of society. When they show or imply that social injustice against minorities (still) prevails, realist films are able to pass criticism on the culture they stem from, and its discrimination against minorities in particular, by taking up their perspective.

Pride's characters all have to face the struggles of their time, the 1980s in Britain. The Welsh mining towns are heavily affected by the miners' strike, "the longest and most significant dispute in modern British industrial history" (Towers 8). Moreover, the 1980s in Britain, as well as all around the globe, saw an increasing threat in what Cvetkovich pointedly calls a "national trauma . . . having a profound impact on history and politics" (376): the outbreak (or, rather, the growing awareness) of AIDS. Because AIDS is "connected to the insidious and everyday forms of trauma generated by sexism, racism, and other forms of oppression" (ibid.), it can be used to mirror the experiences of the miners. As such, *Pride* foregrounds the relationship between minorities and society. It focuses on those marginalized by society and represents them in a realist manner. This furthermore implies a comment on society itself. As Waugh asserts, "for those marginalized by the dominant culture," which applies to both the working class and queer individuals, "a sense of identity as constructed through impersonal and social relations of power . . . has been a major aspect of their self-concept" (3). In that respect, queer social realism shifts the focus from the cultural hegemony to the margins of society and gives voice to the heretofore silenced. In Linda Hutcheon's words:

> When the center starts to give way to the margins, when totalizing universalization begins to self-deconstruct, the complexity of the contradictions within conventions—such as those of genre, for instance—begin to be apparent. . . . Cultural homogenization too reveals its fissures, but the heterogeneity that is asserted in the face of that totalizing (yet pluralizing) culture does not take the form of many fixed individual subjects . . . but instead is conceived of as a flux of contextualized identities: contextualized by gender, class, race, ethnicity, sexual preference, education, social role, and so on. (59)

The genre of social realism cannot but address these categories; queer identities, as part of a minority, are a necessary component of society's dynamic within these categories. That is to say, hegemony in any area does not exist without marginalization and vice versa. However, this does not mean that the pursuit of social justice dies. The social realist film becomes the breeding ground of what Dave calls an "ethics of solidarity, an ethics capable of reviving the social" (19), a concern that is also close to the heart of the LGBTQ community. In that respect, *Pride* posits itself as a hybrid between queer cinema and the genre of social realism. The marriage of two forms of neglected cinema—queer cinema which is "linked to negative values within a reproductive aegis" (Roof xxvii) and social realism which often focuses on grim subject matter, e.g., themes such as "the demise of the traditional working class" (Lay 14)—mirrors the solidarity between marginalized and neglected groups in society. As the following examples will show, the miners' strike and AIDS, although *Pride* depicts them quite differently, are used to show that both are omnipresent and therefore inevitable during the 1980s in Britain.

While "AIDS movies produced and released during the first two decades of the pandemic regularly reinforced the persistent representational link between gay men and AIDS" (Hart 84), *Pride* depicts AIDS as a hidden danger. For example, at the end of the film, it is revealed that Mark dies only a few days after his diagnosis with HIV, aged 26. The film mirrors the disease's insidiousness by gradually making its references to AIDS more explicit. In the beginning, AIDS is not talked about by members of LGSM. Mark runs into his ex-boyfriend at a club who has not been home for four days and is on a "farewell tour." Should the spectators not have understood at this point that the ex-boyfriend is dying of AIDS, they can infer it in the following scene, in which Mark looks at a poster saying "AIDS KILLS." Hints like this poster stress that AIDS is a ubiquitous threat, especially within the queer community, which, however, is not spoken about. It is not until the end of the film that AIDS is addressed explicitly by members of LGSM. In hospital for getting beaten up, Gethin asks Sian to keep an eye on Jonathan for him: "He needs to take care of himself. . . . If you could just make sure he has some groceries in. . . . He's HIV positive, Sian. He's not supposed to smoke and he needs to eat properly." This does not mean, however, that *Pride* erases the traces of AIDS. Outside of the queer community, AIDS is addressed more directly, for example when Maureen refuses to host members of LGSM because she is "concerned about AIDS." This shows that in public discourse, AIDS is frequently evaluated as a threat that is inextricably linked with LGBTQ characters. Maureen's prejudice and ignorance are mirrored by Joe's family, who do not accept him for being gay. Watching one of the infamous AIDS spots from the 1980s on TV, Joe's future brother-in-law makes fun of AIDS and claims that the acronym stands for "anally injected death sentence." This illustrates that AIDS is indeed a substantial, though asymmetrically expressed concern of society in *Pride*: it correlates with explicitly voiced prejudice by outsiders, while it is mostly not spoken about by LGBTQ characters who might be affected. The omnipresence of AIDS and the inescapability of this incurable disease result in a feeling of powerlessness—a feeling that is used to construct a parallel to the miners' experience during their strike.

In contrast to AIDS, the miners' strike is thematized more explicitly throughout the film. When Dai gives a speech at a gay club in London, thanking LGSM and all those who donated money to their cause, he jokes that speaking in front of people is one thing that he has learnt during the strike, besides standing in a picket line. This is just one of many examples of how *Pride* incorporates humour to approach the miners' strike. The representation of the strike in *Pride* relies on accounts like this one by the characters, since, apart from a few short scenes shot at the pit, the film does not show the strike itself. We only get to know that men are participating in the strike, and we see women who, for example, pack parcels with food at the Welfare Hall. The focus is on the effects of the strike on the miners' and their families' lives. The large-scale impacts of the strike are communicated through public media such as television or radio. For example, the TV report in the beginning of the film reveals that, because of pit closures, 20,000 people will lose their jobs. As a BBC report announces, "the strike entered its 42nd week. The union responded with a renewed attack on the government's latest cuts to benefits for the families of those on the strike. They're calling it an attempt by Mrs Thatcher to starve the miners back to work." After listening to the report, LGSM witnesses these effects on a more personal level in the town of Onllwyn. The windows of some houses are bricked up because their gas is cut off. In addition, their bus (which the miners refer to as a "lifeline," since it is the only way of transporting food between the villages and pits) has broken down. However, *Pride* again includes humour to enliven the situation: for instance, Dai jokes about the fact that their heating does not work and states that it has benefits because the beer is always cold. It seems as if humour is the only way he can cope with a situation that is, otherwise, inescapable. *Pride* also incorporates individual stories the characters narrate themselves. For example, Cliff tells LGSM how he lost his brother to the pit and resignedly utters: "Without the mines the villages are finished, the pit and the people are one and the same," something he would also like to say to Thatcher. Indeed, *Pride* shows a community threatened by the pit closures because their lives depend on the mining industry, and their repugnance against Thatcher, whom they hold responsible for their poor living conditions.

As such, *Pride* evokes comparisons to films of the social realist genre such as *Brassed Off* (1996) or *The Full Monty* (1997). The film makes use of representational realism not only in its depiction of the miners' strike but also in the negotiation of AIDS, two themes that place emphasis on marginalized groups in society. *Pride* thus emerges with a clear signposting as the hybridized genre queer social realism on the levels of content and presentation which elucidates that, even though the two represented minorities suffer individually from their own misfortunes, it is in fact a majority of society that struggles on a daily basis. This is probably best explicated using another prevalent theme of the film: Because marginalization always raises questions about a dominating force, the marginalizing group, the theme of prejudice becomes the harsh reality of both miners and LGBTQ characters.

Although a Gay Pride demonstration—and queer cinema, for that matter—is supposed to be a place of utmost inclusiveness and tolerance, celebrating diversity, its public siting also provides a stage for prejudice and hate. *Pride* shows a variety of prejudiced reactions, ranging from skinheads insulting Joe as a "faggot" and throwing a can of beer at him to a woman who, walking by with her daughter, calls the demonstration and its participants "disgusting." If nothing else, the old woman with the "Burn in Hell" sign shows that prejudice permeates, and is deeply rooted in, society. Again, similar to AIDS, this is not addressed directly at this point. Instead, Mark highlights society's cruelty towards the miners and starts collecting money for them: "It's a show of solidarity. Who hates the miners? Thatcher. Who else? The police, the public and the tabloid press. Sound familiar?" Prejudice and hate are evaluated as the problem of an entire society (including the government) rather than an individual disposition.

In several instances, the film parallels the experience of the miners and LGBTQ characters in order to illustrate the extent of prejudice in society without explicating it. For example, after the Pride parade and first collection, Mark notes:

> Is it me? Or are the police getting soft? . . . My guess is they went somewhere else. To pick on someone else. . . . Now these mining communities are being bullied. Just like we are. Bullied by the police. Bullied by the tabloids. Bullied by the government.

Even the miners (at first) do not accept the help of LGSM because of their prejudices against homosexuals. Right after their decision to donate money to the miners, LGSM's request gets rejected by the National Union of Mine-Workers. Sian's husband reckons: "I'm not prejudiced. I'm a realist. I know what small towns are like." And the miners of Onllwyn, accordingly, leave the Welfare Hall after Mark's speech. Prejudice against LGBTQ characters seems to be internalized to a degree where it is not recognized as such. Instead, their condemnation is perceived as natural because, as has already been addressed, in the opinion of the people in Onllwyn, homosexuality correlates with AIDS. Furthermore, deviations from heteronormativity are considered as perversion. However, most of the people in Onllwyn gradually shed their prejudice and learn that the members of LGSM are regular people. *Pride* ridicules prejudice when conversations turn to stereotypes, simply to repel them. For example, during a get-together at the Welfare Hall, Gail asks a gay couple: "So you live together, like husband and wife. But what I want to know is . . . Which one does the housework?" The first sentence induces the obvious stereotypes of the female and male part of a homosexual relationship. Her question, however, eradicates stereotyping since she treats the gay couple like a heterosexual one—to the surprise of the couple.

Prejudice and discrimination in *Pride* occur on various levels. On the one hand, both can be considered as institutionalized and instrumentalized by the government and the police. *Pride* uses comparisons between the miners and LGSM to express their scope. On the other hand, prejudice is evident on a personal level. The miners' first reaction to LGSM is just one of many examples in the film. Most instances of prejudice, however, rather stay on the sideline. For example, we see Gethin removing a graffito saying "QUEERS" from his bookshop, which is not commented on at all. It is simply another instance the film uses to illustrate the omnipresence of homophobic discrimination. With its rather humorous engagement with stereotypes and the subversion of prejudice under the banner of solidarity, *Pride* passes criticism on society. It shows that prejudice is ultimately illogical and that the government, police and media are biased, which makes large-scale discrimination possible. *Pride*'s negotiation of prejudice is therefore symptomatic of its hybrid generic status: while prejudice constitutes a very typical theme of the social realist genre, it is linked to the idea of activism, a potential frequently highlighted in queer cinema.

Since queer characters are often perceived as "an anomaly in a homogeneous heterosexual world, [queer cinema] may obscure the fact that everyone is affected by social systems of sexual regulation, and that a very small minority of people are well served by them" (Saxey 45). The cultural construct of the closet, as theorized by Sedgewick, is "the defining structure for gay oppression" (71). Since miners and LGBTQ characters are both outsiders/minorities in society, their experiences can be paralleled; their union highlights the fact that it is not just one group who suffers from prejudice, discrimination, and regulation, be it governmental or sexual, but instead that the extent of adversity in society is much larger. That is also the reason for the emergence of solidarity between both groups. *Pride*'s negotiation of activism is closely linked to the idea of solidarity; the metaphor of the closet not only shows how underrepresented groups can gain representation but moreover draws attention to the fact that coming out is only necessary because of the existence of the closet. In other words, activism is only necessary because of oppression in society. *Pride* thus criticizes a culture of oppression and, especially in the case of the miners, abusive power of the government.

While LGSM collects money for the miners, the support they receive in return is centred around a Pride demo, which openly exhibits queerness and mirrors the very speech act constituted by coming out. Although Joe (who is still closeted) does not "want to be too visible," he ends up carrying a banner, thus coming out by showing that he belongs to the gay community. The banner has the caption "Queers! Better blatant than latent." On the one hand, this signifies the importance of community regarding activism. Just as it takes more than one person to carry a banner, it takes a group of people to achieve a goal. On the other hand, the banner reveals *Pride*'s critical attitude towards society: *Pride* gives voice to marginalized groups in society whose interests are neglected. This applies to LGBTQ characters and miners alike. Hence, miners have to come out of their own 'closet' of oppression as well, which they try to do in the course of their strike. Club secretary Cliff's actual coming out as gay functions as a catalyst in the eventual figurative 'coming out' (which ultimately means taking action) of the miners as a collective. The people of Onllwyn come out to London for a second Pride parade, now supporting the gays and lesbians who supported them before. As Joe points out, "the important thing is that we march together. All of us. That's what this whole thing has been about since the beginning. And that is absolutely how it is going to end. Together. Us. United." This act of solidarity is emphasized by the use of the miners' traditional banner which shows a handshake. The political agenda that resonates here seems to speak for *Pride* in its entirety: As a hybrid, *Pride* qua essence demonstrates the coalition of two distinct genres; the film follows the solidarity it represents in its generic form and gives voice to the forms of neglected cinema it merges—showing that there is indeed "power in a union."

Although, as has been shown, *Pride* is concerned with the realisms of both the miners and the LGBTQ community in 1980s Britain, it is not as explicit about the downsides of life such as the miners' strike, AIDS, and prejudice as most social realist films. However, just because these issues are rarely addressed explicitly or, in case of the miners' strike, approached rather wryly, does not mean that *Pride* omits criticism against society completely. The film provides a lot of visual cues—posters, banners, TV spots—that signify the omnipresence of these issues. Indeed, it is *Pride*'s attention to detail that gives expression to serious topics like death, the poor living conditions during the miners' strike, and discrimination. It therefore requires rather attentive spectatorship—for instance, most of the prejudice or even violence perpetrated against miners and LGBTQ characters has to be reconstructed by the viewer since the film often only shows its results, for example, Gethin in hospital. The film uses its generic status as a hybrid between social realist and queer film in order to represent *both* minorities faithfully, which rarely happens on the silver screen; while mainstream cinema often mirrors the marginalization of these groups in society or draws on stereotypes, *Pride*'s realism can be read as an attempt of society coming to terms with inequality. As such, *Pride* passes criticism on a bygone era as well as present-day society: on the one hand, *Pride* is straightforward in its criticism of the Thatcherite government which it holds responsible for the poor conditions of the miners and also for discrimination. Since *Pride* foregrounds the union of those oppressed by the government and society, on the other hand, it counterposes and criticizes a society of passivity and looking away, showing that community is much stronger than exclusion and ignorance. The film advocates the more inclusive model of a society where solidarity for one another prevails, where coming together, to quote the recurring song "Solidarity Forever" by Pete Seeger, "can break their haughty power" and enable those oppressed to eventually "gain [their] freedom."

Works Cited

Cvetkovich, Ann. "Aids Activism and Public Feelings: Documenting ACT UP's Lesbians." *The Routledge Queer Studies Reader*. Eds. Donald E. Hall and Annamarie Jagose. London: Routledge, 2013. 373-397.

Dave, Paul. "Tragedy, Ethics and History in Contemporary British Social Realist Film." *British Social Realism in the Arts Since 1940*. Ed. David Tuker. London: Palgrave MacMillan, 2011. 17-56.

Griffiths, Robin. "Introduction: Queer Britannia – A Century of Sinema." *British Queer Cinema*. Ed. Robin Griffiths. London: Routledge, 2006. 1-19.

Hart, Kylo-Patrick. *Queer Males in Contemporary Cinema: Becoming Visible*. Lanham, MD: The Scarecrow Press, 2013.

Hutcheon, Linda. *A Poetics of Postmodernism: History, Theory, Fiction*. New York and London: Routledge, 1988.

Lay, Samantha. *British Social Realism: From Documentary to Brit Grit*. London: Wallflower, 2002.

Lee, Alison. *Realism and Power: Postmodern British Fiction*. London: Routledge, 1990.

Pride. Dir. Matthew Warchus. Screenplay by Stephen Beresford. BBC Films, 2014. DVD..

Roof, Judith. *Come as You Are: Sexuality and Narrative*. New York: Columbia UP, 1996.

Saxey, Esther. *Homoplot: The Coming-Out Story and Gay, Lesbian and Bisexual Identity*. New York: Lang, 2008.

Sedgwick, Eve. *Epistemology of the Closet*. Berkeley: University of California Press, 1990.

Towers, Brian. "Posing Larger Questions: The British Miners' Strike of 1984-85." *Industrial Relations Journal* 16.2 (1985): 8-25.

Warhol, Robyn, and Susan Lanser. *Introduction. Narrative Theory Unbound: Queer and Feminist Interventions*. Eds. Robyn Warhol and Susan Lanser. Columbus: Ohio State University Press, 2015. 1-20.

Waugh, Patricia. *Feminine Fictions: Revisiting the Postmodern*. New York and London: Routledge, 1989.

White, Hayden. "Historiography and Historiophoty." *The American Historical Review* 93.5 (1988): 1193-1199.

Notes on Contributors

Argha Banerjee is currently the Dean of Arts, St Xavier's College, Kolkata, India, and is part of the faculty of the Department of English. He was a Commonwealth Research Scholar to the Department of English, Sussex University (2004-07) and a Charles Wallace Fellow to the UK in 2012.

Fanny Beuré is a French scholar with a PhD in Film Studies and is a Lecturer at University Paris Diderot—Paris 7 and at University Paris Ouest Nanterre La Défense. Her PhD thesis focuses on the classic Hollywood musicals and the notion of 'entertainment.' Her work focuses on American cinema and TV series (classical and contemporary), from cultural and gender studies standpoints, the sociology of audience and the economics of cinema.

Subashish Bhattacharjee is an Assistant Professor of English, Munshi Premchand College, India and UGC-Senior Research Fellow at the Centre for English Studies, Jawaharlal Nehru University, India. His areas of interest include comparative architecture, architectural theory, gender studies, gender and urbanity and philosophy of technology. He is the Editor (Literary Articles and Academic Book Reviews) of *Muse India* and Co-editor of *The Apollonian: A Journal of Interdisciplinary Studies.*

Fernando Gabriel Pagnoni Berns works at Universidad de Buenos Aires (UBA)—Facultad de Filosofia y Letras (Argentina) as Professor in "Literatura de las Artes Combinadas II". He is director of the research group "Grite". Among his many publications in the area are chapters in books such as *To See the Saw Movies: Essays on Torture Porn and Post 9/11 Horror* and *Dreamscapes in Italian Cinema.*

Rohit K. Dasgupta is lecturer in Global Media at Winchester School of Art, University of Southampton. He has co-edited the volume, *The World of Rituparno Ghosh: Texts, Contexts and Transgressions* (Routledge, 2015).

Anna Fahraeus is Director of Studies, Department of English Literature and Language at the School of Education, Humanities and Social Science, Halmstad University. She has obtained her PhD from Gothenburg University on black and white masculinity in Renaissance revenge tragedies.

Canela Ailen Rodriguez Fontao holds an MA from the Facultad de Filosofia y Letras at Universidad de Buenos Aires (UBA), Argentina. She integrates the research group on cinema CIyNE and has published articles on Argentinean and international cinema and television in books such as *Bullying in Popular Culture: Essays on Film, Television and Novels, and Representations of Cruel Children in Popular Texts.* She is a lecturer specializing in horror TV and cinema.

Elke Krasny is an Austrian curator, urban researcher, cultural theorist and art educator. She teaches at the Academy of Fine Arts, Vienna, in the areas of art and cultural educations, didactics of the visual, didactics architecture, space and environment as well as art and public. Along with Cynthia Schwertsik she founded the group Plan B.

David Klein Martins holds an MA in English and American Studies with a specialisation in Queer Theory. His research interests include Gender and Queer Studies, Film Studies, and American Popular Culture. He is presently preparing for his doctoral research on queer representations in American independent cinema.

Lara S. Narcisi is Associate Professor of English at Regis University, USA. Her areas of interest include ethnic literatures of the United States, modern and contemporary American Literature and literary theories.

William J. Simmons graduated from Harvard University with a Bachelor of Arts in art history and LGBTQ studies. He is currently a student in the art history Ph.D. program and the women's studies certificate program at the Graduate Center of the City University of New York, as well as an adjunct lecturer in art history at the City College of New York.

Mariana Zárate holds an MA from the Facultad de Filosofia y Letras at Universidad de Buenos Aires (UBA), Argentina. She has published chapters in *Gothic and Racism* (Universitas) and *Projecting the World* (Wayne State University Press).

Florian Zitzelsberger is currently tutor for English and American Literary Studies at the University of Passau, Germany. He has published articles on environmentalist children's literature and American popular culture. His main research interests include self-reflexivity and metareference across media with a focus on the American film musical, American literary realism and naturalism, gender and fan studies, as well as queer culture.

Universitas Press

Books that make sense of the world

Also from Universitas Press:

Charles Dickens - American Notes
Antonia Palacios - Ana Isabel: a Respectable Girl
My Own Land's Sins: An Anthology of Victorian Poetry
John Cleland - Memoirs of a Woman of Pleasure
(the original text and the updated text in a single volume)
Oscar Wilde - The Portrait of Dorian Gray
Jane Austen - Pride and Prejudice
Jane Austen - Sense and Sensibility
Mary Shelley - Frankenstein
(the 1818 edition with the 1831 introduction)
Goody Two-Shoes and Other 18th-Century British Stories
These Immortal Creations:
An Anthology of British Romantic Poetry
Dracula: The Postcolonial Edition
Specialists: Passions and Careers
Dragos Moraru - Histopias: From the Bible to Cloud Atlas
Gothic and Racism
Monsters and Monstrosity in 20th-Century Film and Television
Dracula: A Study of Editorial Practices
Dracula Invades England:
The Text, the Context and the Readers

www.ingramcontent.com/pod-product-compliance
Lightning Source LLC
LaVergne TN
LVHW020717110826
845149LV00012B/2297

* 9 7 8 0 9 9 5 0 2 9 1 3 2 *